Welsh Yeomanry at War

Welsh Yeomanry at War

A HISTORY OF THE
24TH (PEMBROKE AND GLAMORGAN
YEOMANRY) BATTALION,
THE WELSH REGIMENT

Steven John

Pen & Sword
MILITARY

First published in Great Britain in 2016 by
PEN & SWORD MILITARY
an imprint of
Pen and Sword Books Ltd
47 Church Street
Barnsley
South Yorkshire S70 2AS

Copyright © Steven John, 2016

HB   ISBN 978 1 47383 362 3
TPB ISBN 978 1 47386 793 2

Printed and bound in England by
CPI Group (UK) Ltd, Croydon, CR0 4YY

Typeset in Times New Roman
by CHIC GRAPHICS

Pen & Sword Books Ltd incorporates the imprints of
Pen & Sword Archaeology, Atlas, Aviation, Battleground, Discovery, Family
History, History, Maritime, Military, Naval, Politics, Railways, Select, Social History,
Transport, True Crime, Claymore Press, Frontline Books, Leo Cooper, Praetorian Press,
Remember When, Seaforth Publishing and Wharncliffe.

For a complete list of Pen and Sword titles please contact
Pen and Sword Books Limited
47 Church Street, Barnsley, South Yorkshire, S70 2AS, England
E-mail: enquiries@pen-and-sword.co.uk

Contents

Introduction

Until moving to Shropshire from my native Laugharne some years ago, I had no interest in the happenings of the Great War, as my only knowledge of any ancestors who had served was of my grandfather and great uncle during the Second World War. Shift working left me with plenty of spare time to fill, so I began carrying out some research on my family tree. After struggling to find out about my paternal grandfather's side of the family, I discovered that his father, David Thomas John, a coal miner, from Halfpenny Furze, near Laugharne, had run away to Australia in 1913 after he had been forced to marry his then pregnant girlfriend. My grandfather was born around the same time that David disappeared, and his mother later remarried; as a result the true story of my great grandfather was never relayed to my generation. David's younger brother, John James John, also a coal miner, was due to join him in Australia, but when war broke out it left the two brothers on opposite sides of the globe, with David working as a miner in the Bulli Colliery, New South Wales.

Whether it was a sense of patriotism or desperation will never be known, but David enlisted at Randwick and became one of the original members of the newly formed 4th Battalion, Australian Imperial Force (AIF). His brother John volunteered for service with the Pembroke Yeomanry. Neither man would live to see the end of the war, although they did meet briefly in Egypt in 1916. David would survive the infamous campaign in Gallipoli, taking part in the famous Battle of Lone Pine, and later fought in the successful Australian assault on Pozières during the Somme battles. He was killed while leading a reconnaissance patrol at Mouquet Farm on 18 August 1916. John served throughout the Pembroke Yeomanry's campaign in Egypt and Palestine, then embarked with the 24th Welsh for France in May 1918, only to be killed during the Battle of Épehy on 18 September 1918. The two brothers and close friends, lie just thirty miles apart on French soil.

Because of this discovery, and the immense pride I feel about having these two men as my immediate ancestors, I started on the road to researching their battalions. While half-way through writing a book on the history of the 4th Battalion AIF, I was disappointed to discover that an Australian author, Colonel Ron Austin, had beaten me to it, and was about to publish his own book. A cheeky telephone from me to Ron led to the exchange of my research and material on the battalion, and resulted in a few paragraphs of his book being written about the death of 244 Lance Corporal David Thomas John. His death, along with a photograph of him, was printed in the book *The Fighting Fourth*, so my intention of getting my great grandfather commemorated in print was realised.

The next project of mine culminated in the publication of my first book, *Carmarthen Pals*, a history of another local unit, the 15th (Service) Battalion, Welsh Regiment. While writing *A Township in Mourning*, which I self published, I was told of the existence of a photograph of my mother's uncle, Harry Allen, a Whitland man. Harry was killed while serving with the 15th Welsh at Mametz Wood. While researching his story, enough material was found to complete the book, which I dedicated to Harry.

With *Carmarthen Pals* published, I was commissioned by Pen & Sword to write another book, which would be part of their 2014 Great War Centenary list, entitled *Carmarthen in the Great War*, which chronicles how the war affected the county of Carmarthenshire, and was published on 1 June 2014. With that completed, I embarked upon this book, in order to commemorate my great uncle, John James John, who was killed in action at Gillemont Farm, during the battle of Épehy. For this reason this book is being written both in his memory and in memory of the other men of the former Pembroke and Glamorgan Yeomanry battalions who fought and died after being amalgamated into the newly created 24th Battalion, Welsh Regiment.

The Welsh Regiment was originally raised from the merging of two of the old Regiments of Foot, the 41st and the 69th. The 41st Regiment of Foot was raised on 1 March, 1719 by Colonel Edmund Fielding, and consisted of a core nucleus of Outpatients from the Chelsea Military Hospital (Chelsea Pensioners). It moved to Portsmouth as garrison troops, enabling existing units to be able to serve overseas. This led to the early regimental nickname of the 'Invalids', a somewhat unfortunate name that proved hard to shake off.

On 11 December 1787 the 41st Foot became a Line Regiment of the British Army. It saw active service for some years throughout the Americas, and also against the French at Quebec. In 1815 the 41st moved to France, seeing service in the campaign against Napoleon under Lord Wellesley, and through the remainder of the nineteenth century fought in wars throughout the Empire: in Burma, Afghanistan, India and the Crimean Wars. In 1857 the Regiment moved to Jamaica on garrison duties, and after a three year spell there returned to Britain. The Regiment was renamed after the Cardwell Reforms in 1881, and became the Welch Regiment. Two Battalions were formed, the 1st Battalion from the 41st Foot and the 2nd Battalion from the 69th.

The 69th Regiment of Foot was originally raised on 20 September 1756 as a second battalion of the 24th Foot. It spent the early years of its life at sea with the Royal Navy, and during the next 123 years of its history served throughout the British Empire, until being turned into the 2nd Battalion the Welch (sic) Regiment under the Cardwell Reforms.

The 1st Battalion began this next stage of their life in South Africa, where they saw service against the Zulus, before moving to Egypt in 1886. After seeing action there the Regiment spent time on garrison duty back in Britain before embarking again for South Africa, where it fought throughout both of the Anglo-Boer Wars. In July 1904 it returned home but was back on the borders of the Empire at the outbreak of the Great War, stationed at Chakrata, India.

The 2nd Battalion meanwhile had spent most of its time in the years before the war on garrison duty in Britain. From 1892 to 1906 it was in India, before moving to South Africa and then to Pembroke Dock. In August 1914 the 2nd Battalion was sent to France as part of the 1st Division of the British Expeditionary Force, and remained on the Western Front for the remainder of the war, gaining for Wales its first Victoria Cross of the war, when the actions of Lance Corporal William Fuller of Laugharne, during the rescue of his captain, Mark Haggard, under heavy German machine-gun fire during the fighting at Chivy-sur-Aisne, led to his being awarded this most sought after of gallantry awards.

In the meantime the British army was rapidly expanding and gearing up for war. Territorial battalions were called up, and the first of the Territorial Welsh battalions, the 1/6th Welsh, arrived on the Western Front in October 1914.

The Welsh Regiment expanded rapidly throughout August of that year. The 2nd Battalion was in France, the 1st was on its way back from India, and the Territorial battalions, the 1/4th (Carmarthenshire), the 1/5th (Glamorgan), the 1/6th (Glamorgan), the 1/7th (Cyclists) and the Pembroke and Glamorgan Yeomanry Battalions (which were later to become affiliated to the Welsh Regiment as its 24th Battalion) had mobilised ready for war.

As well as these regular and territorial units, Service, or war-time only, Battalions were raised throughout the recruiting grounds of South Wales during the opening months of the Great War. These Battalions were the 8th (Pioneers), 9th (Service), 10th (1st Rhondda), 11th (Cardiff City), 12th (Reserve), 13th (2nd Rhondda), 14th (Swansea City), 15th (Carmarthenshire), 16th (Cardiff City), 17th (Glamorgan), 18th (2nd Glamorgan), 19th (Glamorgan Pioneers), 20th (3rd Rhondda), 21st (Reserve), 22nd (Reserve), and 23rd (Reserve) Battalions. As well as these, the Territorial battalions often had Reserve battalions attached; for example the front-line unit of the 4th Welsh was the 1st/4th Battalion. The reserve battalion was the 2nd/4th.

This book is written to commemorate the achievements of one of these magnificent battalions of the Welsh Regiment, the 24th (Pembroke and Glamorgan Yeomanry) Battalion, the Welsh Regiment, and in memory of my great uncle, John James John.

*This book is dedicated to Private John
James John (320374), of Laugharne. Killed
near Gillemont Farm on 21 September 1918.*

Chapter 1

The Origins of the Battalion

The 24th Battalion of the Welsh Regiment was officially formed in Egypt on 2 February 1917 from two dismounted Yeomanry Regiments: the Pembroke Yeomanry and the Glamorgan Yeomanry, which had both previously seen service with the 4th Dismounted Brigade of the South Wales Mounted Division. Both of these Regiments had a long and interesting history prior to the outbreak of the Great War, and were formed on a similar basis to the 'Pals' Battalions of that war. The Yeomanry Regiments were locally raised, and comprised troops of men from different parts of their respective counties, many of whom had enlisted together, thus forming an unbreakable bond of friendship and comradeship that was to stand them in good stead throughout the coming trials.

The two constituent parts of the 24th Battalion, the Welsh Regiment were:

The Pembroke Yeomanry (Castlemartin)

The Pembroke Yeomanry was raised in 1794 by Lord Milford as part of the national response to the threat to the country following the French Revolution. In 1797 the Republican *Légion Noire* landed off Carreg Wastad Point near Fishguard, only to surrender to a much smaller force hastily assembled under Lord Cawdor, which included his own Castlemartin Troop of the Pembroke Yeomanry. Two of the French frigates involved were captured, one of which was subsequently re-commissioned as HMS *Fisgard*. In 1853 Queen Victoria bestowed the battle honour 'Fishguard' upon the Pembroke Yeomanry. The unit became the first volunteer unit to receive a battle honour and remains the only one still serving in the British army to bear the name of an engagement on British soil.

From 1839 to 1843 the Pembroke Yeomanry took part with Regular forces in controlling the unrest that began with the Rebecca Riots.

During the first Boer War the Pembroke Yeomanry provided the 30th Company of the Denbighshire Hussars, 9th (Welsh) Battalion of Imperial Yeomanry, landing in South Africa in 1890 to fight as mounted infantry. A second company of the Pembroke Yeomanry replaced them in 1901, and they both saw considerable action during the two Boer Wars.

The Glamorgan Yeomanry

The Glamorgan Yeomanry formed in 1794, when Britain was faced by a French nation which had recently executed its King, and possessed a revolutionary army numbering half a million men. The Prime Minister proposed that the English counties form a force of volunteer yeoman cavalry that could be called on by the King to defend the country against invasion or by the Lord Lieutenant to subdue any civil disorder within the country.

The Glamorgan Yeomanry provided troops for the 4th Company, 1st Battalion of the Imperial Yeomanry force, and arrived in South Africa between February and April 1900, to take part in the Second Boer War, fighting alongside their Pembrokeshire counterparts.

In 1908 the Territorial Force was brought into being, and the various Yeomanry regiments became a part of this force, attending camps every year where the part time soldiers would assemble and train. For the men of the mainly rural county of Pembrokeshire, this annual camp became their only chance of a holiday, getting them away from the boring routine of work on the farm, and allowing them a chance to earn some much needed extra pay. Likewise, for the men of the industrial county of Glamorgan it was a good chance for some time away from the coal mines and the copper, iron and tinplate works where many of them toiled.

At the outbreak of war, on 4 August 1914, the Yeomanry were at such a camp. Their intended role during war was to act as guard units within Britain. The Yeomanry were not intended, nor were they signed up, to serve overseas, and the Pembroke and Glamorgan Yeomanry Regiments found themselves being mobilised for this purpose of home defence, for now at least.

The Pembroke Yeomanry formed three battalions during the war:

1/1st Pembroke Yeomanry.

Formed on 4 August 1914 at Tenby, as part of the South Wales Mounted Brigade. On 12 August 1914 the Brigade concentrated at Hereford, and then at the end of August moved to the Thetford area, joining the 1st Mounted Division. They then moved to Aylsham and were stationed at Haveringham and Heydon in Norfolk. During October 1915 the Battalion moved to Cromer. It was here, in November 1915, that the Pembroke Yeomanry was dismounted. In March 1916 the 1st Mounted Division sailed for Egypt, and, on 20 March 1916, the South Wales Mounted Brigade became absorbed into the 4th Dismounted Brigade.

2/1st Pembroke Yeomanry.

The Battalion formed in 1914 and in early 1915 was stationed at Carmarthen in the 2/1st South Wales Mounted Brigade, before moving first to Llandeilo and then Dorchester. In September 1915 the Brigade moved to Yoxford, joining the 1st Mounted Division. In 1916 the Brigade became the 4th Mounted Brigade. In July 1916 it became a cyclist unit in the 2nd Cyclist Brigade, 1st Cyclist Division. During November 1916 the Division was broken up and it merged with the 2/1st Glamorgan Yeomanry to form the 2nd (Pembroke and Glamorgan) Yeomanry its Cyclist Regiment, in the 1st Cyclist Brigade. During March 1917 the Battalion resumed identity, and moved to Aldeburgh and then in July 1917 to Benacre. By the end of the year the Battalion was at Lowestoft, where it remained in the 1st Cyclist Brigade, seeing action during the German naval raid on Lowestoft.

3/1st Pembroke Yeomanry.

The Battalion formed in 1915 at Carmarthen, before moving to Brecon. In the summer of 1915 it became affiliated to a reserve cavalry regiment in Ireland. During the summer of 1916 the Battalion dismounted and became attached to the 3rd Line units of the Welsh Division, based at Park Hall Camp, Oswestry. Early in 1917 the Battalion disbanded, with its personnel moving to the 2nd Line unit and the 4th (Reserve) Battalion Welsh Regiment at Milford Haven.

The Glamorgan Yeomanry also formed three battalions during the war:

1/1st Glamorgan Yeomanry.

The Battalion formed on 4 August 1914 at Bridgend, attached to the South Wales Mounted Brigade. On 12 August 1914 it moved with the brigade to Hereford, and at the end of August to Thetford, joining the 1st Mounted Division, before moving again to Aylsham. During October 1915 it moved to Cromer, where in November 1915 the Battalion became dismounted. In March 1916 the Battalion moved to Egypt and, on 20 March 1916, the South Wales Mounted Brigade was absorbed into the 4th Dismounted Brigade.

2/1st Glamorgan Yeomanry.

The Battalion formed in 1914 and in January 1915 joined the 2/1st South Wales Mounted Brigade. In July 1915 it moved to the Dorchester area, then in September 1915 to East Suffolk, joining the 1st Mounted Division. During March 1916 the brigade became the 4th Mounted Brigade. During July 1916 the 1st Mounted Division became the 1st Cyclist Division and the unit became a cyclist unit in the 2nd Cyclist Brigade of the Division at Yoxford. In November 1916 the Division was broken up and the Battalion merged with the 2/1st Pembroke Yeomanry to form the 2nd (Pembroke & Glamorgan Yeomanry) Cyclist Battalion in the 1st Cyclist Brigade. In March 1917 the Battalion resumed its identity, now based at Leiston. By July 1917 they were at Benacre. By the end of 1917 the Battalion had moved to Worlingham, near Beccles, where it remained, in the 1st Cyclist Brigade, until the end of the war.

3/1st Glamorgan Yeomanry.

The Battalion was formed in 1915 and in the summer was attached to a reserve cavalry Regiment at the Curragh. During the summer of 1916 it dismounted and was attached to the 3rd Line Groups of the Welsh Division. Early in 1917 the unit was disbanded, with the personnel going to the 2nd Line unit and to the 4th (Reserve) Battalion, Welsh Regiment, at Milford Haven.

As can be seen, the two front line Battalions of the Pembroke and Glamorgan Yeomanry Regiments were in Egypt by the end of March 1916, where they took up positions on the Suez Canal Defences. They merged on 2 February 1917, forming the 24th (Pembroke and Glamorgan Yeomanry) Battalion, the Welsh Regiment.

Upon its formation, the new Battalion was attached to 231 Brigade, 74th (Yeomanry)

Division. This Division was to gain much credit for itself during General Allenby's campaign against the Turkish Forces in Palestine in 1917, before being hurriedly recalled to the Western Front in May 1918, after the German Offensives on the Somme and on the Lys had seriously threatened the front of the British Expeditionary Force.

The 74th (Yeomanry) Division arrived at Marseilles on 7 May, and thereafter fought through until the Armistice on 11 November 1918, when they stopped their great advance at the Belgian town of Ath.

This book will, hopefully, rekindle the memory of this gallant battalion of the Welsh Regiment, which was never to be re-formed again.

Chapter 2

Mobilisation and Home Service

The yeomanry and territorial units which were stationed around Britain consisted of men who had volunteered to serve at least four years; a requirement of their service was to attend a two week Territorial camp each summer. This camp was, for the majority of the men, a rare break from the toil of their everyday working life. Many of the men were poor farm workers who could not afford to go away, and so this was an ideal opportunity for two weeks 'holiday' with a group of friends, and a good chance also to earn some extra cash: at that time five pounds if you provided your own horse! For men with the ability to ride, and with a horse in their possession, this was really a deal not to be missed in those days of toil and hardship, and many groups of friends enlisted for this reason.

During the years leading up to 1914, these summer camps for the Pembroke and Glamorgan Yeomanry were held throughout Wales. For example, the Pembroke Yeomanry held camps at: Garth (Brecon) in 1906, Pembrey in 1907, Penally in 1908, Llandovery in 1909, Penally in 1910, Builth Wells in 1911, Penally in 1912, Llandeilo in 1913 and Penally in 1914. The Glamorgan Yeomanry held camps at: Margam in 1906, Penally in 1907, Margam in 1908, Llandovery in 1909, Porthcawl in 1910, Builth Wells in 1911, Brecon in 1912, Llandeilo in 1913 and Porthcawl in 1914. Camp was a big part of the lives of the young men who attended, but one camp in particular, at Penally in the summer of 1914,

Llandovery Yeomanry Camp in 1909.

Some fun loving members of the Glamorgan Yeomanry at Llangammarch Wells Camp in 1913.

was to remain etched in the memory of these young men for the rest of their lives due to the news they received while there.

At the beginning of the twentieth century, the European powers were in the midst of a struggle for power. The mighty British Empire was at its peak, and an up and coming Germany, led by Kaiser Wilhelm II, was intent on building an empire of her own. A rapid rise in industrialisation in Germany provided the money, whilst the Kaiser devised a much stronger, deep water navy, threatening the domination of the Royal Navy. This led to an arms race, with Britain resolute in her decision to have a navy at least twice the size of her two nearest rivals combined. During the years 1908 to 1913 this arms race gathered momentum, fuelling distrust among the peoples of both countries, and unnerving France, who was still reeling from her defeat by Germany in 1871.

In mid 1914 Europe was a tinderbox of rivalries, and the spark that ignited it was the assassination of the Austrian Archduke Franz Ferdinand and his wife, on 28 June 1914 while on a visit to Sarajevo. After a great deal of gesturing by Germany, Austria-Hungary declared war on Serbia on 28 July 1914, which prompted Russia to mobilise her vast army. This in turn dragged Germany into war alongside her ally, and set into place the chain reaction which led to the British declaration of war on Germany and her allies on 4 August 1914 when the first German troops crossed the Belgian frontier.

The German plan was simple, following a concept conceived by Count Alfred von Schlieffen after the Franco Prussian War of 1870. Its aim was simply to sweep through Holland and Belgium, and enter France by its northern border, before brushing past the channel ports to Paris, where it was believed the French would capitulate. The devastating speed of the campaign would keep Britain out of the war.

The capture of key places in Belgium, vital for the maintenance and support of the advancing armies, proved to be a bigger stumbling block than had been anticipated; the cities of Liege and Namur were defended by a ring of (admittedly obsolete) forts and proved to be more than just a minor irritant. Elsewhere, the French war plan, involving an attempted push across the Rhine, fell into disarray and at the cost of vast casualties.

Joffre, the French Commander in Chief, however, understood what the Germans were trying to achieve and began to build up substantial forces on his left flank. These early battles involved numbers of men far greater than the hundred thousand or so men of the British Expeditionary Force who were despatched from home and who started to arrive just after the middle of August. The small force was despatched to join the left of the French line near Maubeuge and was to advance with them against the German right flank. By 23 August the two corps of the BEF had taken up their positions, with II Corps, under Smith-Dorrien, on the left and spread thinly along the line of the canal north of Mons.

The anticipated offensive was soon turned into an urgent need to withdraw as German forces in strength, two armies forming the left part of Schlieffen's 'sweep', pushed against the British line. Thus began the long, hot days of the Retreat from Mons, ending on the Marne, south east of Paris. As well as losing significant numbers at Mons (mainly as prisoners) there was a hard fought action at Le Cateau on the 26th – again, expensive in casualties – before the BEF was able to continue to move southwards, largely unhindered by German operations.

The fight back of the allies came at the battles of the Marne and the Aisne; the German plan had been foiled. Both sides sought to outflank each other to the north. In October the BEF was moved to the northern flank once more and suffered at the battles of La Bassee and Ypres. By Christmas the front was in stalemate; but the BEF – frequently reinforced as it had been – was a shadow of its former self. With the regular army reserves almost exhausted, increasing numbers of Territorial units were sent to bolster the British army on the continent.

After the declaration of war the Pembroke and Glamorgan Yeomanry were also mobilised and, along with the Montgomery Yeomanry became part of the South Wales Mounted Brigade. The Pembroke Yeomanry, were still in their annual territorial camp at Penally on 4 August 1914, and were filled with excitement at the news.

As a mainly rural county, Pembrokeshire could not raise a full regiment, so recruiting had also taken place in Carmarthenshire and Cardiganshire. Pembrokeshire had two

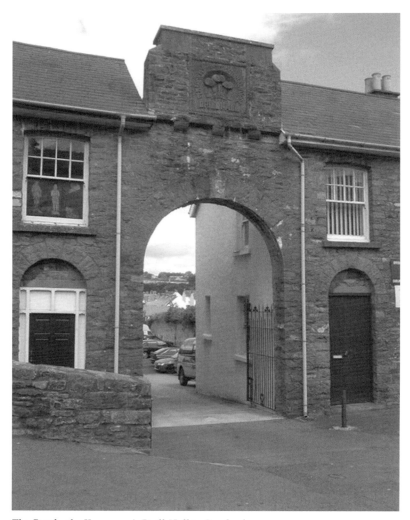

The Pembroke Yeomanry's Drill Hall in Pembroke.

squadrons; A Squadron based at Yeomanry Headquarters in Tenby, with drill stations at Tenby, Maiden Wells, St Florence, Jeffreystone and Kilgetty: and B Squadron at Haverfordwest, with drill stations at Clarbeston Road, Newport and Johnston. C Squadron was based at Carmarthen, along with the 4th Welsh, and later the 15th Welsh, with drill stations at Whitland, Llandeilo, Ferryside and Llanelli. D Squadron was at Lampeter, with additional drill stations at Aberystwyth, Aberaeron, New Quay and Llandyssul. It was commanded by Lieutenant Colonel Owen Hird Spear Williams TD, and had a complement of 469 men. The Honorary Colonel of the Regiment was Colonel Sir Owen Henry Philipps Scourfield TD, a long standing Territorial officer.

The Glamorgan Yeomanry had life a little easier, with a much larger population to draw upon. It had a complement of 596 men organised in three squadrons: A Squadron based at Swansea; B Squadron based at Bridgend; and C Squadron based at Cardiff. It was commanded by Lieutenant Colonel Charles Venables-Llewelyn, with its honorary colonel being Colonel The Right Honorable the Earl of Plymouth, CB. Not only did the Regiment quickly reach its full strength but it also had the luxury of a lengthy waiting list of men wanting to join. The officers of both regiments were recruited mainly from the county gentry, whilst other ranks were mostly farmers' sons, tradesmen, coal miners and businessmen. Most of the officers and men of each squadron knew each other socially, as did the officers across the squadrons. This led to a much less formal relationship than in the regular army, although discipline was not generally sacrificed as a result and in reality made the yeomanry regiments a form of 'Pals' unit.

All of these yeomen had attested for home service only, as they were classified as Territorial soldiers. Their attestation forms required them to enlist initially for four years' service at home, and so for the moment this is where they would be bound, although most of the men would sign disclaimers to this, stating their willingness to serve overseas. Those not willing to do so would, in the coming months, be replaced by men who were willing and so would move to the Second Line Regiments, the 2/1st Pembroke Yeomanry and the 2/1st Glamorgan Yeomanry.

Within two weeks of mobilisation, the various yeomanry squadrons in Pembrokeshire, Cardiganshire, Carmarthenshire and Glamorgan packed up, and began their move to assemble for entraining to Hereford. The Pembroke Yeomanry left their local depots for Carmarthen on 10 August 1914, with much public adulation and ceremony. Once assembly was completed at Carmarthen, the units entrained for Hereford that same day, while the men of the Glamorgan Yeomanry had assembled at Cardiff preparatory to their short train ride to Hereford. A report in the *Carmarthen Journal* of 12 August described the scenes in the town:

Penally Camp 1914: a group of men from the Llanddowror, St Clears and Laugharne area.

Members of the Pembroke Yeomanry leaving Penally for Norfolk (Sergeant Morgan on the left-hand leading horse).

'The Pembrokeshire Yeomanry, who were called up last Wednesday evening, were billeted in the town until Monday morning, when they left for Hereford. At a later stage, it is believed, they will be drafted to Scotland. The men were aroused before 2 am, and by dawn the streets were ringing with the clatter of hoofs and the bustle of troops hurrying hither and thither. Half the men left on horseback, and the other half entrained to Whitland, where they rejoined their squadrons. Great activity prevailed in the town all day Sunday. The Yeomanry paraded in the morning and marched out to the country for several miles for exercise. All day long the town bore a martial aspect. Horses were continually arriving, and the work of shoeing proceeded at rapid pace. Everything seemed to be carried out with marvellous precision.'

At Hereford the men were asked to sign up for overseas service, with much speculation in local newspapers about the numbers of men who had refused. Within two days of the departure of the men, rumours were rife at Carmarthen and Haverfordwest about the lack of enthusiasm among them to attest for overseas service, and that less than 120 men had answered the call. The men of the Glamorgan and Montgomery Yeomanry reportedly attested en-masse, making matters even worse. In a very patriotic Britain, many of its people were disgusted by the grossly exaggerated stories of large numbers of yeomen who had declined to sign up for overseas service. This later prompted the second in command of the Pembrokeshire Yeomanry, Major Spence-Jones, to publish a list of the 'non volunteers' from within the ranks of the Pembrokeshire Yeomanry: this amounted to some forty eight men, and included their names, service numbers and addresses, causing some distress to the mens' families. Spence-Jones wrote:

'From time to time I have seen quoted in various South Wales papers the number of the Pembroke Yeomanry who have not volunteered for service abroad. As these numbers have invariably been incorrect I should be glad if a correct version might be made known. I enclose a roll with addresses of those men who have not volunteered, and should be glad if these might now be published. From the attached Roll it will be seen that Pembrokeshire provided 42 non-volunteers: Carmarthen 3, Cardigan 3, total 48. Any other men sent to the Reserve units are men who are medically unfit for service abroad.'

It can only be speculated what repercussions this public humiliation brought to this small band of men; in some cases, condemnation was not deserved. Some, notably Staff Quartermaster Sergeant Thomas Picton Davies, of Rhoswell, Haverfordwest, were middle-aged (he was 49 years old in 1915), and had seen prior active service during the Boer War; others, such as Trooper John Henry John of Haverfordwest, were to die due to the strain of army life on home service, so would most likely not have been fit for overseas service anyway (he died on 30 October 1915, aged 37). Widespread condemnation of the publication of these names even reached Parliament. Matters were not helped when news that every single member of the 4th Welsh had volunteered for overseas service, and news of this spread throughout west Wales after the initial publication in the local press on 2 September.

While this furore was in full swing in south and west Wales, the yeomen moved from Hereford to Norfolk where, as far as they knew, they were to serve in their traditional role as cavalry, guarding the Norfolk coastline against invasion. The Pembroke and Glamorgan Yeomanry were billeted in various farms, homes and public houses at and around Heydon Hall and Haveringland Hall near Norwich. Here they were attached to the South Wales Mounted Brigade, 1st Mounted Division. This was a particularly beautiful part of England, and the yeomen enjoyed their time here, exploring the countryside on horseback, decked out in their impressive Yeomanry uniforms and regalia.

A local Pembrokeshire newspaper in September 1914 printed a small article on the local unit:

Lieutenant Colonel Owen Hird Spear Williams, Commanding Officer the Pembroke Yeomanry until his tragic death.

'The Pembroke Yeomanry is now split up into three Squadrons around Aylsham, Norfolk. The active service squadron is quartered in Heydon Hall, near Norwich. Horses on lines and men undercover in stable yard, with plenty of wheaten straw to sleep on. Food good and well cooked. Bread limited but plenty of capital biscuits. Weather good, men drilling.'

Bad luck was to hit the Pembroke Yeomanry just weeks after settling into their duties at Norfolk. Their Commanding Officer, Lieutenant Colonel Owen Hird Spear Williams TD, was killed after he fell out of his bedroom window on the morning of 9 December, while attempting to clear out a gutter. He was fifty-two years old, and was buried with full military honours in Llawhaden Churchyard in Pembrokeshire. (Another newspaper erroneously reported that Williams was killed while riding on the estate at Haveringland.) Promoted to take his place was a member of the west Wales gentry, Cecil John Herbert Spence-Jones. He had married Aline Margaret Colby in 1908, the elder daughter of Major John Vaughan Colby, JP DL, late 4th Battalion, Worcestershire Regiment, of Ffynone, Boncath, Pembrokeshire. The marriage cemented his position in the officer ranks of the Pembrokeshire Yeomanry; he later assumed the name of Spence-Colby.

Nevertheless, the military machine ground on, preparing the volunteers for life overseas. During the coming weeks of training the men were given their first batch of inoculations. Many of the men were taken ill after these jabs and were sent home to recover. John James John travelled by train back to St Clears, where he walked the two miles back to his home at Halfpenny Furze. Here he recuperated, before saying a swift farewell to his friends and family, leaving Laugharne for the very last time at the end of October 1914.

By the time John arrived back at Thetford, other recruits had moved there. John Lewis and William Coyens of Lamphey had enlisted at Carmarthen at the outbreak of war and, after attesting for overseas service, were posted as part of a draft of ninety-five men to replace a similar number who had refused service overseas. They spent their last night in Carmarthen in relative comfort at the Lammas Hotel, before entraining at Carmarthen for Norfolk. On their arrival, the men were issued with two blankets and billeted in a massive barn on the Haveringland estate.

Trooper Bert Douglas, of Barry, a member of A Squadron, Glamorgan Yeomanry, wrote a series of long letters to his parents describing camp life in Norfolk, many of which touched on the deep impression that the Welshmen made on the locals, who must have been engrossed by the various concerts and rugby matches which took place to help entertain the men. The prowess of C Squadron, Pembroke Yeomanry, in the singing stakes was outweighed by the prowess of the Glamorgan men on the rugby field, however: a prowess that would gain a reputation that preceded the 24th Welsh to France in 1918 where the battalion rugby team became the first team to beat the Welsh Guards.

While the original groups of yeomen were busying themselves in Norfolk, the 2nd/1st Pembroke Yeomanry was being raised in Carmarthen, and the 2/1st Glamorgan Yeomanry in Bridgend. These battalions were destined to take the place of the Active Service Squadrons on their eventual move to Egypt late in 1915. Recruiting officers for the home-service squadrons appealed for recruits: 'All strong healthy lads 5ft 3 and upwards who can ride are eligible.' These units were first based at Dorchester and then moved to Suffolk to join the 2nd/1st South Wales Mounted Brigade, which would take the place of the 1st/1st, which was to shortly leave for Egypt.

The Welsh yeomanry battalions were proving to be popular among young adventure-seeking men. Over the coming months men entrained to the barracks at Carmarthen from Yorkshire, Manchester and London, with the intention of serving in a distinguished mounted regiment. One such volunteer, a Jew from Manchester, was Lawrence Marks, the son of Louis and Jessie Marks of Cheetham Hill. His most memorable taste of Carmarthen

The impressive fascade of Heydon Hall, in Norfolk, a billet for many of the officers of the Pembroke and Glamorgan Yeomanry.

came in his first meal while billeted with an old lady in Lammas Street, when he was served a pie baked with pure lard: 'strictly non-kosher', as he later wrote in his memoirs.

From October 1914 onwards the Pembroke and Glamorgan Yeomanry trained, while also providing a garrison force around the Norfolk Coast, to help shield it from the possibility of invasion. Apart from Harwich and Felixstowe, which had batteries of modern guns, the rest of the Norfolk coastline was undefended. Although it was generally accepted by the government that any invasion would be held off by the might of the Royal Navy, it was nevertheless decided to set a second line of defence in case the Germans did manage to breach the naval defences and land. As a precaution, Essex, Norfolk and Suffolk was each defended by one Infantry brigade, one mounted Yeomanry brigade, a brigade of Royal Field Artillery and two battalions of cyclists. In addition to this force, Harwich Fort had six battalions of infantry. Because large stretches of the coast were unsuitable to landings in strength, these troops were concentrated in the most likely landing places: the North Norfolk coast between Cley and Sheringham, the open beaches south of Lowestoft and the stretch of coast between Walton on Naze and the mouth of the river Colne. A series of defence lines were planned to bar the advance on London from any landings in Norfolk or Essex. The London Defence Position was put into operation in 1915 on a line from Epping to the Thames, with an outer position at Brentwood and, later, a third line, running from Chelmsford to Maldon. In 1915 an armoured train was stationed in Norfolk based at North Walsham, ready to move at a moment's notice.

On the dawn of Christmas Day 1914, the South Wales Mounted Brigade, following news of an imminent German landing, was roused from its sleep to man the coastal defences. After a nervous day's wait, the men were stood down as it was realised that this was a false alarm. The members of the 2/1st Pembroke Yeomanry were to get a proper taste of a German assault the following year, though, when they were stationed at Lowestoft, guarding the North Sea port. During the morning of 25 April 1916 a German fleet had

Men of the Pembroke Yeomanry from the Lampeter area posing outside the Bell Inn at Cawston, with the Landlord, Alfred Thrower, and his daughter Annie.

positioned itself off-shore and began a heavy bombardment on the town. The main aim had been to support the Irish Easter Uprising, which it successfully carried out, causing damage to over 200 houses, before being driven off by the Royal Navy. The Pembroke Yeomanry aided in the rescue of people from collapsed houses and in stemming fires over the remainder of the day, helping to minimise the damage to the town and the disruption to an important fishing port.

Back at the HQ of the South Wales Mounted Brigade at Carmarthen, recruits continued to pour in. On 29 February 1915 a young Yorkshireman travelled by train to Carmarthen. Gerald Marston Owen had worked at a YMCA Camp at Scarborough and had keenly observed the soldiers of different regiments who frequented the hospitality of the camp, before making his mind up to join a cavalry unit. He chose the Pembroke Yeomanry and arriving at Carmarthen Station on a cold, blustery day was to have his first meeting with a Welshman:

'After a ten hours journey I arrived at this neat little Welsh market and agricultural town. On stepping out of the train my first question was to ask for the nearest way to the recruiting office. This I asked of an old porter who took my ticket. To my surprise he stared at me in dumb amazement, at the same time shaking his head and uttering some terrible oaths. What he said I never knew, but to hear him speak made me wonder whether I had already arrived in a foreign land. This was then my first encounter with the Welsh language and I shall never forget the impression it gave me on that dark, cold night of February. Everywhere people were chattering in this awful language. I have heard many since, but never one so terrible as this.'

His experience got better as he was led to his billets with an elderly woman and her teenage daughter and Gerald tasted the best of Welsh hospitality over the coming days. Carmarthen at that time was buzzing, and absolutely packed with soldiers and men wishing to join the colours. The town was the Headquarters of the South Wales Mounted Brigade, but was also home to the local Territorial battalion, the 4th Welsh. In October 1914 it also housed recruits for one of the new Service battalions of the Welsh Regiment, the 15th Welsh, or Carmarthen Pals. Camaraderie between the men of each unit abounded, but there was also friction in the air when it was discovered that the townspeople who were billeting troops got more for a Pembroke Yeoman that they did for one of the Welsh Regiment men. (17s 6d compared to 23s 7d – *The Welshman,* 16 April 1915).

During February, a court case involving the Pembroke Yeomanry was headline news. At Tenby, a local newspaper proprietor, Frank B. Mason published an article in *The Tenby Observer* on 20 January 1915, condemning the yeomanry for remaining on home service while the future of the Empire was at stake. A similar article the following week led to the prosecution, under the Defence of the Realm Act, of Mason and his editor. Three charges were brought against them:

'(1) That on January 20th, in the issue of the Tenby Observer of that date that the defendants made statements likely to prejudice the recruiting, training. discipline and administration of certain of His Majesty's forces, to wit, the Pembroke Yeomanry, and did thereby contravene Regulation 27 of the Defence of the Realm refutations:
(2) That on January 20th the defendants made similar statements with regard to His Majesty's army, and:
(3) That on the 27th January he made similar statements with regard to the Pembroke Yeomanry.'

Mason had alleged that the officers of the Pembroke Yeomanry were unwilling to go overseas and fight, and that they were falsely declaring their men as unfit for overseas

A group of Pembroke Yeomen, from the collection of W. J. Jenkins PIY.

service: serious and damaging allegations. However, Mason lost the case, and was heavily fined.

In Norfolk, the men of the South Wales Mounted Brigade were readying themselves for a possible move overseas. On 25 April 1915 the British, Australians, New Zealanders and French landed forces on the Gallipoli Peninsula, at the mouth of the Dardanelles Straits. A fresh front had been opened here to attempt to force the passage of the Dardanelles, with the aim of sending a Royal Navy force into the Black Sea to bombard Constantinople, and force Turkey out of the war. The Turks were Germany's ally, and had a strong influence in the Middle East, with the territory occupied by the old Ottoman Empire holding vast reserves of oil, essential to the Allied war effort. The Turkish forces were potentially powerful, ably commanded by German Officers, and so this was thought to be an easy way out of fighting a prolonged war with Turkey.

In fact this easy victory was not to materialise. The Turks had been forewarned of the invasion by a failed naval bombardment of the various forts dotted on the peninsula, and had moved troops into the area as a precaution. The landing forces of that first day failed to get more than a few hundred yards from their beaches, and the campaign was to bog down into the same stagnant warfare as had the fighting on the Western Front.

Second Lieutenant Elydyr Lewis, of Carmarthen.

As an attempt to break the stalemate, troops were diverted from the Western Front, to the disgust of Sir John French, the British Commander in Chief, and rumours spread amongst the yeomen of the possibility of their moving to the Mediterranean to reinforce the Garrison on Gallipoli. On 19 July 1915 the 53rd (Welsh) Division was sent to the Mediterranean. Amongst their units were the 4th and 5th Battalions of the Welsh Regiment, recruited in south and west Wales alongside the Pembroke and Glamorgan Yeomanry. A young officer of the 4th Welsh, Second Lieutenant Elydyr Lewis of Llanwrda, wrote home to his sister to inform her of his departure aboard the S.S. *Huntsend* on 19 July 1915. Among the men aboard *Huntsend* were friends and family of many of the Yeomanry and they were destined to cross paths in the future once more and fight together in the Holy Land.

Trooper John Evan Phillips, of Robeston Wathen, who drowned in Norfolk on 12 August 1915.

Throughout the summer of 1915 the South Wales Mounted Brigade remained in Norfolk. The officers and men posed for group photos, and became well known locally, attending church services on Sundays, and taking parts in local sports events. On 12 August a party of men of the Pembroke Yeomanry machine-gun section had the afternoon off, and went swimming at Mundesley. The tide began to ebb, and Private John Evan Phillips, of Robeston Wathen, got into difficulty. A friend, James James, swam to his aid, and tried to bring him ashore, but began getting into difficulty himself and let go of Phillips, who drowned, despite the additional efforts of Lieutenants Penn and De Rutzen, who had also waded out to try and rescue him. His body was recovered several days later, and he was brought home for burial at Robeston Wathen Churchyard.

During November 1915 the 1st Mounted Division became a dismounted formation. Now the men were essentially infantry and the majority were not to use their horses again. By this time it was obvious that the Gallipoli campaign was doomed to failure, and the prospect of the evacuation of the Peninsula had been decided. After a visit by Earl Kitchener to Gallipoli, he deemed the situation impossible, and so on 6 January 1916 the final phase of the evacuation of the troops began, and was complete within three days, with the loss of just two lives.

Trooper William Grove, Glamorgan Yeomanry. A survivor of the Porteynon Lifeboat disaster.

In the meantime, many of the yeomanry were given leave to return to Wales and visit their families. One of the men had a very interesting tale to tell when he returned. Private William Grove was a member of the Glamorgan Yeomanry, from Porteynon, a seaside village near Swansea, and returned home on leave at the end of December. On New Year's Day 1916, a great storm brewed up in the Bristol Channel and a steamer, *Dunvegan*, ran aground at Pennard. The Cox of the Porteynon lifeboat, *The Janet*, Billy Gibbs, struggled to find a crew, so Grove volunteered, as two of his uncles were already part of the crew. They boarded *The Janet*, and after the horse team had pulled the boat into the water, the crew rowed out into Porteynon Bay, past Oxwich Point. At around 1.30 pm a huge wave struck *The Janet*, capsizing her, and throwing her crew into the sea. After what must have seemed like an eternity, the mast snapped off *The Janet*, and she righted, allowing the crew to get back aboard, however two men were missing; 2nd coxswain William Eynon and lifeboatman George Harry. The stricken lifeboat then began a frantic search for the men, but capsized again, and in the effort to right the boat, Coxswain Gibbs was washed away. The survivors spent a terrible night huddled together in the helpless *Janet*, and on the following day managed to land at Porteynon. The three men are commemorated on a memorial in the village.

Chapter 3

The Middle East – Egypt and the Suez Canal

In August 1914 the British garrison troops in Egypt were the 2nd Devonshire, 1st Worcestershire, 2nd Northamptonshire, 2nd Gordon Highlanders, the 3rd Dragoon Guards, a battery of Royal Horse Artillery, a Mountain Battery and a Field Company of Royal Engineers. The situation on the Western Front required the recall as son as practicable of these troops; they were relieved on 27 September 1914 by the East Lancashire Division, Territorial Force. In October, Indian troops began to arrive.

Egypt, even after years of British administration, was still a province of the Ottoman Empire. The Khedive was actively pro-Turk, and when war was declared on Germany he went to Constantinople. Until Britain declared war on Turkey on 5 November, Germans could roam about Egypt at will and German ships could use its harbours. The aim of the British government was to suppress any rising that might break out and to defend Egypt from invasion, as it was imperative that the Suez Canal would be kept open, to allow vital access to the Indian Ocean and beyond. Egypt as a base for operations against the Turks was the last thing they contemplated.

Egypt was declared a protectorate on 18 December; the reigning Khedive, Abbas Hilmi, was deposed, and his uncle, Prince Hussein Kamel Pasha, was raised to the position with the title of Sultan. On the opposing side was the Turkish Army: Djemal Pasha had been appointed Commander-in-Chief in Syria and Palestine, and his plan was to invade and conquer Egypt. The operation was placed in the hands of Colonel Djemal Bey, who had the German General Kress von Kressenstein as his Chief of Staff.

The Germans and the Turks hoped to provoke an Arab rising against the British through their allies, the Sultan of Darfur and the Grand Senussi. The first serious enemy attempt was in January 1915, when the Turks tried to cross the Suez Canal. However from then until July 1916, when they again crossed the Sinai Desert, all of the British military operations consisted in the pursuit of a few tribesmen.

Some of the troops who were evacuated from Gallipoli at the end of the campaign were rested in Egypt before moving to the Western Front, in particular the Australians

The German General Friedrich Freiherr Kress von Kressenstein.

and New Zealanders (Anzacs), who sailed from Egypt to Marseilles, and took up positions in Flanders. Many more were to remain in Egypt, and so the Egyptian Expeditionary Force (EEF) was built up from March 1916 onwards to counter the threat of the Turkish backed Senussi tribesmen and to safeguard the Suez Canal, coming under the command of Sir Archibald Murray, who arrived in Egypt on 9 January 1916. Murray arrived to find that a defensive scheme for the Suez Canal was already in place, after the attempt by the Turks to capture it in January 1915. The area had quietened down after the centre of the fighting shifted to Gallipoli but, with Gallipoli evacuated, Egypt again became a potential crisis point.

Included in the plans for the EEF was the 1st Mounted Division, which had embarked by train from Norfolk for an unknown destination. Sergeant E. Howells Evans, of Aberdare, wrote:

'After a rush we left yesterday afternoon, and joined a special troop train. We have just left and we are eight in a compartment, Ben Moss amongst them. Where our next stop will be I don't know, but we are told it will be about 10.30 to-night. At Swindon a Canon treated us to bread, butter and buns, and at Exeter the Mayoress provided us with hot tea and buns. These were very acceptable. The Mayoress had about twelve women on the platform serving the things out. It was very good of them to be up at two in the morning in the pouring rain to look after our comfort. The boys sang to them, and gave them three rousing cheers on leaving, and we in out compartment have written to the Mayoress expressing our thanks on behalf of the boys of the various regiments. We arrived at the port this morning at about 4.30 am, and were immediately shown our quarters on the transport, after which we

The SS Arcadian*, the troopship that ferried the Yeomanry to Egypt.*

were put on shipping mules for the A.S.C. It was jolly hard work getting them on board, but it was huge fun and the methods adopted for the most stubborn ones aroused our admiration and amused us at the same time. Our transport ship is about 250 yards long.'

It was 4 March 1916. Men of the Division had embarked aboard the transport ship HMT *Arcadian*, bound for Alexandria. The ship was packed, and contained the full complement of men of the Pembroke and Glamorgan Yeomanry, as well as the Shropshire Yeomanry. Their journey was fraught with danger, with German submarines known to be operating in the waters of the Mediterranean, but the *Arcadian* safely reached port on 14 March 1916. (*Arcadian* in her pre-war days was a luxury liner, and was the ship on which Sir Robert Baden Powell fell in love with his future wife. *Arcadian* was later sunk by the German submarine UC74 on 17 April 1917 while bringing troops to Salonika. The UC74's captain was Wilhelm Marschall, who went on to take charge of the Battleship *Scharnhorst* in the Second World War.

An article published in the *Western Mail* of 22 March 1916 lists the following Officers of the 1st/1st Pembroke Yeomanry as being on active service overseas:

Lieut.-Colonel	C. J. H. Spence-Jones.
Majors	D. W. C. Davies-Evans.
	J. A. Higgon.
	L. Partridge.
Captains	J. W. Bishop.
	E. G. Jones.
	E. Lambton.
	J. B. H. Woodcock.
	J. H. L. Yorke.
Lieutenants	C. G. S. Barnes.
	T. C. Jones.
	F. S. Morgan.
	A. F. J. de Rutzen.
2nd Lieutenants	H. J. Barclay.
	G. A. Burge.
	J. F. A. Lewis.
	D. L. P. Morgan.
	S. H. E. G. Owen.
	L. W. Penn.
	L. D. C. Rose.
	G. A. S. Sheddon,
	C. H. Williams.
AdjutantCaptain	M. L. Hutchison.
Quartermaster	Lieut. G. M. Rumball.
Medical Officer	Captain C. D. Mathias, R.A.M.C.
Veterinary Officer	Captain H. L. Anthony, A.V.C.
Chaplain	Rev. R. Jenkyn Owen.

The Army List of 1915 named the officers of the Glamorgan Yeomanry:

Lieut.-Colonel	D. Venables-Llewellyn, C.L
Majors	G. T. Bruce
	O. R. Vivian, M.V.O.
	J. D. Nicholl
	C. F. T. Wyndham-Quin
	J. G. Moore-Gwyn
Captains	W. Cope
	E. Helme
	R. G. M. Prichard
Lieutenants	Sir F. C. R. Price
	G. S. N. Carne
	Hon. J. H. Bruce
	R. W. Lewis
	R. H. P. Miers
Second Lieutenants	J. J. B. Harvey
	O. Fisher
	C. L. Aylett-Branfill
	E. J. C. David
	P. Fisher
	G. R. P. Llewellyn
	R. C. Wilson
Adjutant	Captain A. G. L. Astley
Quarter Master	Lieutenant A. S. Barratt
Medical Officer	Captain R. J. R. C. Simons, R.A.M.C.
Chaplain	Rev. H. S. Nicholl, A.C.L.D.

Upon disembarkation, the sea weary troops marched to camp and some of the men settled down to write their first letters home from foreign soil. The *Arcadian* had also transported reinforcements bound for the 4th and 5th Welsh, who had been so badly damaged at Gallipoli that the units had been merged temporarily into the one battalion, the 4/5th Welsh. A delighted John James John bumped into two of his relatives who were part of this batch of recruits, as well as two old school friends from Llanddowror. In his first letter home to his uncle, Ben John, of Parsons Lays Lodge, Laugharne, John wrote of the chance meeting and a résumé of the letter was printed in the local newspaper, *The Welshman*:

'During the nine days and ten nights voyage he met onboard his uncle, Trooper W. Jenkins, late of Cross Inn, Also his cousin Trooper P. J. Saer, and Ptes Evan and John Hughes of Pantymenin, Llanddowror - now of the 4th Welsh. He says that they are encamped in a desert of sand with no sign of any village or town. The weather is so hot that they do nothing between the hours of 11 am and 4 pm. Still, we are all in the pink, and whilst not knowing what is in store for us in this far off country, we feel confident of doing our duty.'

Shipping in the Suez Canal.

Now safely encamped in Egypt, the 1st Mounted Division joined up with four other brigades of Yeomanry who had fought at Gallipoli: the Highland Mounted Brigade the South-Western Mounted Brigade, the Eastern Mounted Brigade and the South-Eastern Mounted Brigade. The strategic importance of Egypt lay in its location, guarding the vital Suez Canal and the north African oil fields, so Britain felt that it had no option but to make Egypt a protectorate; this is the role that these newly arrived yeomen now settled into.

Dudley Ward's book, *74th (Yeomanry) Division In Syria And France*, includes the following description, written by Napoleon, of the journey taken by French troops through the deserts in their campaign of 1798-1801 and gives a good idea of what was facing the Allies:

> 'The desert which separates Syria from Egypt extends from Gaza to Salhiya: it is seventy leagues (over 190 miles). Caravans march eighty hours to cross it. Gaza is one hundred leagues from Cairo (250 miles). The desert is divided into three parts: first from Salhiya to Qatia there are sixteen leagues of arid sand; one finds no shade, no water, and not a vestige of vegetation: the caravans march for twenty hours. The French troops covered the distance in two days, but three are necessary for the camels, wheeled vehicles and artillery. Near Qatia are moving sands, very tiring for transport. Qatia is an oasis: there were two wells of water, rather bitter, but, nevertheless, drinkable: there were about a thousand palm trees which could provide shade for four or five thousand men... It is a very exhausting and delicate operation to cross the desert in summer. First the heat of the sand; second, the lack of water; third, the lack of shade, are all capable of perishing an army, or of weakening it, or of discouraging it more than it is possible to imagine.
>
> 'Of all obstacles which can cover the frontiers of empires a desert, similar to this, is incontestably the greatest.'

A little over one hundred years later little had changed and these were the conditions that the yeomen would be operating in for the coming months, a far cry from the lush, green farmlands of south and west Wales.

The great dividing line in the Sinai Desert was the Suez Canal; Sir Archibald Murray divided the Canal into three zones of defence, under the command of Major-General

Map of the Sinai Desert (courtesy David John).

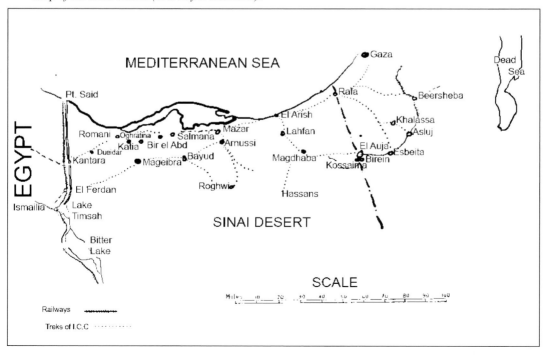

Alexander Wilson, with centres at Suez, Ismailia, and Qantara. The greatest threat here came from the Senussi tribesmen. Prior to 1906 the Senussi had been a relatively peaceful religious sect, who roamed the Sahara Desert, opposed to fanaticism. They had then become involved in resistance to the French occupation. In 1911 the Italians invaded Libya, occupying the coast, while the Senussi maintained resistance inland and in Cyrenaica. During this period they generally maintained friendly relations with the British in Egypt.

The outbreak of war raised the tension. The Turks made strenuous efforts to persuade the Senussi to attack British occupied Egypt from the west. In the summer of 1915 Turkish envoys, including Nuri Bey, the half brother of Enver Pasha, and Jaafar Pasha, a Baghdadi Arab serving in the Turkish Army, managed to gain influence over the Grand Senussi, Sayed Ahmed, and convinced him to begin hostilities against the British with Turkish support. The original plan was for a three pronged attack on the British forces stationed here. The Senussi would mount attacks along the narrow strip of fertile land on the Egyptian coast, heading towards Alexandria, and on the band of oases one hundred miles west of the Nile. At the same time the Emir of Darfur would launch an attack on the Sudan. In the event the three campaigns were fought separately and were defeated in turn.

The coastal campaign began first, in November 1915. The British withdrew from Sollum and Sidi Barrani and concentrated their forces around Mersa Matruh. The Western Frontier Force, under Major General W. E. Peyton, was created from the garrison of Egypt, consisting of one cavalry and one infantry brigade, supported by a battery of horse artillery. They were outnumbered by the Senussi, who had 5,000 men trained to fight as infantry, supported by a larger number of irregular troops and with a small number of Turkish

The Senussi going to war.

Prince Feisal, with T. H. Lawrence (Lawrence of Arabia) behind his left shoulder.

artillery and machine guns. Despite their advantage in numbers, the Senussi were defeated in encounters at Wadi Senba (11-13 December 1915), Wadi Majid (25 December 1915) and Halazin (23 January 1916).

The Senussi were finally defeated at Agagia (26 February 1916), on the coast close to Sollum. The Western Frontier Force had been reinforced by the South African Brigade, under Brigadier General H. T. Lukin. A column under his command was sent west to recapture Sollum, encountering and defeating the Senussi on their way west. Jaafar Pasha was captured during the battle, Sollum was reoccupied on 14 March 1916 by a mixed force of South African and Yeomanry troops. Jaafar was kept in captivity in Egypt, but later in the war volunteered to join the forces under Emir Feisal, became commander of the Arab regulars during the revolt and then served as Minister of War and Prime Minister of Iraq under the then King Feisal. Feisal was famously aided in his campaign by a renowned army officer, Thomas Edward Lawrence, better known as *Lawrence of Arabia*, or *El Aurens*, who was the British liaison officer serving with Feisal's Arab army. However, small bands of Senussi tribesmen continued their fight. A fresh campaign against the oases started in February 1916. Sayyid Ahmed occupied the oases at Baharia, Farafra, Dakhla and Kharge, and forced the British to keep a sizable garrison in Upper Egypt while a mobile force was organised to push him back.

On 20 March 1916 the South Wales Mounted Brigade became part of the 4th Dismounted Brigade and was attached to the Western Frontier Force. After a short stay at Wardan, on the banks of the Nile, it moved to the Wadi El Natrun, west of the Nile Delta, and was tasked with guarding the coastal strip, the gateway to Alexandria and to the Nile Delta, an area known as the Baharia front. The role of these newly arrived troops was a simple peace keeping one for the time being, and as garrison troops on the Suez Canal Defences.

The loss of the first officer of the Pembroke Yeomanry on active service occurred on 28 March 1916, when Captain Edward Lambton, a member of a well known Pembrokeshire family, died in hospital in Cairo. He was born on 5 February 1877, the son of Lieutenant Colonel Francis William Lambton, of Brownslade, Pembrokeshire, late Scots Guards, and Lady Victoria Alexandrina Elizabeth, the eldest daughter of John Frederick Campbell, second Earl of Cawdor. He was educated

Captain Edward Lambton, Pembroke Yeomanry. Died in Cairo on 28 March 1916.

at Wellington College and Cooper's Hill, prior to taking up a post as Director of Public Works for the Egyptian government in Cairo. Edward trained with an Egyptian cavalry regiment prior to the war. He returned to England, where he became a captain with the Pembroke Yeomanry. Two of his elder brothers were killed in South Africa during the Boer War.

The distribution of troops administered on the Suez Canal Defences by April 1916, temporarily under the command of the 53rd (Welsh) Division HQ, was:

ALAMEIN	1st Welsh Field Coy. Royal Engineers (Detach.).
	53rd Division Signal Coy. R.E. (Detach.).
MOGHARA	1st Denbighshire Yeomanry.
ABBASSIAH.Q.	53rd Division and 53rd Signal Company.
WADI EL NATRUN	158th Brigade (less Transport Details).
	1st Welsh Fid. Coy. R.E. (Detach.).
	3rd Welsh Field Ambulance (Section).
	53rd Division Train (Detach.).
BENI SALAMA	53rd Divisional Artillery (Less one Battery.).
	Details 53rd Division R.E.
	159th Brigade.
	Transport Details 158th Brigade.
	1st Pembroke Yeomanry.
	1st Montgomery Yeomanry.
	2nd Welsh Field Ambulance.
	3rd Welsh Field Ambulance (less one Section)
	53rd Division Casualty Clearing Station.
	53rd Division Train Details and Bakery.
	53rd Division Mobile Veterinary Sect.
FAIYUM	160th Brigade.

	1st Welsh Field Ambulance.
	53rd Division Sanitary Sect. (less Detachment)
	2/1st Welsh Field Coy. R.E.
	53rd Division Train Details.
	53rd Division Cyclist Coy.
MINIA	4th Dismounted Brigade.
	4th Glamorganshire Battery Royal Field Artillery
SOHAG	2/1st Cheshire Field Coy. R.E.
SUEZ	53rd Divisional Train.

In the meantime, the British were forming a regiment of mounted infantry. Members of the Australian Light Horse, which had been badly handled and severely damaged during a futile charge across open ground at the action on the Nek in Gallipoli on 7 August 1915, had been moved to Egypt after the evacuation, and had successfully taken part in mounted campaigns against the Senussi. With the extra horsemen now available to them, due to the arrival of the Yeomanry Brigades, the Imperial Camel Corps was established in January 1916, with a core of six companies of Australian Light Horsemen from New South Wales. Formed alongside them were six British companies, all drawn from the yeomanry brigades. New Zealand personnel formed two additional companies. Later in the campaign motorised units were also formed, using men from the Imperial Camel Corps, to which a detachment of Pembroke Yeomanry and one of Glamorgan Yeomanry were attached. During July a detachment of thirty men under Lieutenant De Rutzen left the Pembroke Yeomanry to join the 6th Company, Imperial Camel Corps. With them went the Regimental Signal Officer, Lieutenant F. S. Morgan, to become Brigade Signal Officer to the Imperial Camel Brigade.

The war seemed a distant thought for some members of the yeomanry who were struggling to deal with life in Egypt. On 4 April 1916, a Pembroke yeoman wrote to the *Llanelly Star*:

'Sir, On behalf of the Llanelly boys now with the Pembroke Yeomanry forming part of the Egyptian Expeditionary Force, it is with much pleasure that I write to give our friends at home some idea of how matters are progressing with us in this part of the world. We have been here for some time, and all we see is sand, sand, sand. There are a few canteens in our locality but things are twice as dear as they are at home. The pay we receive, I can assure you, does not last very long, amounting as it does (if we make an allotment, and most of us do) to only 5d a day. By about Tuesday in each week, therefore, we have very little left and are often without even a Woodbine to smoke. We shall be very pleased if you will publish in the "Star" that we will be very grateful for any comforts from the public in Llanelly. The friends at home have been very kind to the boys in many places, and we would much appreciate anything they would do for us in the same way. I am, etc., 1st Troop, B. Squadron, R.D.J. Pembroke Yeomanry, Egyptian Exp. Force, April 4th, 1916.'

The loss of the first officer of the Glamorgan Yeomanry on active service occurred soon afterwards: Capel Lisle Aylett Branfill was born on 29 August 1884, the son of Capel Aylett

Branfill and Gwladys Gwendoline Branfill (née Miers), of The Plas, Crickhowell. He lived at Ynistawe, Clydach, with his wife prior to the war. He was initially commissioned into the Glamorgan Yeomanry on 19 April 1909 and by the time the regiment landed in Egypt had been promoted captain. He took ill due to the adverse desert conditions and succumbed to pneumonia in hospital at Cairo on 11 May 1916, aged 31. He is buried in Cairo War Memorial Cemetery. Capel's short life was full of tragedy. His wife, Susannah Hamilton Williams, was so distressed at the thought of him going to the front, that she drowned herself and their infant child, Gwendoline, in a pool near her parent's home at Upton upon Severn on 24 January 1915.

Captain Capel Lisle Aylett-Branfill, Glamorgan Yeomanry. Died in Egypt on 11 May 1916.

The main body of the Pembroke and Glamorgan Yeomanry were responsible for patrolling huge swathes of desert, either through the manning of outposts and blockhouses, or by the use of converted Roll Royce armoured cars. Although this routine was relatively safe, it was difficult and dangerous work, in a climate which bred ideal conditions for sickness. By night the men froze, by day their blood almost boiled in the arid heat, and then they had to contend with sand, dust and the myriad flies. On top of all these unpleasantries, the Turks were building up a powerful force in the Middle East, which by mid 1916 had reached a strength of forty-three divisions, all in all over 650,000 men. On 19 July reconnaissance aircraft from the Royal Flying Corps discovered that a large body of the enemy had moved from El Arish; on the morning of the 20th cavalry patrols reported that Oghratina was held by strong forces of the enemy, who were entrenching.

The Turkish 3rd Division, a strong formation, commanded and partly manned by Germans which had Austrian heavy artillery units attached, advanced under the command of Kress von Kressenstein. On the night of 2 July he had pushed his line forward to Sabkhet el Amya - Abu Darem; and on 2 August, he made a strong reconnaissance towards El Rabah – Qatia - Bir el Hamisah. His troops were driven back after several sharp encounters.

Until now, Sir Archibald Murray had been uncertain as to whether the enemy would make the first move, but on 3 August von Kressenstein advanced his line again to a semi-circle from the immediate west of Hill 110, past the high ground east and south-east of Qatia, to the high ground north-west of Bir el Hamisah. Both in order to contain this Turkish threat and also in order to change their own position from the defensive to the offensive, throughout 1916 the British drove out further outposts in the direction of Qatia, following up this drive with the building of a standard gauge railway and a line of blockhouses.

The Aberdare Leader published a letter from one of the Glamorgan yeomen on 24 June 1916:

'Sir, A few of the local lads in the 1/1 Glamorgan Yeomanry, Egyptian Expeditionary Force, have asked me to write you a few lines to let our numerous friends know how we are faring. After remaining so long on the East Coast we are at last actually on service, and although we have not seen action we find that soldiering abroad is far different to that at home. It is terribly hot, and considering that when we left England it was very cold, we have all stuck it very well, and have not a man in hospital with any serious illness. For a time we were in the same camp as the 5th Welsh. We are out in the desert this last month, right away from any town. We have no amusements of any sort except what we try and make ourselves.

'I wonder if any friend could rummage out a few old [oddly censored out!]. It would be a boon to us, and at night we could sit and sing to our hearts' content. There are about 20 of us (Aberdare boys) here, among them Sid and Charlie Pontin, Bert Davies (G.W.R. parcels), Percy Morgan (tailor), and Sergeant Jack Allen (Town Brewery). It may interest you to know that I met Lieut. Mostyn George some time ago at Alexandria, and had a long chat with him. He looks exceptionally well, and has grown into quite a big fellow. I also came across Harry Coates (K.S.L.I.). Although he joined our ship at Malta I did not see him until we had disembarked. Thanking you for allowing me valuable space, and hoping that we will receive the [censored].

'Yours, etc. (for the boys), 1197 Corporal Ben Moss, D Squadron, 1/1 Glamorgan Yeomanry, E.E.F. P.S. Our Squadron D are nicknamed the "Dare Devils". Why, I will leave your readers to guess.'

Officers of the yeomanry were in the main well trained and highly educated. As a result there was much movement of officers to other units. During June 1916 Captain John Arthur Higgon left the Pembroke Yeomanry to join the 32nd Battalion AIF prior to its move to France, being promoted to become second in command of the battalion. He was killed in action during the futile Battle of Fromelles on 20 July 1916, while commanding the battalion during its attack on the Sugarloaf Salient.

The first major contact with the Turks was on 4 August 1916, when a large Turkish force under von Kressenstein attacked towards Romani, a strategically important railhead and oasis, eighteen miles from Qantara. The

Major John Arthur Higgon, Pembroke Yeomanry. Killed in action at Fromelles whilst serving with the 32nd Battalion AIF.

Some of the Imperial Camel Corps members of the Pembroke Yeomanry in Egypt.

Turks had prepared successive lines of defence as they moved towards Romani. Sir Archibald Murray's plan was to make a stand at a mound called Katib Gannit, and ordered the 1st and 2nd Light Horse Brigades, under General Chauvel, to cover the position between Katib Gannit and Hod el Enna, on the edge of an area of sand dunes that cropped up along the edge of the flat desert.

The Battle of Romani commenced at 3.30 am on 4 August, when the Turks attacked this position. Murray's troops counter-attacked them in flank from Dueidar and the Canal Defences, whilst a mobile column swung behind, catching the Turks in the rear and cutting the attacking troops off from the main Turkish forces. Soon after 5.00 am four German aircraft attacked Romani Camp, dropping around thirty bombs. By the end of the day, around 4,000 Turkish troops had been taken prisoner, out of a total of 18,000, but von Kressenstein had managed to escape, falling back on the successive lines he had prepared. This first engagement marked the last enemy attempt to advance on the Suez Canal.

The only Yeomanry element involved at Romani was the Imperial Camel Corps; one of the few British casualties suffered was a Pembroke Yeomanry officer, Baron Alan De Rutzen, who was killed on 7 August 1916. His obituary was published in *The Sphere*:

> 'Lieutenant Alan Frederick James, Baron De Rutzen, son of the late Sir Albert de Rutzen, the famous Metropolitan Magistrate at Bow Street, was born in 1876. He was educated at Eton and became a member of the Stock Exchange. He succeeded his uncle as Baron de Rutzen in 1915. At the outbreak of the war he joined the Pembroke Yeomanry, being gazetted in August 1914, and went with them to Egypt in March 1916. Whilst there, he volunteered for and became attached to the Imperial Camel Corps, with which he was serving at the time of his death. He fell leading a company of the Camel Corps against the Turks near Qatia.'

Lieutenant Alan Frederick James, Baron De Rutzen.

The following extract, testifying to his great ability as an officer and leader of men, is from a letter of an officer of the Camel Corps to Lieutenant Colonel Spence-Jones:

> 'You will probably have heard, before this reaches you, that Baron de Rutzen was killed yesterday. He was in command of this company and the amount of confidence he put into his men helped considerably towards holding a very tight corner. A brave man and a real topper in the field and out of it. His men simply adored him, as did all his brother officers.'

Baron de Rutzen had travelled extensively. He was greatly interested in horses, hunting and agriculture, and was a keen fisherman. He married, in 1908, Eleanor Etna Audley, the only child of Captain Pelham Thursby Pelham, of Abermarlais Park, Carmarthenshire, and Ridgeway, Pembrokeshire.

News of the award of the Victoria Cross to a former member of the Pembroke Yeomanry also reached Egypt during September. Major Stewart Loudon Shand was the son of John Loudon Shand, of Dulwich, London. He had served with the Pembroke Yeomanry during the Boer War. On 12 December 1915 he became second in command of the 10th Battalion, Yorkshire Regiment. His award of the Victoria Cross was published in the *London Gazette* of 8 September 1916:

'For most conspicuous bravery. When his company attempted to climb over the parapet to attack the enemy's trenches, they were met by very fierce machine gun fire, which temporarily stopped their progress. Major Loudoun-Shand immediately leapt on the parapet, helped the men over it, and encouraged them in every way until he fell mortally wounded. Even then he insisted on being propped up in the trench, and went on encouraging the non-commissioned officers and men until he died.'

He was killed during the opening assault on the Somme on 1 July 1916 and is buried in Norfolk Cemetery, Bécordel-Bécourt.

In Egypt, the British line had advanced further still after the withdrawal of the Turks, and the railway line extended further in the direction of El Arish in preparation for the following year's offensive. Apart from minor skirmishes against small bands of Senussi during the remainder of the summer, there does not seem to have been a lot to report. There were comings and goings of officers from both regiments; notable in 1916 was the departure of Major Delmé Davies Evans when, on 19 September, he left the regiment behind to head for France, after being given command of the 5th Battalion, Lincolnshire Regiment. Delmé went on to forge a well earned reputation as a good battalion commander, having been a popular and efficient commander of C Squadron, the Cardiganshire detachment of the Pembroke Yeomanry, for many years.

Lieutenant Colonel Delme William Campbell Davies-Evans.

John James John wrote another letter home to his Uncle Ben during the summer of 1916. He spoke in it of meeting the Australian troops for the first time and had briefly managed to meet up with his brother David, who was about to move to the Somme, to take part in the assault on Pozières Ridge with the 1st Australian Division. The Australians were a breath of fresh air in the British army. Officers had to earn respect in their eyes, and routine discipline was treated rather informally. Their spirit and joviality went down well with the young men of the Pembroke and Glamorgan Yeomanry, and great friendships were formed.

A further letter from John to his Uncle Ben John, which was published some months later, in *The Welshman* of 22 September 1916, read:

'Dear Uncle Ben, just a few lines to let you know that I am still in the land of the living, and very much alive too. I am in the best of health and perfectly happy doing my bit. I suppose that you must have been busy at the hay lately, and hope that the harvest is now over. I learn that you had good weather there for it, and that some were falling in the fields through the heat. Well old chap, if they were out here I expect they would fall and never get up again, it being so warm here! We are however getting used to it and are thoroughly enjoying ourselves. Please write soon with all the news from the old home and district, which will be very welcome in this far off country. Give my kind regards to all old friends, and especially to old 'Llwynog'. I will conclude this time with best wishes,
Your affectionate nephew, Jack.

By this time John had not yet heard the news of his brother's death on the Somme, during the final stages of the battle of Pozières on 18 August 1916. David was buried at Mouquet Farm Cemetery after the fighting to capture the fortified complex was over, but his grave was later lost and he is today commemorated on the Villers-Brettoneaux Memorial. John was not to find out about his brother's death until the spring of 1917, after an enquiry had been held on the disappearance of the four man patrol that David was leading.

In a sense, this must have felt like a phoney war for many of the troops on the ground, the majority of whom had, as yet, seen no sign of the enemy. It was exciting for the men to be stationed in such an exotic part of the world, and the feeling of bathing in the warm waters of the Mediterranean while off duty must have invoked a feeling of being on holiday.

The main obstacle for the forthcoming offensive was the supply of fresh water for the troops, camels and horses, but by November 1916 this, too, had reached the front, with a newly laid pipeline supplying water from the sweet-water canal. This pipeline was increased again as the front was pushed further east, until it reached Bir el Abd. West of

Swimming in the Mediterranean.

Natives pipeline laying; they were also used to construct roads and railways.

Bir el Abd there had been water for horses, mules, and camels, but to the east there were few wells, and they were widely separated. A desert railway was also being constructed by units of the Royal Engineers who utilised large numbers of native labourers. This railway and the water pipeline would prove vital for the success of the planned operations in Palestine.

At the end of November Sir Archibald Murray wrote in his despatches:

> 'Every tactical preparation for the offensive had been made, naval co-operation planned, and arrangements made for the landing of stores and construction pipes as soon as El Arish was in my possession. But the difficulty of water supply, even with my advanced railhead, was immense. The enemy was so disposed as to cover all available water in the neighbourhood of El Arish and Masaid. Between his position and ours and south of his position, no water could be found.
>
> 'If, therefore, he should be able to force us to spend two days in the operation of driving him from his position, it would be necessary to carry forward very large quantities of water on camels for the men and animals of the formations engaged. This entailed the establishment of a very large reserve of water at railhead, and the preparation of elaborate arrangements for the forwarding and distributing of water.
>
> 'The water supply for the striking force was not adequately secured until the 20th December.'

In the meantime the yeomen were still carrying out the same routine of manning outposts, detachments, route marches and regimental drill. During this time there were several detachments on a multitude of courses. One Squadron was always on outpost duty at El Garr, and there were detachments to Bir Victoria, Khataba, Sidi Bishr, Sidi Gobbu and Alexandria. There were also many transfers out to the Camel Corps and the Machine Gun Corps during this period, which also saw an end to the Senussi threat, and thus the freeing up of over 30,000 troops. The defeat of the Senussi in Egypt fatally undermined Sayyid Ahmed's position; it was his being forced out of power in favour of his nephew, Sayyid Mohammed el Idris, who had opposed the campaign, which led to the end of the Senussi threat. He went into exile in Constantinople. Idris would soon be recognised by the British and Italians as Emir of Cyrenaica, and would eventually become King Idris I of Libya.

Conditions were still comfortable for many of the officers. An officer in the 53rd (Welsh) Division wrote:

'From Qantara we went occasionally to Port Said for the day. As we journeyed home the sun was setting. In the foreground was just the huge expanse of lake, scrub and salt pans. One laughs at the gold, sapphire and ruby idea, but I tell you the colours were deeper and beyond description. Yellow and orange sky, silver and blue water, green and grey scrub. Then, as the light changes, flame coloured sky, a silver band of water in the distance, a great tract of purple scrub, and the nearer expanses of water partly pink and gold reflections, and partly Cambridge blue.

'The hospitable French Club at Ismailia! Ismailia itself is a perfect little French township, with appropriate two storied houses, plainly but tastefully built, tree shaded, with deep verandas over which climbed innumerable plants. Bougainvillea, hibiscus and roses splash the gardens with rich colours. Through the trees is a glimpse of the Lake Timsah, a deep blue bounded by blazing golden sand. On moonlit nights, as one dined at the Club, or the Café Beige, the trees were silhouetted in filigree against the sky, sweet scents came stealing over from the gardens, and peace and content drove away the troubles of the moment.

'At Qantara, the town of tents, huts and dumps, bathing in the Canal and riding along its banks were the chief antidotes to care. Passengers on passing liners used to throw tins of cigarettes to the men in the water below.

'One curious duty was the keeping of the "swept track". This was a broad track in the sand along the canal bank, and was produced by dragging a very wide brush of branches by mules up and down to meet our next door neighbour. This was done each evening, and each morning a patrol proceeded along it to see if it had been crossed during the night by nefarious feet. The authorities were afraid that a very small enemy patrol might get through with camels and a mine and drop it in the Canal.'

With this threat removed, the troops guarding the western front of the MEF were now free to reinforce the eastern front, to counter the growing threat of the Turks. At the start of the new year of 1917, the three Dismounted Brigades on the western front began to move east. The 2nd Dismounted Brigade was at Moascar by 5 January, El Ferdan on the 15th, Qantara on 5 March, and El Arish (by rail) on the 6th. The Lovat Scouts dropped out of this brigade in August 1916 and were replaced by the Ayr and Lanarkshire Yeomanry Regiments in January 1917. The brigade was renamed 229 Infantry Brigade. The 3rd Dismounted Brigade went to Sidi Bishr on 2 April and to Deir el Belah on the 9th. It was renamed 230 Infantry Brigade. The 4th Dismounted Brigade moved to Assiut on 1 January

Officers Mess of the 24th Welsh, in the Managers House of the Salt and Soda Company.

1917, Zeitoun on 1 March, Helmia on 1 April, and Khan Yunus on the 10th, and became 231 Infantry Brigade which, under Brigadier General Philip Chetwode, was attached to XX Corps. Part of the new 231 Brigade were the Pembroke and Glamorgan Yeomanry Regiments, which had been merged to form a new battalion, the 24th, of the Welsh Regiment. These three new infantry brigades became part of a newly formed 74th (Yeomanry) Division, with their divisional emblem, the broken spur, to mark the previous cavalry role of the Yeomanry. This emblem was worn as an embroidered cloth patch on the right upper arm of the service tunic, and also on, for example, divisional vehicles.

This new division joined a powerful force under the command of Sir Archibald Murray, which comprised the 52nd, 53rd, and 54th Divisions, the New Zealand and Australian Mounted Division, the Imperial Mounted Division, and the Imperial Camel Corps on the Syrian Front. He organised this force into the Desert Column, under Sir Philip Chetwode, and the Eastern Force, under Sir Charles Dobell. The 53rd Division was a Welsh Territorial division; and among its infantry units were the 4th Welsh from Carmarthenshire, and the 5th Welsh from Glamorgan. The former Yeomanry men were to be fighting alongside their South Welsh compatriots at last. By the time of this merger, the two Yeomanry Regiments had lost sixteen men dead between them: the Pembroke Yeomanry fourteen of these, and the Glamorgan Yeomanry two, all of whom had succumbed to sickness or accidental death bar three: Private Harry Brown, of the Pembroke Yeomanry, had been posted to France with the 13th Welsh, and was killed at Boesinghe (Belgium). Private William James Collins was posted

An unidentified soldier of the 74th (Yeomanry) Division. Note his broken spur divisional shoulder patch.

from the Glamorgan Yeomanry to the 10th Royal Welsh Fusiliers, and died of wounds suffered at Boesinghe. Both served with the 38th (Welsh) Division, and fought at Mametz Wood during July 1916.

The make-up of this new 74th (Yeomanry) Division was as follows, under the command of Major General E. S. Girdwood, CB, late Scottish Rifles:

229 Infantry Brigade
Commanded by Brigadier General B. Hoare, DSO, late 4th Hussars.
16th Bn. Devonshire Regt. (Royal West Devon and Royal North Devon Yeomanry).
12th Bn. Somerset Light Infantry (West Somerset Yeomanry).
14th Black Watch (Fife and Forfar Yeomanry).
12th Bn. Royal Scots Fusiliers (Ayr and Lanark Yeomanry).
4th Machine Gun Company and 229th Light Trench Mortar Battery.

230 Infantry Brigade
Commanded by Brigadier General A. J. McNeil, DSO, Lovat Scouts.
10th Bn. The Buffs (Royal East Kent and West Kent Yeomanry).
16th Bn. Royal Sussex (Sussex Yeomanry).
15th Bn. Suffolk (Suffolk Yeomanry).
12th Bn. Norfolk (Norfolk Yeomanry).
209th Machine Gun Company and 230th Light Trench Mortar Battery.

231 Infantry Brigade
Commanded by Brigadier General B. A. Herbert, Somerset Light Infantry.
10th Bn. King's Shropshire Light Infantry (Shropshire and Cheshire Yeomanry).
24th Bn. Royal Welsh Fusiliers (Denbighshire Yeomanry).
25th Bn. Royal Welsh Fusiliers (Montgomeryshire and Welsh Horse Yeomanry).
24th Bn. Welsh Regiment (Pembroke and Glamorgan Yeomanry).
210th Machine Gun Company and 231st Light Trench Mortar Battery.

Royal Artillery
Commanded by Brigadier General L. J. Hext, CMG.
117th Brigade R.F.A. (A, B, 366th and D Batteries).
44th Brigade R.F.A. (340th, 382nd, 425th, and D Batteries).
268th Brigade R.F.A.
X74 and Y74 Medium Trench Mortar Batteries.
74th Ammunition Column.

Royal Engineers
Commanded by Lieutenant Colonel R.P.T. Hawksley CMG, DSO.
No. 5 (Royal Monmouth) Field Company.
No. 5 (Royal Anglesea) Field Company.
439th (Cheshire) Field Company.
74th Divisional Signal Company.

Army Service Corps
Commanded by Lieutenant Colonel J.G. Needham.
447th, 448th, 449th, 450th Companies A.S.C.

Divisional Troops
261st Machine Gun Company, 74th Employment Company, 69th Mobile Veterinary Section, A Squadron, 2nd County of London (Westminster Dragoons) Yeomanry. This squadron was moved to act as the Corps Cavalry Regiment on 23 August 1917.

Chapter 4

The First Battle of Gaza

he new battalion, the 24th (Pembroke and Glamorgan Yeomanry) Battalion, Welsh Regiment, was officered by a mixture of Pembroke and Glamorgan Yeomanry, but the Pembroke Yeomanry held the upper hand. The Commanding Officer was Lieutenant Colonel C. J. H. Spence-Jones of the Pembroke Yeomanry, with Lieutenant Colonel G. T. Bruce of the Glamorgan Yeomanry his understudy, due to seniority. The remaining officer staff were a mixture from the two units, with the Medical Officer being Lieutenant C. D. Mathias, the Chaplain, Reverend H. S. Nicholl, and three company commanders, J. B. H. Woodcock, J. W. Bishop and J. H. L. Yorke, and all of the Company sergeant majors being Pembroke men. The men themselves were intermingled, creating a truly homogenous unit.

This is how the new battalion was described in the *History of the Welsh Regiment*, by T. O. Marden:

'A word must now be said about the 24th Welsh. This Battalion was formed from the dismounted Pembrokeshire Yeomanry and Glamorgan Yeomanry, and brigaded in January, 1917, with the 24th R.W.F. (Denbighshire Yeomanry), 25th R.W.F. (Montgomeryshire Yeomanry and Welsh Horse), and 10th K.S.L.I. (Shropshire and Cheshire Yeomanry) in the 231st Brigade of the 74th Division, under the command of Major-General E. S. Girdwood. The whole Division was composed of men of superior education and very well officered. The 24th Welsh were commanded by Lieutenant-Colonel J. Spence-Jones, Pembrokeshire Yeomanry, and though they bore the territorial title of "Welsh," drew their reinforcements from Yeomanry sources and not from the Reserve Battalions of the Welsh Regiment.'

The first ever entry in the new battalion's war diary, entered on 4 January 1917, was basic in the extreme and simply reads: 'Two farrier sergeants proceeded to yeomanry base Alexandria.'

On the following day a party of men from the battalion relieved troops from the blockhouses, thus starting life together for the first time as a battalion of the Welsh Regiment.

The third entry in the battalion War Diary mentions the death of Private Robert Scott, the son of Robert and Mary Scott, of Lazenby, Cumberland, and the husband of Amy Scott, of Burry Port, who had been wounded whilst attached to the 6th Company, Imperial Camel Corps. He died in the 3rd Australian Light Horse Casualty Clearing Station on 6 January, and is buried in Qantara.

A lot of shuffling of personnel was still going on throughout the first months of the

Part of a tented camp of the 74th (Yeomanry) Division. (Shropshire Archives)

The massive base camp at Kantara.

battalion's existence. Reinforcements arrived in dribs and drabs, while several NCOs were commissioned. The battalion came in existence officially at midday on 2 February 1917, according to a note in the war diary, and remained at Shousha for most of the month, preparing to join the remainder of the brigade at Zeitoun. An advanced party of officers and NCOs from the 24th Welsh left for Zeitoun on 18 February. Four days later, notification of the award of the Distinguished Service Order to Major Llewelyn Partridge was received. The award, gazetted on 26 March 1917, read:

'For conspicuous gallantry and devotion to duty. He displayed great judgment and skill in the leadership of his three light patrols, and showed inexhaustible resource in overcoming the most serious physical obstacles. Later, in action he proved himself a dashing and competent leader.'

On 27 February the battalion marched to Samalut station, and entrained at midnight for Zeitoun. The first three weeks of March were spent on the rifle range, and carrying out route marches in the desert, with the only item of note being the trial by court martial of Private Philip Rees Beynon for theft, and the awarding of forty days Field Punishment No. 2. Beynon was later killed at the Third Battle of Gaza, on 8 November 1917.

At the beginning of March Lieutenant General Chetwode, commanding the Desert Mounted Corps, had his headquarters at Sheikh Zowaiid and his troops were covering the construction of the railway along the coast to Rafah. Sir Charles Dobell had the Eastern Force in the neighbourhood of El Arish. By the middle of the month, the railway and pipeline had reached Rafah, and Sir Archibald Murray decided that the time had come to strike a blow at the Turks, who had withdrawn to a strong defensive line running from Gaza on the coast to Beersheba, thirty miles inland, securing the only reliable water supplies.

Palestine has a series of four geographical parallel features. Between the sea and the Arabian Desert lies a long maritime plain, a central range of mountains, the Jordan Valley and the eastern range of mountains. There is a break in the central range, where the Plain of Esdraelon connects the maritime plain with the Jordan Valley. The Turks had their left flank on Beersheba at the foot of the central range and on the edge of the desert, while Murray's troops were on the coast, with their lines of communication running back through the Province of Sinai along the coastal route. He decided that an attack along the coast towards Gaza was the safest proposition, as lines of communication would be more easily protected along the coast and water would be more readily available. Murray re-formed the Desert Column, which comprised the Australian and New Zealand Mounted Division, the Imperial Mounted Division and the 53rd Welsh Division. With his other two infantry divisions, the 52nd and 54th, in support, the stage was set for the First Battle of Gaza, the objects of which were: to seize the line of the Wadi Ghuzze and cover the advance of the railway; to prevent the enemy from retiring without a fight; and to capture Gaza by a *coup de main*, and cut off its garrison.

On 24 March the 24th Welsh crossed the Suez Canal to Qantara. The 74th Division would not be involved in this first stage of the campaign, however the following abbreviated account is necessary to give some understanding of the effect on the whole.

During the night of 25-26th March, Dobell's troops moved into position in readiness for the battle; two mounted divisions and the 53rd Division moved to Deir el Belah, the

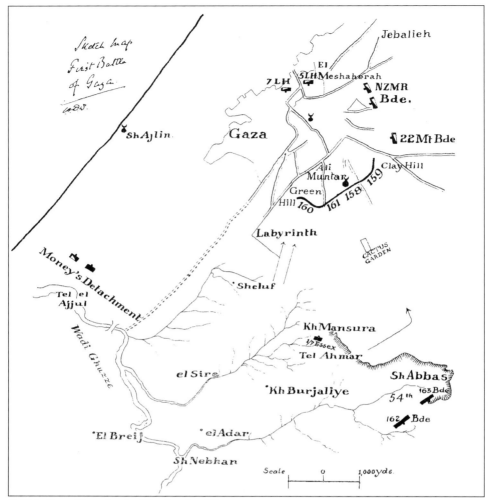

British dispositions for the First Battle of Gaza.

camel brigade to Abassan el Kebir; the 54th Division to the el Taire hill; and the 52nd Division to Khan Yunis, with one brigade at In Seirat.

During the early hours of 26 March the troops began to move out, covered by a thick mist that had fortuitously rolled in from the sea. The Australian and New Zealand Mounted Division left Deir el Belah, crossed the Wadi Ghuzze, followed by the Imperial Mounted Division, and headed for Beit Durdis, five miles east of Gaza, while the Imperial Mounted Division made for el Menclur, on the Wadi Sheria. The leading troops then deployed to the sea, thus closing the exit from Gaza. At the same time the 54th Division crossed the Wadi Ghuzze and occupied the Sheikh Abbas Ridge; while on the left the 53rd Division advanced towards Ali Muntar.

The initial stage of the battle was a success and by the end of the day Gaza was surrounded. The 53rd Division had taken the strategically important Ali Muntar position,

Laying the tracks for the Sinai Desert Railway.

and the Australians and New Zealanders were fighting in the streets of Gaza. With night falling and Gaza still not captured, Dobell began to worry about watering his troops and horses and, after consulting with Chetwode, decided to withdraw his mounted troops from the town. Dobell had not received the news of the capture of the position at Ali Muntar and Gaza itself was on the verge of capitulation, so this withdrawal of his troops proved to be a costly error which allowed von Kressenstein to reinforce Gaza. The battle ground to a close by 27 March, the Allies withdrawing to Deir el Belah and Khan Yunus. In an attempt to mitigate the failure, Murray over-estimated the Turkish losses, stating in his despatches:

'The total result of the first Battle of Gaza, which gave us 950 Turkish and German prisoners, and two Austrian field guns, caused the enemy losses which I estimate at 8,000, and cost us under 4,000 casualties, of which a large proportion were only slightly wounded, was that my primary and secondary objects were completely attained, but the failure to attain the third object, the capture of Gaza, owing to the delay caused by the fog on the 26th, and the waterless nature of the country round Gaza, prevented a most successful operation from becoming a complete disaster to the enemy.'

Chapter 5

The Second Battle of Gaza

On 28 March 1917 all of the officers and men of the 24th Welsh were inoculated for cholera, in preparation for their entry into the campaign. The elements of 231 Brigade assembled at Khan Yunus; the 10th Shropshire's on 3 April, the 24th Royal Welsh Fusiliers and 24th Welsh Regiment on 4 April, the 25th Welsh Fusiliers and 210th Machine Gun Company on 5 April. Headquarters joined them on 6 April. From Khan Yunus the Division moved to Deir el Belah, where units took over sections of trenches and where 230 Brigade assembled.

As they entered Sinai, the men of the 24th Welsh found the climate to be hotter than they had encountered in Egypt and that water was much more of a problem, even with the pipeline. In a similar move to that made by the Germans during their withdrawal to the Hindenburg Line in March 1917, the Turks had destroyed the desert railway as they retreated east and the 74th Division had to march for long distances over deep sand while repairs were made to the tracks. A novel solution to the problem of marching thousands of men and mules through the soft sand was to lay rolls of wire netting in front of the advancing army; this greatly helped to make the terrible conditions somewhat easier.

In the meantime, Murray had been ordered to advance on Jerusalem without delay and as a result had got to work planning the next attempt to take Gaza. The Turks had now reinforced Gaza, so a different plan was drawn up. The attack was planned to be carried out by the 52nd, 53rd and 54th Divisions, with the 74th in reserve, as it was still assembling and had not yet received its artillery. Along with the artillery supporting the other divisions, however, was a detachment of eight tanks, and the Anzac Mounted Division and the Imperial Mounted Division would provide the mobile element.

Troops of the 74th Division on a route march.

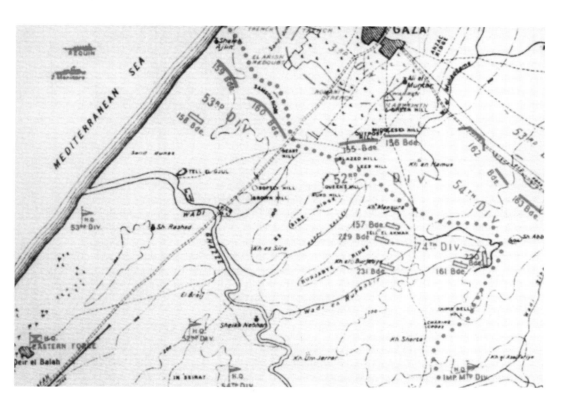

During April the 74th Division took its place in the line at Khan Yunus, relieving the 54th Division. On 14 April General Girdwood issued his orders for the second attack on Gaza although, because the division was in reserve, it played no real part in the battle. 229 Brigade took over the line held on the right sector by 162 Brigade, 54th Division, on 7 April, while 230 Brigade concentrated east of In Seirat and 231 Brigade assembled close up to the Wadi Ghuzee, ready to counter-attack any enemy movement against the right of the 53rd or the left of the 52nd Divisions, as required.

The Second Battle of Gaza opened at 5.30 on the morning of 17 April with the launching of a bombardment on the Turkish positions. British heavy guns south of Gaza were joined by gunfire from the French coastal defence ship *Requin* and two British monitors *M21* and *M31*. The heavy guns fired on selected strong points, the *Requin* on Ali Muntar Ridge, one monitor on the Labyrinth, the other on the Warren. The 201st Siege Battery turned its 6-inch guns on Outpost and Middlesex Hills, and its 8-inch on the Labyrinth and Green Hill. The 91st Heavy Battery dealt with the El Arish redoubt and Maghdaba trench, which affected the front of the 53rd Division, and the 10th and 15th Heavy Batteries on other points opposite the 54th and 52nd Divisions. The bombardment also saw the first use of gas shells in Palestine. From right to left, on the right of the British line lay the Desert Column, with an outpost line stretching from el Gamli to the right of the 54th Division, At Sheikh Abbas the 54th and 52nd divisions then carried on the line through Mansura to Kurd Hill; and the 53rd Division held positions stretching from the sand dunes to the sea. Zero hour for the infantry attack was set at 7.30 am.

A lumbering British tank, not a pleasant place to be in the baking Palestinian sun.

At zero hour, the two mounted divisions advanced with the object of engaging the enemy in the direction of Abu Hureira and along the Gaza to Beersheba road. On the right flank, one brigade of the Anzac Division went to Tel el Fara, one towards Abu Hureira, and two were held in reserve. The Imperial Mounted Division attacked on foot, and successfully advanced towards Abu Hureira, occupying the Kh Sihan in conjunction with the Camel Brigade on the right of the 54th Division. Their attack diverted the enemy towards them and the Desert Column played a role of protecting the main infantry division's flanks during the battle.

The 54th Division attacked down the slopes of Sheikh Abbas and Mansura and had to cross a bare plain towards the enemy trenches. There was not sufficient artillery available to cover the advance, and so the enemy artillery reaked havoc among the advancing troops, causing heavy casualties. The men kept moving on and reached the far side of the plain where they were met with Turkish machine-gun and rifle fire.

Ottoman machine gunners on the Tel el Sheria to Gaza Line.

It was only on the extreme left of the 54th Division that the attack gained some success, with the 11th Battalion, London Regiment capturing a Turkish trench astride the Gaza to Beersheba road. The remainder of the divisions attack faltered 200 metres away from the Turkish lines; even with the support of tanks, the enemy artillery had proved too accurate.

In the meantime the 53nd Division, led by 155 Brigade, had advanced along the Es Sire Ridge and, when sufficient ground had been captured, 156 Brigade wheeled around to attack Green Hill and Ali Muntar with the aid of a single tank. This attack faltered due to the inability of the brigade to capture and hold Outpost Hill, which was a vitally important position, and heavy fighting raged here throughout much of the day.

Major General Mott, commanding the 53rd Division, sent two of his brigades into the attack, and so 159 Brigade and 160 Brigade moved up along a strip between the coast and the Gaza road, passing through the front line, which was held by 158 Brigade. The former attacking brigade moved towards the high ground between Samson Ridge and Sheikh Ajlin, while the latter attacked Samson Ridge, with one battalion of 160 Brigade keeping in touch with the 52nd Division on the right flank. Each brigade was supported by a female tank. (Tanks were classified as 'male' or 'female' depending on the armaments carried. The male was armed with a six pounder gun in each sponson together with four machine-guns; the female was armed with machine guns only and was used mainly for anti infantry work).

The attack of 160 Brigade was carried out in full view of the defenders of Gaza and as a result the men came under heavy machine-gun and rifle fire. In support, the 266th Field Artillery Brigade targetted Samson Ridge and the gardens around the outskirts of Gaza with gas shells, while the French battleship *Requin* also covered the advance with her 16.5 inch guns from her offshore position. Despite this support, by 10 am the assault on Samson Ridge had petered out and Brigadier General Butler reacted by sending in the 2/4th Battalion, the Queen's into the attack to support the 2/10th Battalion, Middlesex Regiment, which had become bogged down.

The Queen's found the enemy rifle and machine-gun fire to be heavy and accurate, and suffered heavy casualties, although the battalion machine guns did good work after moving up onto Heart Hill to defend the flank.

The situation was getting desperate for the Allies. The 2/4th Battalion, Royal West Kent Regiment had lost their Commanding Officer wounded and their Adjutant killed, and as a result Major Arthur Preston Hohler, later to command the 1/4th Welsh, assumed command, only to find that the enemy fire was too intense to continue any advance for now.

By 12.45 pm the Middlesex, West Kents and the Sussex had began to advance again and stealthily moved forward to within 200 meters of Samson Ridge, which they then rushed and captured. Beyond the ridge the ground was partly cultivated and was interspersed with cactus hedges and scrub. The main enemy defences were beyond this ground, comprising deep trenches covered by scrub; the ridge had only been an outpost line, so the 1/1st Battalion, Herefordshire Regiment were ordered forward and occupied a ridge running southeast from Samson Ridge.

159 Brigade had fared better during its attack, as the Turkish troops in front of them had fled when Samson Ridge was taken; the brigade occupied its objective with little opposition. Corporal William Jones, of 29, Water Street, Carmarthen, recounted this moment in a letter home to his father;

'The Turks were entrenched on a hill and we had to cross an open plain to get to them. They stuck there and peppered us until we got to within 20 yards of their trenches. Then the order was given to fix bayonets. That did the trick. As soon as they saw the gleam of our bayonets they jumped out of their trenches, dropped their rifles, and went like the wind. But we were soon after them, and we killed, wounded, and captured thousands of the blighters. The night suddenly came on or we might have been in Constantinople by now as nothing would have stopped us! Our regiment made a great name for itself.'

General Mott then moved up the 5th, 6th and 7th Royal Welsh Fusiliers of 158 Brigade, but it was soon realised that it would be futile for the 53rd Division to attempt any further advance with the ground well defended by Turkish riflemen and German machine gunners.

On the Es Sire Ridge the survivors of 155 Brigade were still barely holding onto Outpost Hill. The situation had now become deadlocked, necessitating reinforcements to enable any further advance. However, Sir Archibald Murray decided not to send the reserve brigade up but to wait and to continue the attack the next morning.

Sir Archibald Murray wrote in his despatches;

"Middlesex Hill, and a large area of extremely broken ground west and north-west of it, had been made by the enemy exceedingly strong. The nests of machine guns in the broken ground could not be located among the narrow dongas, holes and fissures with which the locality is seamed. Partly owing to this, and partly owing to the extent of the area, the artillery fire concentrated on it was unable to keep down the enemy's fire when the Brigade on Outpost Hill attempted to advance... The reserve brigade of the 52nd had not been employed, and the remaining brigade was in a position to attack Green Hill and Ali Muntar as soon as the progress of the brigade on Outpost Hill on its left should enable it to do so. Up to this time, therefore, only one brigade of the 52nd Division was seriously engaged. The conformation of the ground, however, was such that the attack on Outpost Hill and Middlesex Hill could only be made on an extremely narrow front. It is possible that if the General Officer Commanding Eastern Force had now decided to throw in his reserves, the key of the position might have been taken with the further loss of between 5,000 and 6,000 men... As it was the General Officer Commanding Eastern Force, in view of the information received that our attack had not yet succeeded in drawing the enemy's reserves, decided that the moment had not come for an attempt to force a decision by throwing in the general reserves."

Casualties had been heavy during the battle: the 52nd Division had lost 1,365 men; the 53rd Division 584; the Camel Brigade 345; the Anzac Division 105 and the Imperial Mounted Division 547. The 74th Division had remained unused and as a result had escaped any losses; after deliberating with Dobell, Murray decided to cancel the attack and to consolidate the ground which had been won and as a result the British dug in.

Effective Turkish and Austrian artillery fire had concentrated on the attacking troops, and the assault was brought to a halt well short of the objectives, with heavy casualties having been sustained. The Turks had won the Second Battle of Gaza, suffering casualties themselves of 48 officers and 1,965 other ranks.

Conforming to its part in the plan of attack that day, the 24th Welsh had moved to Deir el Belah, taking up positions on Raspberry Hill, and in subsequent days; moved onto Tel el Ahmar and Charing Cross, before reaching outposts along Sharia Ridge on 23 April. By the end of the month the division had reached Tel el Jemhi, in front of Khan Yunus. No resistance was encountered, although a Turkish scout was captured on the morning of the 25th. The 24th Welsh lost just one man, Private Fred Southgate, killed on 21 April. Southgate was born in Ipswich in 1895; he had worked as a farm labourer for Mr. James Davies, of Abercwm, Llanllwni, prior to enlisting into the Pembroke Yeomanry in Carmarthen.

Private Frederick Southgate (320271), of Llanllwni. Killed at Gaza on 21 April 1917.

The men had been keen observers as the battle raged, and had watched the attack suffer under accurate Turkish artillery fire, which destroyed all of the supporting tanks. The men suffered from the *khamsin*, or *sirocco*, which blew throughout the 19th and 20th, causing much discomfort to men, camels and mules, with several cases of heat stroke suffered among the men and dozens of pack animals killed.

With the battle deemed another failure, Murray and Dobell were both relieved of their commands. In the reorganisation which followed, Sir Philip Chetwode took over the command of the Eastern Force from Sir Charles Dobell, and Sir H. G. Chauvell took over the Desert Column. The front, between Sheikh Ajlin and Tel el Jemmi, was divided into two sections; to the right, patrols of mounted troops took charge.

Sir Archibald Murray's fourth and final despatch of 28 June 1917 contained a lengthy account of the Palestinian campaign during his time in command and attempted to offer some excuses for the two failed attacks on Gaza:

'It is perhaps possible that if General Dobell had at this stage pushed forward his reserve (the 52nd Division) to support the 53rd, the result would have been different, but the difficulty of supplying water for men and horses would have been immense and impossible to realise by those who were not on the spot.' (The First Battle of Gaza)

'It is possible that if the General Officer Commanding Eastern Force had now decided to throw in his reserves, the key of the position might have been taken with the further loss of between 5,000 and 6,000 men, but this would have left my small force, already reduced, with a difficult line of front to hold against increasing reinforcements of the enemy, who, owing to the conformation of the terrain, could attack from several directions.' (The Second Battle of Gaza)

Murray had in fact achieved a vital success that had been overlooked. Under his command the EEF had conquered the Sinai Desert and the foundations for the campaign had been laid down securely, with the establishment of the water pipeline, railway and efficient lines of communication and supply that would prove vital in the coming months.

While the 24th Welsh were digging trenches along the ridge at Sheik Abbas on 6 May, a hostile aircraft dropped a bomb on the men, killing twenty three year old Private David Lloyd, a farm worker from Llandovery. He is buried in Deir El Belah War Cemetery. The battalion in fact spent most of the month digging trenches, in awfully hot conditions, plagued by heat and swarms of flies, problems which would characterise the campaign. The conditions were taking their toll on the men. On 12 May 1917 Private Alcquin Christmas Evans (320495), the son of David and Harriet Evans, of Caefadog, Llanarthney, a 23 year old farm worker, died of enteric fever at Qantara. His brother Evan was killed in Belgium just three months later, on 10 August 1917, aged 28, and is commemorated on the Menin Gate Memorial in Ypres. Lieutenant S. H. Kirby was detached to command the 321st Light Trench Mortar Battery on 15 May, but apart from these items of news, the month was just one of hard work, digging trenches and road building.

Private Alcquin Christmas Evans (320495), of Llanarthney. Died at Kantara on 12 May 1917.

June followed a similar pattern, interspersed with drafts of reinforcements to the 24th Welsh, with 156 men and three officers joining the battalion at Deir-el-Belah during the month: the most important news came on 27 June, when General Murray was replaced by General Sir Edmund Allenby.

A regular pattern now developed, with the 74th Division in the line, two brigades would hold their positions, while the third would be training and at rest. On 9 July the 24th Welsh was relieved by the 1/7th Scottish Rifles, and marched to Regent's Park for training, reorganisation and rest. Much of the spare time was devoted to sport and, as well as football and swimming, the 24th Welsh played a series of rugby matches against the 4th and 5th Welsh. Throughout this period the division had begun receiving its artillery at long last, and a new branch of railway was laid from Rafah to Shellal, running along the road towards Beersheba on the south of the plain, interspersed with watering places, readying for the next move on Gaza.

A route march in the Judaean Hills. (Shropshire Archives)

Chapter 6

The Third Battle of Gaza

The battalion lost its long serving medical officer on 13 July when Captain C. D. Mathias left to join the staff of the hospital at Giza. Lieutenant J. Fehily, Royal Army Medical Corps, took over his duties. The month was again uneventful, with a series of batches of men rejoining from hospital and other men falling ill and being sent to hospital. As well as the heat and flies, the desert abounded with scorpions and spiders, and any open wounds festered in the arid conditions. Spence-Jones and G. T. H. Bruce returned home on leave that month, with Major J. B. H. Woodcock taking over temporary command of the battalion. Woodcock was a solicitor's clerk prior to the war, and had served with the Pembroke Yeomanry since his commission in 1906. He was an able substitute to his two senior officers, taking command of the 24th Welsh at several periods throughout the war.

Major John Burrell Holme Woodcock DSO MID, of the Pembroke Yeomanry.

According to Dudley Ward in *74th Yeomanry Division in Syria and France*, General Allenby soon got to grips with the situation facing him:

'He found the Turkish Army covering a front of, roughly, thirty miles, from the sea and along the Gaza - Beersheba Road. Gaza was heavily entrenched and wired; the remainder of the line was held by strong works at Sihan, Atawineh, Baha, Abu Hureira, and Beersheba. There was a gap of four miles and a half between Hureira and Beersheba, and the other positions were about a mile apart. The British lines lay between the sea and Gamli, a distance of twenty-two miles. General Allenby decided to attack the left of the Turkish positions, and his divisions were set to work, readying for the next assault on Gaza.

'Beersheba was not an attractive place. East of it was the most God-forsaken country, and the Dead Sea. To the north was Jerusalem, but between that place and Beersheba were the heights of Hebron, and the Judean Plateau, an arid, waterless, and mountainous tract of country. But the defences of Beersheba were less formidable than elsewhere, and were easier to approach - and Beersheba had water! With Beersheba in his hands, General Allenby would have an open flank against which to operate, and he was superior in mounted troops.

'His plans, of course, included an advance on Jerusalem, and it would be as well to consider the nature of the country between the Wadi Ghuzze and that city...'

Allenby was known to the men of the Glamorgan Yeomanry who were serving in the battalion. On Tuesday 26 May 1914 he had inspected the Glamorgan Yeomanry in camp at Porthcawl. Allenby was not the only noteworthy commander in Palestine, however, as in the summer the Prussian officer, Erich von Falkenheyn, arrived from Verdun, following a short spell in Transylvania, to take command of the Ottoman army.

Trooper Frederick Charles Rees, of 6 Park Grove, Barry.

Spence-Jones returned from leave in August, and on the 3rd marched his battalion into a training area in the desert, west of the railway, where they undertook training in platoon formation and field firing. Another court martial took place that month, when Private Archibald H. Collins was charged with casting away his rifle in the face of the enemy. The charge was, however, dropped, and he was instead offered the lesser charge of losing his rifle and bayonet, resulting in the sentence of ninety days Field Punishment No. 2.

Several new drafts of men also joined the battalion during the month, with Second Lieutenant J. O. Rees arriving from the Officer's School of Instruction at Zeitoun. On the 28th, news of a number of men of the 24th Welsh being mentioned in Murray's despatch of 18 March 1917 was received by Spence-Jones, who proudly noted all of the men concerned in the battalion war diary: Lieutenant Colonel G. T. Bruce; Major L. Partridge, DSO; Captain R. H. P. Miers; Second Lieutenant C. H. Williams; 320515 Sergeant J. Allen; 320554 Sergeant R. G. Edwards; 320533 Sergeant A. T. Roberts; and 320579 Sergeant J. C. Venables, in the *London Gazette* of 6 July 1917.

On 31 July, the 74th Division carried out a night march, preparatory to being inspected

A group shot of the Imperial School of Instruction at Zeitoun, Cairo, on 20 October 1916.

Ottoman troops, ready to defend Palestine.

on the following day by Allenby. A reorganisation of Allenby's troops also occurred during the month, with the addition of three extra divisions: the 10th (Irish) Division, veterans of Gallipoli and Salonika; the 60th (2/2nd London) Division, veterans of France and Salonika; and the 75th Division, transferred from India.

Three Corps were formed: the Desert Mounted Corps, consisting of the Anzac Mounted Division, the Australian Mounted Division, the Yeomanry Division and the Imperial Camel Corps Brigade, under Lieutenant General Sir H. G. Chauvel; XX Corps, consisting of the 10th, 53rd, 60th, 74th Divisions, under Lieutenant General Sir Philip Chetwode; XXI Corps, consisting of the 52nd, 54th, and 75th Divisions, under Lieutenant General Sir Edward Buffin, with three Brigades of heavy artillery and the 7th Mounted Brigade as Army troops. There was also a composite force of: Imperial Indian Service Troops; 1st Battalion the British West Indies Regiment; a French Contingent; and an Italian Contingent; and the desert air force was also reinforced by the addition of another squadron.

Due to setbacks experienced by the Allies during 1916 at Verdun and the Somme, and in the early part of 1917 at the Champagne and Arras offensives, the Prime Minister, David Lloyd George, saw the need for some good news to bolster morale at home. He realised that Palestine would prove the best chance of this, and his parting words to Allenby had been: 'I want Jerusalem as a Christmas present for the British Nation'. Also by now Russia had collapsed, freeing German troops for the Western Front, and Turkish troops to reinforce Mesopotamia in order to try and recapture Baghdad, which had been captured by Lieutenant General Maude in March. A successful campaign in Palestine would both bolster morale, and draw Turkish troops away from Mesopotamia.

Whilst building up for the forthcoming offensive, the 74th Division was worked hard throughout the remainder of the summer, and became expert in patrolling No Man's Land. The mounted troops carried out daily expeditions towards Beersheba, gathering intelligence

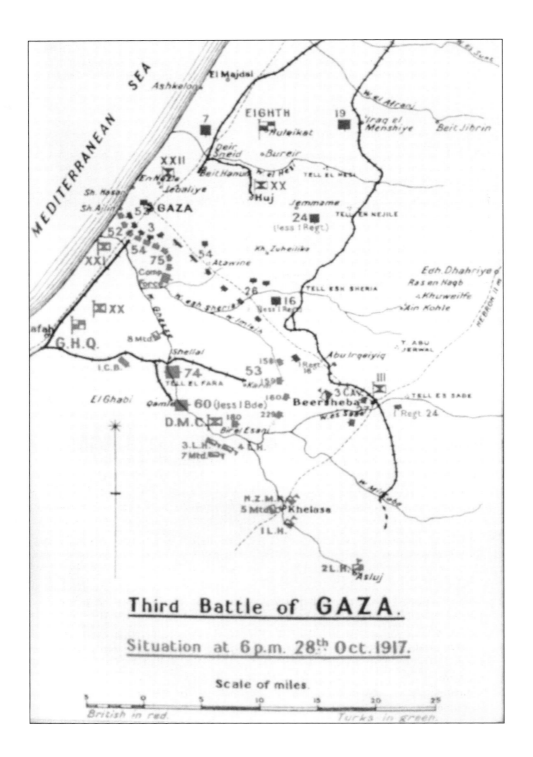

Third Battle of GAZA.

Situation at 6 p.m. 28th Oct. 1917.

Scale of miles.

British in red.   Turks in green.

in readiness for the offensive; the Turks, although building their defensive system, had been fooled into believing that the forthcoming attack would be on the seaward side.

Allenby had realised that a frontal assault would be very expensive, so his plan for the offensive involved deception, to make the Turks believe that the main attack would be on Gaza. It would, in fact, be made towards Beersheba which, once captured, would open up the Hureira - Sharia defensive line, making Gaza undefendable. The date for the attack was fixed as 31 October, and elaborate preparations took place. Forces were moved into place under utmost secrecy; dummy camps were erected; supply lines were planned; motor transport was withdrawn and replaced with camels and mules. Water usage had been calculated at the rate of half a gallon a day per man, and five gallons for each horse, with drinking water to be distributed in copper *fanatis* (vessels), of which great dumps were built up; the artillery plan was laid down to commence on 27 October, and the naval bombardment two days later.

According to Dudley Ward, Allenby's plan was that:

'XXth Corps would deliver the main attack, capture Beersheba, and drive in the enemy's left flank, while the Desert Mounted Corps would make a wide enveloping movement on the outer flank. The XXIst Corps and the Royal Navy were to occupy the attention of the enemy at Gaza during the early stages of the battle by a continuous bombardment, followed by an attack on Umbrella Hill and the defences on the left, to the sea. This attack was to take place between the attack on Beersheba and an attack on the Kauwukah System in front of Tel el Sheria. The idea of the latter phase was to advance in a north-westerly direction, take the Turkish lines in reverse, and occupy the high ground north of Sheria by nightfall so as to get the use of the water supply.'

The role of the 74th Division would be to assault the left hand section of the Beersheba defences, to the south of the Wadi es Saba, and training began in earnest during October. On 6 October the 24th Welsh marched from its rest camp at Regent's Park to Apsley House Camp, and the following day onto Sheikh Nakhrur. Over the coming days the men trained as a brigade, taking part in brigade assaults against the ground east of Wadi Ghuzee. After a day spent on the firing ranges, the battalion moved to Abu Sitta on the 25th, Gamli on the 26th, then onto Khasif on the 29th, taking up its positions in the Black Line at Shropshire Wadi on the 30th.

Major General Girdwood's orders for the 74th Division's attack were as follows:

'The attack will consist of two phases: 1st Phase, attack on 1070 works; 2nd Phase, attack on the main line.

'1st Phase: The attack on the 1070 works will be carried out by the 181st Brigade, 60th Division. The time at which the 1st Phase will commence will be decided by the G.O.C. 60th Division. This operation will commence by registration and wire cutting by the guns of the 60th Division, and by registration and slow bombardment of works Z15 and Z16 by the 268th F.A. Brigade, 74th Division. This operation is calculated to last one hour.

'During this period the 231st and 230th Brigades will co-operate as follows: A screen of infantry, accompanied by machine guns, will be pushed forward and will perform a double role: (a) assist in the advance of the 60th Division on the 1070 works; (b) cover the deployment in depth of the remainder of each brigade.

'The 231st will conform to the advance of the 181st Brigade, and will endeavour to occupy the tributary wadis of Whale Wadi, and will engage by fire the enemy trenches Z16, Z15, and Z7.

'The 230th Brigade will occupy the best available ground along the 960 Ridge.

'Immediately the 1070 System has been captured, three 18-pounder batteries of the 74th Division will move forward to within wire-cutting distance of Z7 and Z6... The remainder of the artillery of the 74th Division will engage the enemy trenches Z7, Z6, Z5, along their entire front.

'While the three 18-pounder batteries are moving forward, the assaulting infantry, accompanied by machine guns, will take every opportunity of advancing to the most favourable positions from which to commence the assault. The time the assault will commence will be decided by G.O.C. 60th Division.

'The 231st Brigade will conform to the advance of the 181st Brigade, on its right; similarly the 230th Brigade will conform to the advance of the 231st.

'When the main objectives of the Division have been captured, and should the enemy still hold on to the trenches north of the Wadi es Saba, the G.O.C. 74th Division will issue orders for an attack to be made on that system of trenches. This attack will be carried out by the 230th Brigade, 74th Division, from the south of the Wadi es Saba in a northerly direction, while the 158th Brigade, 53rd Division, which will come under the command of the G.O.C. 74th Division, will attack on the north side of the Wadi es Saba, from the direction of el Hathira.'

At 6.00 am on 31 October the Third Battle of Gaza was launched and, together with the remainder of 231 Brigade, the 24th Welsh began their assault on Beersheba at 10.30, attacking the town from the south western side, along the Wadi es Saba. The 1070 Works were captured with little fighting, with 24th RWF and 25th RWF leading the way. The 24th Welsh mopped up behind the leading battalions as they moved forward. The country was open, stony and desolate, with little cover except in the wadis, and the 24th Welsh saw considerable fighting during its advance. Within just a few hours the division had captured its objectives, so the 24th Welsh advanced for 2,000 yards in front of the two RWF battalions, and dug into a new defensive position around Wadi es Saba, where it remained for the night. In the wider scheme of things, XX Corps had successfully captured all of its objectives, leaving the town of Beersheba itself to the Desert Mounted Corps, who captured it later that day after a famous charge by the Australian Light Horse. The surviving Turkish forces withdrew.

Casualties had been relatively light in the battalion's attack so far, with one officer, Lieutenant William Armine Edwards and eleven other ranks killed; Lieutenants G. W. Abraham, V. Griffiths and D. R. Smith and fifty six other ranks wounded. One of the wounded died on the following day; Private Christopher Burns, of Dublin and, two days later, Private Jack Llewhellin of Carew died of his wounds. Six other ranks were recorded as being accidentally wounded, and another was evacuated, suffering from shell shock.

William Armine Edwards was a well known Swansea personality. He was born on 3

Remains of a British trench on the Beersheba battlefield.

May 1892, the son of William Henry and Margaret Hannah Edwards (née Williams), of The Hill, Sketty. He was educated at Harrow, and became a well known cricketer, playing for Glamorgan County prior to the war. He married Aerona Sails in 1914. He was mortally wounded during the assault on Beersheba, and died a few hours later. He is buried alongside several of his men in Beersheba War Cemetery.

Among the other rank casualties during this initial attack was Private Sydney Ernest Branfield, a poultry dealer from Llangunnor, who was shot in the heart by a Turkish sniper. His parents both died when he was a schoolboy, and Sydney was brought up by his elder brother at Nantycaws, Llandefeilog. He has no known grave, and is commemorated on the Jerusalem Memorial.

Just after midnight on 1 November, the 24th Welsh was ordered to withdraw from their advanced outposts, back behind Wadi es Saba, where the men commenced work on clearing the battlefield. By the 4th, the battalion was in new positions, readying for its part in the next stage of the attack, while a party of officers from the battalion reconnoitred the country toward Sheria. The khamsin hit the troops that day, and the men spent an uncomfortable day sheltering as best they could.

RSM Teddy White wrote a brief letter home to his family on 4 November, chronicling the battle so far, which they received a month later:

Lieutenant William Armine Edwards, 24th Welsh. Died of wounds suffered at Beersheba 1 November 1917.

'Just a line to let you know I am quite all right and came through without a scratch. Very pleased to say not one of the boys from Haverfordwest was killed or wounded. We lost a few boys from the battle, but not many considering what they went through. They were simply splendid, taking trenches that were considered impregnable and held by large numbers of Turks and Austrians. The 24th showed their mettle by taking the trenches with the point of the bayonet, killing a considerable number and taking many prisoners. They ran away like rabbits; I shall never forget the sight. At night we had to cross the battlefield in the full moonlight to take up rations. I could tell you heaps more, but dare not, though one thing I can say, and that is, you can tell anybody that the Welshmen fought Johnny Turk in his best position and positively wiped the floor with him. One of our boys is worth ten of his, they are very big chaps and have a most awful looking bayonet with a saw-back, but have not the pluck to use it. We shall be in it again very soon, and hope I shall be lucky enough to come out again safely.'

Private Sydney Ernest Branfield, of Carmarthen.

With Turkish attention drawn towards Beersheba, the defences of Gaza were attacked on the 2nd by a strong force comprising the 52nd, 54th, and 75th Divisions, supported by the guns of HMS *Grafton*, the monitors Nos. 15, 29, 31 and 32, the destroyers *Staunch* and *Comet*, and the river gunboats *Ladybird* and *Amphis*.

The original plan after the capture of Beersheba had been for the 53rd (Welsh) Division to make a frontal attack on the Kauwukah System, north of Beersheba, while the 74th and 60th took the whole of the fortified area in flank and reverse. However, the Turks had reorganised, and counter-attacked the 53rd Division, so the 60th Division was ordered to attack the Kauwukah System, and the 74th therefore had the original task of two divisions. As a result, at 6.40 am on 6 November 231 Brigade carried out an assault on the defensive works north of the Wadi es Saba. The 24th Welsh played a full part in the successful attack, capturing the works along with seventeen unwounded prisoners and two machine guns. Spence-Jones then took the battalion forward towards its next objective of the high ground south of the Wadi Sheria, known as the Sheria Heights and, after hand to hand fighting, drove the Turks off. The Welshmen dug into their hard won positions, and during the afternoon beat off several Turkish counter-attacks, all the time suffering from enfilade fire from the right flank. Spence-Jones was forced to swing the right flank of the battalion around to a ridge about 100 yards to the rear to protect the main bulk of the men from attack there, but soon after dusk the 6th Mounted Brigade arrived, straightening the line and easing the pressure from the flank.

The 24th Welsh was relieved during the evening by the Dorset Yeomanry, of the 6th Mounted Division, and moved back into support. Casualties had again been relatively light, at least by Western Front standards, with Second Lieutenant John Thomas Richards killed,

Private John Davies (320373), of Llangain. Killed at Beersheba on 6 November 1917.

Corporal David Robert Jones (320211), of Lampeter. Killed on 6 November 1917.

Lance Corporal David Charles Saer (320122), a postman, from Llanboidy. Killed at Beersheba on 6 November 1917.

along with thirty two other ranks. Wounded were Captain Geoffrey William Pepperall Abraham; Second Lieutenants John Oswald Rees and Arthur William Hunt; and 120 other ranks. Several of these wounded men later died as a result: Second Lieutenant Rees died of his wounds on 8 November 1917, Captain Abraham died on 19 November, and Privates Richard Emlyn Davies (60665), Wilfred George Knight (61614), Philip Rees Beynon (320608), Charles Badam Prosser (320262), Hugh Slader Glanville (320229), David John Thomas (320328) and Harold Clifford Edwards (320779) died of their wounds in the following days.

One of the men killed during the fighting to take the works on 6 November was Private John Davies (320373) of Llangain, near Carmarthen. He worked at his father's woollen mill prior to the war, and left behind a widow and young child. His brother, William Charles Davies, was killed while fighting with the 10th Battalion, Australian Imperial Force in France on 30 May 1918.

Corporal David Robert Jones (320211), was another man killed on the 6 November. He was the son of John and Sarah Jones, of Cefnbryn House, High Street, Lampeter, and had served with the Pembroke Yeomanry for several years prior to the war.

Private David Charles Saer (320122), was born in Llanboidy, the son of Charles and Phoebe Saer. The family later moved to Capelmair Villa, St Clears. 'Dai' worked on the local postal staff pre war and had served in the Pembroke Yeomanry for several years, mobilising in Whitland in August 1914. All three of these men are buried at Beersheba War Cemetery, as are most of the casualties of the battle.

By 8 November the battle had drawn to a close; had fallen on the previous day. The 24th Welsh were employed in clearing the battlefield, salvaging equipment and gathering the dead for burial in Beersheba. Only four of the men killed have no known grave, and as a result are commemorated on the Jerusalem Memorial: Private Moses Jones (320224) of

Llanfynydd, another postman; Private Martin Kane (17335) of Swansea, a former member of the Swansea Pals; Private Ezra Howell Rees (320841) of Nantyfyllon; and Private Joseph Smith (59186) of Durham.

Teddy White wrote a letter home on 8 November to update his family about the latest action:

'Am still all right and going strong, though we have been through a most Hellish fight, the worst we have ever had. Am sorry to say we had heavy casualties, but ended up by taking every trench and redoubt for miles. Our Battalion suffered something terribly. I must not say how many were killed and wounded, but God knows it was too many young lives to be given up. We had our revenge before the end of the day, and a good bit more too. I came across a wounded Turk yesterday while crossing the battlefield, and took out my revolver to shoot him, but bearing his cries for mercy, thought it the better part of valour to take him prisoner instead, though the Turks would not have showed any of us so much mercy. I never expected to write another letter home again, as I thought once it was all over on us, but our boys fought like heroes and drove them out of their trenches at the point of the bayonet when they outnumbered us three to one, but, sad to say, the best and bravest of our boys are gone. I had some narrow escapes, but seemed to have something shielding me all day as we could see nothing but death in front of us, but once we got them on the run, then we had our own back - the cowards! I saw a cavalry charge and shall never forget it, it was grand. We are getting ready for the next fight, but I think we have broken their hearts and have captured a lot of their guns, men and war material. We gave him a top-hole hiding and took all we set out to do. There were many Germans as well as Turks and Austrians among the prisoners we captured. Our boys were simply splendid; nothing could stand in front of them. The old 24th made a name for itself that will never die; the General told us that after it was all over. My word, it was terrible while it lasted. Our boys are hot stuff with the bayonet; the Australians have christened us the Welsh Ghurkhas. I could give you the name of one of the Haverfordwest boys who himself killed eleven Turks and another who with two bombs cleared a trench with twenty Turks in it. My own little bit I'll say nothing about, but I did my duty, and kept the supply good all day no matter what stood in our way. I am so proud to belong to such a Regiment. Some of the positions we took the Turks had been working on for over six months. Our Colonel and Officers were really splendid and there is no doubt that we have really broken the back of our fighting out here.'

A letter sent home by another member of the 24th Welsh just after the capture of Beersheba and which is of interest was printed in the *Aberdare Leader*:

'A Welsh soldier, who has visited Beersheba in Palestine, says that the place did not appeal to him very much. The most interesting item there was a railway with its rails made in Dowlais. And we in Aberdare, which place is illuminated nightly by the Dowlais works, have a tramway with its rails made in Germany.'

The famed Dowlais Steel.

With the fall of the Sheria position, Allenby now had ample water supply for his troops although, during their retreat, the Turks had smashed all of the windlasses and buckets which were used to draw water from the wells. The only substitute, rigged up by the divisional engineers, were canvas buckets suspended on telephone wire. With the Turks in full retreat northwards, the route to Jerusalem lay open. The 24th Welsh moved to Irgeig on the 9th, before marching to Gos El Bazai. Over the coming days the battalion moved on via Shellal (17 November) and Red House (18 November) to El Majdel, and then onto Nahr Sukreir and Junction Station, which had been cleared by advance elements of the EEF after the Battle of Mughar Ridge on 13 November. Junction Station was an important halt, where the branch line to Jerusalem left the main line from the coastal railway. The capture of this was vital to the success of further advances.

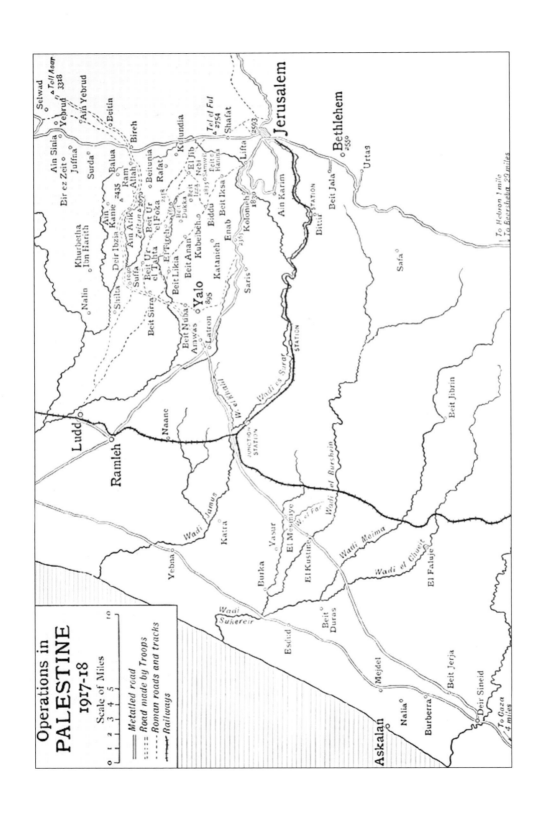

Operations in
PALESTINE
1917-18

Scale of Miles
0 1 2 3 4 5   10

——— Metalled road
:::::: Road made by Troops
------ Roman roads and tracks
—⊢—⊢— Railways

Selwad
▲Tell Asur 3318
Ain Sinia
Bir ez Zeit   Yebrud   ○Ain Yebrud
Juffna
Khurbetha   Surda   Balua   Beitin
Ibn Harith   Ain   Ram   Bireh
Kamie   2435   Allah   Bir ez Zeit
Nalin   Ain Arik   Ram   Beitunia
Deir Ibzia   Zeitun 2679   Beit Ur   Rafat   Kulundia
Suffa   Beit Ur   el Foka 2318   Tel el Ful
Shilta   El Tahta   El Jib   2754
Beit Sirra   El Fughr   Beit Anan   Nebi   Shafat
Beit Likia   Dukk Beit   Samwil   2593
Beit Nuba   Biddu   Beit Iksa
Anwas   Katanieh   Enab
Latron   Saris   Kolonieh   Lifta
Yalo   695   1890
Ain Karim   Jerusalem

Bethlehem
○550

Beit Jala   Urtas
Safa○

Naane
Ludd   STATION   Bittir   To Hebron 1 mile
Ramleh   To Beersheba 29 miles

Wadi el Khalil   Wadi es Surat   STATION

JUNCTION   Wadi el Rurshein
STATION

Katra   Wadi Jamug

Yebna   Burka   El Mesmiye   Wadi Meima
Vasur   Wadi el Far   Beit Jibrin
El Kustine   Wadi el Ghuei

Wadi   Beit   El Faluje
Sukereir   Duras

Eshid   Mejdel   Deir Sineid
Nalia○   Burberra   Beit Jerja   To Gaza
Askalan   4 miles

Chapter 7

The Battle for Jerusalem

The next phase of the offensive would be the drive towards Jerusalem. Dudley Ward described the country the 24th Welsh had now moved into in his book *The 74th Yeomanry Division in Syria and France* and the place names concerned are well known:

'Along the coast, right up to Mount Carmel, 100 miles north of Gaza, runs a very fertile plain of some 10 to 12 miles in width. From this plain there rises a limestone block of tumbled hills, mostly with regular rounded tops, some 3,000 feet at its highest, and 35 to 40 miles in width. To the east of the watershed of this range the ground drops to the Sea of Galilee, the Jordan and the Dead Sea, that curious inland lake 1,200 feet below sea level. Beyond, again, rise the Hills of Moab about the same height as the Judean Hills.

'Hebron, Bethlehem, and Jerusalem stand just to the east of the watershed. North of Jerusalem there is only the one main ridge of hills, south of it there is a lower distinct range called the Shephelah, separated from it by valleys running north and south. The Shephelah Hills are stony rather than rocky, and are terraced for cultivation, but very few roads run through them.

'There are only four practicable approaches to Jerusalem; from the south and west, i.e., by Hebron from Beersheba; by a track leading east from Gaza to Bethlehem and thence to Jerusalem by the Wadi es Sarar in which the railway runs from Junction Station; and by the main Jaffa-Jerusalem road.

'The result of the direction of General Allenby's attack was to force the Turks away from the hills and up the coastal plain. The nearest east and west line on which the divergent forces could rally was the railway to Jerusalem at Junction Station, and this was accordingly the first objective of the pursuing force.'

Allenby's plan had been to capture the coastal plain south and west of Jerusalem before embarking on the next stage of the offensive. On 17 November the important town of Jaffa was captured, opening up the only good road towards Jerusalem from the west. Allenby realised that the Turks could unite their two armies along the Tul-Keram to Nablus road, which ran thirty miles north of the EEF's current positions, so he moved to capture the Nablus to Jerusalem road at Bireh, ten miles north of Jerusalem, preventing Turkish troops from reinforcing the Holy City. With the problems of supply almost solved, Allenby moved his divisions into place for the attack on Jerusalem over the coming days.

On 28 November the 74th Division moved onto Latrun, and the following day marched to Beit Annan. Conditions were awful for the troops, as the way to Jerusalem was now

A view of Jerusalem across ancient ruins.

over ancient cobbled roads, which, after months of marching on soft sand, were proving hard on the feet of the men, and featured in many of the letters sent home by the troops at that time. The roads were also too rough for the wagons, so the infantry marched on while the transport remained behind. The war diary shows the difficulty moving over this country:

'28th November. March to Latrun (Ramleh), seven miles uphill all the way, taking four-and-a-half hours to accomplish. Continued march at night, but transport could not go to Beit Annan, as country too rough. Arrived Beit Annan 4.30 am on 29th November, 26 miles of rocky road - men exhausted. Enormous difficulty in taking over outpost line (from 8th Mounted Brigade) in jumble of steep rocky hills, falling precipitously into deep wadis and rising in places to over 2,000 feet. Only means of progress was by native tracks running up and down sides of mountains and along which only one man could move at a time. Only brilliant moonlight made relief possible.'

By now the Turks had established strong defensive positions on the ridges west of Jerusalem, and were ready to defend the Holy City. On 29 November 321 Brigade was ordered to take up a line from the Wadi Zait to Beit Dukka, on the left flank of the 60th Division. The situation here proved confusing to the commanders of the battalions of 231 Brigade. Hugh Edwardes, Lord Kensington, a prominent landowner in Pembrokeshire, was in command of the 25th RWF, and received several confusing reports of where his battalion was to advance to. Unaware of the situation regarding other units of the EEF and positions of the Turks, he sent a company to capture Hill 1750, which it did soon after midnight. His orders had wrongly informed him that the line his battalion was to take was held by British troops, when in fact it was still in Turkish hands. With dawn breaking, his battalion was in a dangerous position, so Kensington formed his men up around the village of El Foka and attacked it that morning, forcing its garrison of 450 Turks to surrender. All of this gunfire brought about a swift response from the Turks, who sent a force to attack El Foka. A company of the 24th Welsh had been sent up to support the 25th RWF, after Spence-Jones had received a request for aid from Brigade HQ but, in the confusion, the Turks had recaptured the village by 5.00 am before launching an assault on Hill 1750, and had regained that by 2.00 pm. While withdrawing with his prisoners, the remnants of Kensington's unit were allegedly fired at by both Turk and Australian troops.

It was late in the evening by the time the 74th Division HQ had got a grasp of the situation; the 24th Welsh was ordered to fill up the gap between Hill 1750 and the left of the Shropshire's at Kh Jufna, and to capture el Tireh at dawn. After a long march through the night of 30 November, the battalion took el Tireh, but it was found that the position was untenable, as it was open to enfilade fire from Turkish machine-guns on Hill 1750. Spence-Jones ordered the battalion to withdraw to the ridge overlooking the village and to

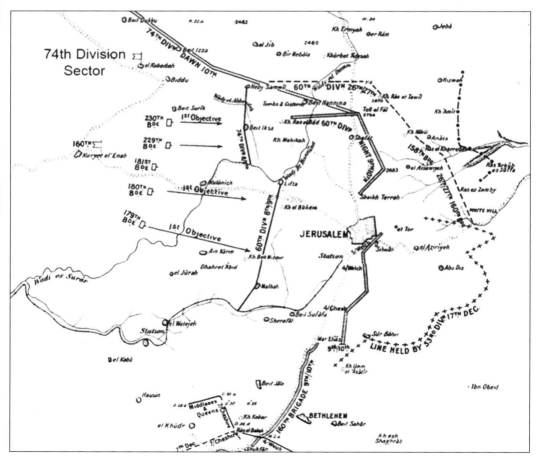

build a line of stone sangars to consolidate the position. During the morning the battalion saw heavy fighting while defending its newly gained positions; throughout the day 231 Brigade suffered 250 casualties, but captured eight officers and 300 other ranks. The 24th Welsh lost fifteen men killed that day, among them James Goss, a former Royal Navy seaman. Goss left the Royal Navy after marrying his wife Jessie Gillard on 4 November 1911, and worked as a collier at Coytrahen Colliery, Tondu prior to joining the Glamorgan Yeomanry. He was a well known rugby player, having played for Pontycymmer. He is buried in Jerusalem War Cemetery, as are most of the other men killed during the day. Two of his cousins from Pontycymmer also fell: Albert Edward Goss, was killed in France on 24 April 1915, serving with the 2nd Battalion, Royal Lancaster Regiment; and Albert's brother, Frederick Robert Goss, was killed in Boesinghe on 22 November 1916, whilst serving on the Canal Bank with the 13th Welsh.

The grave of Private James Goss at Jerusalem War Cemetery.

Spence-Jones wrote home to James' widow at the Malt House, Penyfai soon afterwards:

'I knew your husband well, as he was one of my runners, and was constantly with me, and did many personal things for me and always did them well, and I shall miss him very much. The officers and all the men deeply mourn his loss.'

The 24th Welsh held its positions overnight, and at 7.00 pm on the following day, the battalion was relieved by the 12th SLI, before withdrawing to Wadi Marua. During the day, a young soldier who had been wounded at el Tireh died of his wounds at the nearby 321st Field Ambulance. Arthur Stanley Dayson (320871) was the son of John and Mary Ann Dayson, of Blaengwynfi. He was the manager of the Star Supply Tea Company in Narberth prior to the war, and had served with the Glamorgan Yeomanry before to the merging of the regiments in Egypt. He was thirty two years old when he died of his wounds on 2 December, and is buried in Jerusalem War Cemetery.

Private Arthur Stanley Dayson, Manager of the Star Supply Tea Company, Narberth.

With 231 Brigade now out of the line, it was the turn of 229 Brigade to take up the offensive, and on the 3rd the brigade attacked the Zeitun Ridge. Aggressive Turkish defence, coupled with poor terrain, suiting the defender, made the attack stall, but by now the Turks had realised that Jerusalem would fall.

While the fighting was raging west of Jerusalem, a separate force, comprising the 53rd (Welsh) Division, known as Mott's detachment, was advancing from the south on the Hebron to Bethlehem Road. Outposts at Dahriye, just outside Hebron, were captured by 24 November, and water supplies had been secured there. Included in this force were the

Soldiers of the 74th Division leaving Bethlehem.

4th and 5th Welsh, who had suffered limited casualties. By 5 December Mott's forces were north of Hebron, but were suffering from Turkish artillery fire from Bethlehem. This two-pronged assault on Jerusalem was proving to be irresistible, and as a result of a series of failed counter-attacks which had been launched on 23 November, and the proximity of Allenby's forces to Jerusalem, Erich von Falkenheyn, who had already evacuated his HQ to Nablus from Jerusalem on 14 November, began to withdraw the Turkish troops defending the city.

The position was as yet unknown to the men of the 24th Welsh, who were now busy building and repairing roads in preparation for the advance of the 74th Division into Jerusalem, working through the Wadi Marua and the Wadi Selman to the well at Ain Jufna. On 5 December 231 Brigade, including the 24th Welsh, took over the Nebi Samwil defences, while Spence-Jones made his HQ in a cave below a mosque.

Allenby's plan for the taking of Jerusalem was already laid out, and the 74th and 53rd Divisions were at the centre of it. The Turks held a strong defensive line covering the Hebron to Jerusalem road, which was bolstered by defensive works in the area of Ras Esh Sherifeh. Behind were a network of trenches near el Khudr (now al-Khadr) and also around Bethlehem from Kh Esh Shugbrab, on the south-east, across the road to Kh Kebah and then northward.

The strength of the Turkish troops opposing XX Corps were an estimated 500 to 1,200 along the Hebron Road and around 15,000 from the right of the 60th Division to the left of the 10th Division, which was at Suffa.

It was thought that the worst difficulty facing Allenby's forces would be the terrain, as the Turkish defences were deemed as being of insufficient depth to cope with the assault, and as a result he planned to use two brigades of the 53rd Division, the entire 60th Division, and two brigades of the 74th Division.

The two brigades of the 53rd Division would advance twenty miles towards Jerusalem from a point north of Bethlehem, and would then co-operate in the attack along with the remainder of the Corps. If the enemy were to strengthen the defences in front of the 53rd Division, then the 60th and 74th Divisions would drive straight on to the Jerusalem to Nablus road, the 60th Division securing the flank to the south-east, with the objective being to prevent the escape of the enemy by the Nablus or Jericho roads.

A barrage balloon on the Jerusalem to Nablus Road.

Allenby realised that the enemy might recognise the danger of the aforementioned moves, and also put plans in place to deal with the possibility of attempting a withdrawal from the front of the 53rd Division. This eventuality would require the 53rd Division to directly advance on Jerusalem and for the 60th and 74th Divisions to drive the enemy northwards by pivoting on the Beit Iksa and Nebi Samwil defences and wheel northwards, with the following objectives:

'(a) a position covering the Jericho Road to be occupied by a portion of the 53rd Division; (b) the 60th and 74th Divisions to seize the general line Shafat - Nebi Samwil, or, if possible, the point 2670 - Kh Ras el Tawil - Nebi Samwil.'

The main intention of Allenby's plans was to inflict the severest possibly blow on the enemy by capturing as many troops as possible; and in order to do so the 53rd Division troops had to advance as rapidly as possible once it had began its move from its proposed starting line from Surbahir – Sherafat. Allenby's orders stated:

'Should the enemy retire from before the 53rd Division, or only oppose that division lightly, the general attack will take, roughly, the following form:

'1st Phase. The capture as soon as possible after dawn by the 60th Division of the enemy works from the railway to the main Enab Road, and by the 74th Division of the works covering Beit Iksa, as far north as the Wadi el Abbeideh. After this advance it will be necessary to advance more guns of the 60th Division.

'2nd Phase. The advance of the 53rd and 60th Divisions to the general line Jerusalem - Lifta. It is recognised that difficulties of terrain may prevent the 53rd Division from advancing from Sherafat northwards, and that they may have to work up the main road nearer to Jerusalem before they can gain close touch with the 60th Division.

'3rd Phase. The advance of the 60th and 74th Divisions to the general line of the track running out of the main road one mile north of Jerusalem.

'During this 3rd Phase the left brigade of the 53rd Division, if there is any room, will assist the right of the 60th Division. Otherwise the brigade will drop into reserve. The right brigade of the 53rd will endeavour to place itself in a position covering the Jericho Road, and the east and north-east of Jerusalem.

'4th Phase. The further advance of the 60th Division to a line astride the Jerusalem - Nablus Road about Shafat, and if possible to Point 2670 Ras el Tawil. During this phase the 74th Division will improve its position by throwing its right into Beit Hannina.'

Allenby also made provisions for the 53rd Division in case it was unable to attain its objectives in time due to enemy resistance:

'Should the resistance of the enemy be so great that you are unable to reach this line in time to co operate with the 60th Division, the G.O.C. 60th Division will be instructed to detach troops to advance east, from about Ain Karim, towards the Hebron Road to prevent the escape of the enemy on your front, either by the Jerusalem - Nablus Road or by the Jerusalem - Jericho Road.

'In the more likely case that you are able to break the enemy's resistance south of the line Surbahir - Sherafat, you will advance on 8 December from the line Surbahir - Sherafat in two groups.

'The right group will move at dawn towards Jerusalem, and pass thence south of the town to seize a position to command the Jerusalem - Jericho Road and to protect the XXth Corps from attack from the east and north-east of Jerusalem.

'The left group will advance between the Hebron - Jerusalem Road and the general line Sherafat - Malhah, to co-operate with and protect the right flank of the 60th Division.

'As soon as you are able to pass troops round the southern and south-eastern outskirts of Jerusalem, you will push forward a portion of the Corps Cavalry Regiment to discover whether there are any forward bodies of the enemy on the Jerusalem - Jericho Road within a distance of six miles from Jerusalem.

'The city of Jerusalem will not be entered, and all movements by troops and vehicles will be restricted to roads passing outside the city.'

Spence-Jones was issued with his orders on 7 December for the battalion's part in the attack the following day. According to the plan of attack, 229 Light Trench Mortar Battery (LTMB), 231 LTMB and 209 Machine Gun Company would begin firing from their positions at Nebi Samwil, while the infantry of the 60th Division would attack on the right. The attack began at 5.30 am, but was repulsed after the exhausted 53rd Division failed to safeguard its right flank. The failure forced the 74th Division to withdraw and form an outpost line on the Iksa Ridge. The weather during the day was cold and wet, and conditions were miserable for the troops holding the outposts, as no rations had been brought up due to the state of the roads. Turkish snipers

Ieuan Cranog Jones, of Aberdare.

were very active still, making any movement during the day exceedingly hazardous. The continuous sniping took its toll on the 8th, when Lance Corporal Ieuan Cranog Jones (320797) was shot and killed. He lived at 12, Coychurch Road, Bridgend prior to the war, and is buried in Jerusalem War Cemetery.

At 8.00 pm, Spence-Jones received the welcome news that Jerusalem had surrendered, and early the following morning sent out patrols to verify the location of the Turks. None was encountered. The Turkish Seventh Army had retreated that day, and had left the ancient city undefended. As a result, the Mayor of Jerusalem, Hussein Salim al-Husseini, delivered the Ottoman Governor's letter of surrender of the city to two sergeants of the 2/19th Battalion, London Regiment. The men were part of a scouting party, and brought the mayor to 180 Brigade HQ, where they delivered the letter to Major General Shea, commanding 60th Division.

'Due to the severity of the siege of the city and the suffering that this peaceful country has endured from your heavy guns; and for fear that these deadly bombs will hit the holy places, we are forced to hand over to you the city through Hussein al-Husseini, the mayor of Jerusalem, hoping that you will protect Jerusalem the way we have protected it for more than five hundred years.'

The grave of Lance Corporal Ieuan Cranog Jones, of Aberdare, at Jerusalem War Cemetery

Allenby's men had made history, becoming the first Christian conquerors of Jerusalem in over half a millennium. During 9 December the 60th and 74th Divisions advanced on Jerusalem from the west, while the 53rd Division advanced from the south, reaching the city walls by 8.45 am. The Mayor had fled the city, and the 5th Welsh sent a detachment of men to mount the first guard over the Jaffa Gate, to prevent any troops from entering the city. During the following day, sporadic fighting took place, notably around the Mount of Olives, where the 5th Welsh attacked

The Mayor of Jerusalem, Hussein Effendi al-Husseini

and captured a Turkish machine-gun position. Meanwhile, the 4th Welsh took up positions guarding the eastern side of the city, while the 24th Welsh took up positions on the Beitoun Ridge. Interestingly, with the departure of the Ottoman Mayor of Jerusalem, an Egyptian named Borton Pasha, who served for many years with the Welsh Regiment prior to the war and was working for the Egyptian Civil Service, was appointed Governor of Jerusalem.

The stage was now set for the triumphal entry of Sir Edmund Allenby into Jerusalem.

General Allenby's triumphany entry into Jerusalem through the Jaffa Gate.

At noon on 11 December 1917, two days after the official surrender of the City and six weeks after the fall of Beersheba, to show his respect for the Holy City, Allenby made his entry on foot through the Jaffa Gate, the streets lined by rows of his troops. He had delivered to Lloyd George the Christmas gift he had so longed to give the people of Britain. Inside the Holy City, Allenby marched towards the town hall, where he read out his official proclamation of Martial Law in Jerusalem:

> 'To the Inhabitants of Jerusalem the Blessed and the People Dwelling in Its Vicinity:
>
> 'The defeat inflicted upon the Turks by the troops under my command has resulted in the occupation of your City by my forces. I therefore here now proclaim it to be under Martial Law, under which form of administration it will remain so long as military considerations make it necessary.
>
> 'However, lest any of you be alarmed by reason of your experience at the hands of the enemy who has retired, I hereby inform you that it is my desire that every person pursue his lawful business without fear of interruption. Furthermore, since your City is regarded with affection by the adherents of three of the great religions of mankind and its soil has been consecrated by the prayers and pilgrimages of multitudes of devout people of these three religions for many centuries, therefore do I make it known to you that every sacred building, monument, holy spot, shrine, traditional site, endowment, pious bequest, or customary place of prayer of whatsoever form of the three religions will be maintained and protected according to the existing customs and beliefs of those to whose faith they are sacred.'

PROCLAMATION
OF MARTIAL LAW IN JERUSALEM.

To the inhabitants of Jerusalem the Blessed and the people dwelling in its vicinity.

The defeat inflicted upon the Turks by the troops under my command has resulted in the occupation of your City by my forces. I therefore here and now proclaim it to be under Martial Law, under which form of administration it will remain so long as military considerations make it necessary.

However, lest any of you should be alarmed by reason of your experiences at the hands of the enemy who has retired, I hereby inform you that it is my desire that every person should pursue his lawful business without fear of interruption. Furthermore, since your City is regarded with affection by the adherents of three of the great religions of mankind, and its soil has been consecrated by the prayers and pilgrimages of devout people of those three religions for many centuries, therefore do I make known to you that every sacred building, monument, holy spot, shrine, traditional site, endowment, pious bequest or customary place of prayer, of whatsoever form of the three religions, will be maintained and protected according to the existing customs and beliefs of those to whose faiths they are sacred.

December 1917.

EDMUND HENRY HYNMAN ALLENBY, General,

Commander-in-Chief Egyptian Expeditionary Force.

PROCLAMATION
DE LA LOI MARTIALE A JÉRUSALEM.

Aux habitants de la sainte ville de Jérusalem et à la population des environs.

La défaite infligée aux Turcs par les troupes que je commande a abouti à l'occupation de votre Cité par mon armée. En conséquence, je la proclame d'ores et déjà sous le régime de la Loi Martiale, auquel elle demeurera soumise pour autant que les considérations militaires le rendront nécessaire.

Néanmoins, et afin qu'aucun de vous n'en conçoive quelque alarme du fait de vos expériences passées avec l'ennemi qui s'est retiré, je viens par la présente vous informer que mon désir est que chacun de vous poursuive son légitime travail sans crainte d'interruption.

De plus, considérant que votre ville jouit de l'affection des adhérents des trois grandes religions de l'humanité et qu'au cours de plusieurs siècles son sol a été consacré par les prières et les pèlerinages des pieux fidèles de ces trois religions, je proclame conséquemment que tout édifice sacré, monument, lieu saint, sanctuaire, site traditionnel, dotation, legs pieux ou endroit habituel de prière, relevant de n'importe laquelle des trois religions précitées, sera maintenu et protégé conformément aux coutumes existantes et aux croyances des personnes au regard de qui ces lieux sont sacrés.

Décembre 1917.

EDMUND HENRY HYNMAN ALLENBY, Général,

Commandant en Chef la Force Expéditionnaire d'Egypte.

PROCLAMAZIONE
DI LEGGE MARZIALE IN GERUSALEMME.

Agli abitanti di Gerusalemme la Sacra ed alla popolazione che vive nella sua vicinità.

La disfatta inflitta ai Turchi dall'armata sotto il mio comando ha avuto per risultato l'occupazione della Città vostra dalle mie truppe. Io per conseguenza dichiaro e la pongo sotto la Legge Marziale, e sotto tale forma verrà amministrata per tanto tempo quale le considerazioni militari lo considereranno necessario.

Tuttavia, se mai certuni si fossero allarmati per l'esperienza avuta sotto le mani del nemico che si è ritirato, io vi informo che è il mio desiderio che ogni persona prosegua ai suoi lavori ed affari senza interruzione.

Inoltre, siccome la Città vostra è considerata con affezione dagli aderenti da tre delle grandi religioni dell'umanità, ed il suo suolo è stato consacrato dalle preghiere ed i pellegrinaggi dei devoti popoli di queste tre religioni da parecchi secoli, proclamo che qualunque edifizio sacro, monumento, luogo santo, reliquiario, sito tradizionale, dotazione o pio luogo di culto o abituale di preghiera, di qualsiasi delle tre religioni precitate, saranno mantenuti e protetti conformemente agli usi esistenti ed alle credenze delle persone per le quali questi luoghi sono sacri.

Dicembre 1917.

EDMUND HENRI HYNMAN ALLENBY, Generale,

Commandante in Capo la Forza di Spedizione d'Egitto.

Allenbys Proclamation of Martial Law in Jerusalem on 11 December 1917.

Allenby's political machine had been in full swing. Muslims were allowed to guard sacred Muslim sites, and Christians stood guard over ancient Christian sites. During the advance to, and capture of, Jerusalem, eleven Ottoman infantry divisions had withdrawn after sustaining around 28,000 casualties; some 12,000 prisoners were captured, along with 100 artillery pieces, and countless machine-guns, while the EEF had lost around 19,500 men.

Zeitoun, Palestine.

While this historical moment was taking place, the 24th Welsh was still in position along the Zeitun Ridge, coming under intermittent enemy machine-gun fire from parties of Turkish gunners covering the withdrawal of the main bulk of their forces. Allenby wrote home to his wife later during the day of his entrance into Jerusalem, informing her of the historic moment, but also of the situation of the Turks, who had withdrawn about four miles east towards Jericho, and about eight miles north of Jerusalem. The Biblical town of Bethany was also captured on that same day by the 4th Welsh, and Mott's detachment consolidated east of the town. Welsh troops had played a large part in the capture of Jerusalem, and the men of the 53rd and 74th Divisions were justifiably proud of their achievements. However, they could not afford rest on their laurels: Jerusalem now had to be consolidated, to guard against any Turkish counter-attack. During the 13th and 14th

December, the British shelled the Turkish positions in front of XX Corps: The two Turkish armies had now been split; their Seventh Army was north of Jerusalem, facing XX Corps, part of which was the 24th Welsh.

On 15 December, a special order of the day was circulated amongst the men of the EEF:

'SPECIAL ORDER OF THE DAY
G.H.Q., E.E.F.
December 15th, 1917.

'With the capture of Jerusalem another phase of the operations of the Egyptian Expeditionary Force has been victoriously concluded.

'The Commander-in-Chief desires to thank all ranks of all the units and services in the Force for the magnificent work which has been accomplished.

'In forty days many strong Turkish positions have been captured, and the Force has advanced some sixty miles on a front of thirty miles.

'The skill, gallantry, and determination of all ranks have led to this result.

'The approach marches of the Desert Mounted Corps and the XXth Corps (10th, 53rd, 60th, and 74th Divisions), followed by the dashing attacks of the 60th and 74th Divisions, and the rapid turning movement of the Desert Mounted Corps, ending in the fine charge by the 4th Australian Light Horse Brigade, resulted in the capture of Beersheba, with many prisoners and guns...

'The attack of the XXth Corps (10th, 60th, and 74th Divisions), prepared with great skill by the Corps and Divisional Commanders, and carried out with such dash and courage by the troops, resulted in the turning of the Turkish left flank, and in an advance to the depth of nine miles through an entrenched position defended by strong forces. In this operation the Desert Mounted Corps, covering the right flank and threatening the Turkish rear, forced the Turks to begin a general retreat on their left flank...

'The final operations of the XXth Corps, which resulted in the surrender of Jerusalem, were a fitting climax to the efforts of all ranks. The attack, skillfully prepared by G.O.C. XXth Corps, and carried out with precision, endurance, and gallantry by the troops of the 53rd, 60th, and 74th Divisions, over a country of extreme difficulty, in wet weather, showed great skill in leading, and gallantry and determination of a very high order...

'The Commander-in-Chief desires that his thanks and appreciation of their services be conveyed to all officers and men of the Force which he has the honour to command.

W. DAWNAY,
For Major-General,
Chief of the General Staff,
Egyptian Expeditionary Force.'

On the following morning, Spence-Jones sent a machine-gun crew of the 24th Welsh forward to point 245C and, at dawn, the crew spotted Turkish troops 'Standing To', before opening fire on the startled men. Later that day, he was presented with a list of men of his battalion who had been awarded gallantry medals for the battalion's part in the capture of Jerusalem: Lieutenant Colonel Spence-Jones was awarded the Distinguished Service Order; Captains J. H. L. Yorke, E. J. C. David, Rev. H. Rees-Morgan, and Lieutenant D. L. Popkin Morgan, Lieutenant and QM G. M. Rumball were awarded the Military Cross. Sergeant D. L. Evans (320159) was awarded the Distinguished Conduct Medal, while seven Military Medals were also awarded: Privates Ben Morgan (320351); W. R. Davies (320384); E. W. Maton (320500); W. P. Marks (320932); N. Thomas (320489); W. Beynon (320056); and to Lance Sergeant F. Hindle (320216).

Private Niah Thomas, MM, of Culford Road, Loughor.

The following day was quiet; on 18 December a patrol was sent out by Spence-Jones and found Sh Hasan and point 1910 still held by the enemy. Just one man was killed during the patrol; Private John James Thomas (320114), from the farming community of Llanfynydd, was twenty nine years old. He was the son of David and Mary Thomas of Troedyrhiw, and had served with the Pembroke Yeomanry prior to the formation of the 24th Welsh. He was the fourth man from the small community to fall, and is buried in Jerusalem War Cemetery.

Private William Woodburn (58994), the son of Thomas and Sarah Woodburn, of Rose View, High Harrington, Cumberland, was wounded, and died on the following day, 19 December, at the 231st Field Ambulance. He was a furnace worker before enlisting at Workington on 27 December 1916 and, after being transferred to the Welsh Regiment at Prees Heath on 19 February 1917, he was posted to Egypt in April 1917 with a number of other men destined to join one of the battalions of the Welsh Regiment. Woodburn was originally buried in El Kubeibah Cemetery, east of a monastery, but his grave was relocated after the war to Jerusalem War Cemetery. Woodburn is an example of the changing face of locally recruited battalions during the war, when the neighbourhood identity of the battalion was ever changing due to the necessary replacement of losses.

Private John James Thomas (320114), of Llanfynydd. Killed on 18 December 1917.

During the day further patrols were sent out by Spence-Jones, and again encountered Turkish forces in the immediate front. With Jerusalem and Jericho, the two principle cities of Palestine, in the hands of the British, Allenby now ordered XX Corps to advance its line six miles north of Jerusalem, and XXI Corps to advance eight miles north of Jaffa. The 24th Welsh held part of the line of XX Corps, whose overall line ran across the Jerusalem to Jericho and Jerusalem to Nablus roads, four miles north and east of the city, and continued west through the hills to Beit Ur el Foka and Suffa. As part of the preparations for the advance, Lieutenant General Chetwode ordered the 10th and

Lieutenant General Chetwode.

Generals Chetwode, Chauvel and Royston.

Private William John, of Spring Gardens, Laugharne.

74th Divisions to make tracks for guns and supplies up the valleys which ran eastward from the Jaffa to Jerusalem road. These tracks would prove invaluable over the coming weeks.

On 20 December, XXI Corps launched its attack towards the maritime plain, crossing the River Auja, which was in flood after the rain of the previous days, and captured all of their objectives with little resistance, as the Turks thought the river unfordable and were caught off guard. The weather remained wet over the coming days while XX Corps was making preparations for its attack, but the Turks had decided to launch a counter-attack, and had noticeably begun strengthening their positions, as was noted by Spence-Jones in the war diary entry on 21 December. In the meantime, EEF HQ had intercepted Turkish communications relating to the planned counter-attack, and Allenby ordered his commanders to alter their plans accordingly.

On the front of XX Corps, Chetwode's plan was for the 60th Division to attack northwards, assisted

The memorial stone in Laugharne Churchyard to Private William John, which also marks the grave of his brother John, who died after being struck by lightning.

by part of the 53rd Division on its right, while the 10th and 74th Divisions attacked eastwards along three parallel ridges. The date for the attack was fixed for 28 December. Knowing that the Turks planned to attack, probably on the 26th astride the Nablus road against the 60th Division, and westwards against the 53rd Division in the neighbourhood of the Jericho road, Chetwode planned to allow the Turks to attack, and then carry out his own counter-attack on them from the south and east.

On the night of 26-27 December the situation began to unfold. While the Turks launched their attacks against the 60th and 53rd Divisions, the 24th Welsh launched an assault on Hill 1910, north of Beit Duqqu. After fierce hand to hand fighting, the Welshmen captured their objectives, but a Turkish counter-attack drove them off before they had time to consolidate their gains. Half an hour later, Spence-Jones ordered a fresh attack; and after much fighting the 24th Welsh retook the position, before digging in and consolidating their gains. The left of the battalion also advanced, taking the high ground overlooking the Wadi Imeish. The Welshmen counted over seventy dead Turks in the positions they had gained, but had also suffered themselves: Captain James Hamilton Langdon Yorke MC, of Fishguard, had been killed, whilst Lieutenant Bonnyman and Captain Oakden Fisher had been wounded. Six other ranks were killed, among them Private William John (320285), the son of James and Sarah John, of Spring Gardens Cottage, Laugharne, a former member of the Pembroke Yeomanry, and a cousin to the author's great uncle, John James John, to whom this book is dedicated. A friend of both men, also from Laugharne, Private William Raymond, wrote to his parents after the fighting had ceased:

'I was speaking to Willie John less than an hour before the attack on Jerusalem in which he was killed. He said he hoped to pull through the same as he had done before, and ere we parted we shook hands and wished one another good-bye and good-luck.

'I have made enquiries and am told that he was shot through the eye and died at once, without suffering. He was buried on the Hill which we captured, and a board has been placed with his name, number etc on it. Dai Saer too was buried with his pals where he was killed. Every one of his platoon deserve the VC, for they went through and captured a position which two other battalions failed to take an hour before. I believe I am right in saying that Willie Roberts was one of three who came back safe from there.'

Dai Saer had in fact been killed on 6 November, and is buried in Jerusalem War Cemetery, but Willie John's grave was lost, and so he is commemorated on the Jerusalem Memorial and also on the grave of his younger brother John, in Laugharne Churchyard. John was just fourteen years old when he was struck by lightning and killed whilst playing in Laugharne in 1914.

James Hamilton Langdon Yorke is the only man of the battalion who was killed on Hill 1910 that day to have a known grave. He was the son of James Charles Yorke JP and Katherine Ellen Yorke (née Langdon), of Langton, Durnbach, Pembrokeshire. He married Violet Mary Vincent, of 8 Argyll Mansions, Chelsea, London on 1 December 1910. Educated at Haileybury and Oriel College Oxford, James joined the Pembroke Yeomanry while still a graduate, and at the outbreak of war was employed by the British South Africa Company. Yorke resumed his service in the Pembroke

Captain James Hamilton Langdon Yorke, Pembroke Yeomanry.

The grave of Captain James Hamilton Langdon Yorke MC, of Fishguard, at Jerusalem War Cemetery

Yeomanry, and was awarded the Military Cross prior to his death. He is buried in Jerusalem War Cemetery.

Later that evening, Spence-Jones received orders to advance the battalion to relieve the 24th RWF, who had suffered heavy casualties during their assault on the hills at Kh El Dreihemeh, and by 10.00 pm the relief was completed. The Turkish counter-attacks had by now faltered due to heavy casualties, and although some outposts held by the 60th and 53rd Divisions had been lost, the divisions had stood firm and broken up the Turks' last ditch attempt to retake Jerusalem. The attack of the 74th Division had been successful: 229 Brigade had captured the Zeitun Ridge, including Hill 2450, and this was the position onto which the 24th Welsh had now moved.

Now it had become clear that the Turkish attacks were spent, Allenby ordered a general advance. On 28 December the 74th Division received orders to co-operate with the advance of the 60th Division on its right, and 229 Brigade was to co-operate with the 10th Division and capture Beitunia and Hill 2435. As the advance began, 231 Brigade moved into reserve, and the 24th Welsh moved to positions south of Beitunia, where the men were put to work on battlefield clearance and road repairing. The unsavoury part of clearing the battlefield was the collecting and burial of dead soldiers, and the men were obliged to bury dozens of Turkish dead.

By the end of December the fighting had all but petered out, and the Turks found themselves to be seven miles further from Jerusalem than they were when they launched their counter-attack. The 24th Welsh had lost during the month one officer (JHL Yorke) and twenty other ranks killed; four officers and forty eight other ranks wounded. On 29 December Spence-Jones received a telegram from Chetwode, congratulating 231 Brigade on its part in the successful operations. Only two more gallantry awards were received by the 24th Welsh for its part in the capture of Jerusalem: Sergeants G. D. Nott (320801) and V. E. Llewellyn (320527) were both awarded the Military Medal.

Ottoman dead after the attack on Jerusalem on 26 December.

Chapter 8

The 74th Division's Final Affairs in Palestine

By the time that the New Year came the 24th Welsh were still in reserve, and in torrential rain carried on with road making duties. One man from the battalion, Private Arthur H. Palmer, was comfortably in hospital, after being wounded during the Battle of Beersheba; he wrote to his father in Llanelli;

'I'm in hospital with a slight wound in my left leg – a little beauty of a wound which hasn't done any harm as it is in the fleshy part.

'I suppose you have seen the news of the fights we've had in Palestine and of the success that has attended our efforts. I went through the first battle for Beersheba; the manner in which our lads drove the Turks back was positively great. Subsequent to our taking their trenches the Turks fought desperately with the view of regaining them, but the British Tommies were too good a match for them. I also went through the second battle, and just as I was thinking the job was over I got wounded. The second fight was infinitely better than the first as we had to fight a jolly sight harder, every inch of the ground being contested from start to finish.

'When we had driven the enemy back about three miles, he resorted to a counter-attack with a Division of fresh troops whom we fought a good time before retiring a little, after which we resumed the attack, but our energy was flagging when the cavalry dashed up to reinforce us, and my God, dad, we needed the reinforcement as we were only about a dozen and a half left fighting where the counter attack was made. You can imagine how we had to fight, but never mind, Dad, we did the trick, and it was mainly through our efforts that Gaza was taken on the left. Sad to relate though, as the result of these two battles nearly all our Battalion has been wiped out, and the other Regiments as well who participated in it have sustained some nasty knocks. It is consoling to think that the Turks suffered in casualties three or four times as much as we did without taking into account the prisoners we captured on the whole front. I know the prisoners numbered far more than the number reported. I am right by the hospital that Harry is in and I sent him a note this morning telling him I am here and asking him to come and see me.'

His brother, Sergeant Harry Palmer, was in the same battalion; however, by the time the letter was being penned, he was back with the 24th Welsh after a spell in hospital in Alexandria, quite unbeknown to Arthur.

A British Hospital at Gaza.

Another Llanelli man, Quartermaster Sergeant Emlyn Williams, of the 4th Welsh, also wrote home to his parents at Llanelli:

'I am now discharged from hospital and back with the regiment. I left Beersheba on a motor lorry on December 23rd, and had a most interesting ride, driving through Hebron, which is now a large town built in terraces and abounding in vineyards. I was charmed with Bethlehem which possesses large and beautiful buildings and good cultivation. On the site where Jesus was born is a tremendous church, on top of which is a marble statue of Christ.

'Later, we passed King Solomon's Wells and then reached the Holy City of Jerusalem (Jaffa Gate). I walked into Jerusalem and found several of our staff quartered in an empty room, and I joined them. Yesterday I spent a most profitable day in sight-seeing. Not two minutes' walk is Golgotha, or Calvary. I paid a visit to the tomb of Joseph of Arimathea, where Christ was laid, and saw the stone that was rolled away. I afterwards saw the Mount of Olives and the Garden of Gethsemane. Inside the inner walls of Jerusalem no soldier is allowed without a permit, and must he accompanied by an officer. The quartermaster and I succeeded in getting inside in the afternoon and saw Old Jerusalem. We saw the sites where Christ was tried by Pilate, the prison He was in, and the five stations where He halted with the Cross. The Omar Mosque is about as fine a building as I have seen, all decorated with mosaic work.'

On 2 January 1918 the 24th Welsh moved into billets in the village of Beitunia, in an attempt to escape the miserably wet weather. Road making continued over the coming days, interspersed with various courses for officers at Heliopolis. While the men of the 74th Division were busy road building, Allenby was pressing on with further plans for an advance through the Jordan Valley; the road building that the 24th Welsh was employed in

The Omar Mosque.

Heliopolis School of Instruction Staff 1917.

was a necessary part of the plans. A welcome break from this backbreaking work came with a torrential downpour on 13 January, making the ground too wet to continue. In the meantime, Spence-Jones had received verification of his recommendation of the Military Medal to Lance Corporal George Henry Redler (320563) for operations before Hill 1910. Redler was a native of Bristol, who had found work as a collier at Ynysybwl prior to the war, and was a member of the Glamorgan Yeomanry. He served with the Royal Engineers after the war, also being awarded the Territorial Force War Medal, and died in 1965, aged eighty.

On 19 January a party of men of the battalion attended a parade where Sir Edmund Allenby presented decorations to several men from the EEF. One was the award of the Distinguished Conduct Medal to Sergeant Rhys Thomas (320160), the son of Evan and Margaret Thomas of 26 College Street, Lampeter, which was for operations before Hill 1910. The citation was printed in the *London Gazette* of 1 May 1918, and reads:

'For conspicuous gallantry and devotion to duty. He was on several occasions instrumental in establishing his portion of the line when driven back by superior numbers of the enemy, who were counterattacking. During the third counterattack, after his company commander had become a casualty, he led the line most gallantly, reorganised the defence of two companies, and held his ground, personally accounting for seven of the enemy with the bayonet. His gallantry and disregard of danger proved a fine incentive to the men.'

The award was for his actions on the night of 26–27 December, during which Captain Yorke was killed. Thomas's younger brother, David Roderick Thomas, was killed in Salonika on 27 February 1917. While Sergeant Thomas was receiving his DCM, the remainder of the battalion took up a line at Kh Er Ros, where it took part in a brigade outpost scheme. While the 74th Division was on manoeuvre, the 60th and 53rd Divisions pushed the line further to within half-a-mile of Am Yebrud, in readiness for future operations against Jericho. Conditions remained wet and miserable throughout January, with dozens of men taking ill. One of the members of the 24th Welsh succumbed to illness on 30 January, after suffering from the weather. Private Thomas Henry Jones (52907) was the son of Thomas and Selina Jones, of 7, Ordell Street, East Moors, Cardiff, and was forty years old. He is buried in Jerusalem War Cemetery.

On 31 January the 24th Welsh marched from Beitunia, and bivouacked for the night before marching onto Latrun the following day. Conditions were still poor, and supplies were scarce, as the railway had suffered from flood damage and camels could not be used on stony roads that were slippery when wet. The battalion stayed at Latrun for the next few days, spending the 5th disinfecting and washing their tattered uniforms. Eighty two men rejoined the battalion from hospital, and Second Lieutenant H. S. Pryce of the 5th Welsh transferred into the battalion. The weather remained stormy all the while, but on 8 February the battalion marched to Enab, where it bivouacked for the night, and on the following day marched to Jerusalem, encamping in Abraham's Vineyard in heavy rain. The main Jerusalem to Bireh road was flooded, so on the 11th the men were ordered to begin work on building a parallel road, which ran from Jerusalem to Ramallah, work which continued over the coming days.

Empty trucks on a Palestinian Railway.

While preparations for the advance into the Jordan Valley were taking place, on the Western Front optimism was falling away. During the autumn of 1917 the Third Battle of Ypres had ground to a close after heavy casualties had been suffered by the Allies, and the Battle of Cambrai, which had began so promisingly, ended in an inconclusive result, with honours even. Russia had collapsed, freeing many German troops, who were moved to France, while the Italians had suffered a heavy defeat at the Isonzo in October/November. Throughout February 1918 it was beginning to become clear that the Germans were getting ready for an offensive on the Western Front, but noone as yet knew exactly where.

Other units of the EEF had continued their movement forwards. By the end of February the Turks were holding a line along the high ground on the north of the Wadi Aujah, and a bridge-head on the west bank of the Jordan, which covered the bridge at El Ghoraniyeh over which ran the road to Es Salt, which was in turn connected to Nablus and Amman by road and by railway. While the remainder of the 74th Division was in action, aiding the 60th Division in the push towards the Jordan Valley, the 24th Welsh spent the remainder of February continuing their work on the road to Ramallah, and also supplied a number of men to mount guard in Jerusalem. Major Ogilvie of the Fife and Forfar Yeomanry, who were also working on the road, wrote:

'We had to make a new road to link up with the Ramallah Road at Tattenham Corner. It was a most picturesque Wadi, covered with olive trees and, what was more important, with any amount of stones suitable for road-making to hand. On the Latron - Beit Sira Road stones were scarce, and had to be man-handled in limbers, or in baskets often quite a distance, but here there were stones of decent size, and within a few yards of the road. It was a 16-foot road, bottomed with large stones, then two layers of smaller stones, and blinded with gravel. Everyone went at it like a schoolboy on a holiday, and we completed our road two days before scheduled time, on one occasion actually doing 1¹/₄ yards of road per man.'

Standing guard over Jerusalem.

Trenches along the shore of the Dead Sea.

Between 19 and 21 February, Jericho was captured, after a move eastwards from a line running north-east of Jerusalem southwards to Beersheba by the 53rd (Welsh) Division, 60th (2nd London) Division, and the Anzac Mounted Division. The western coast of the Dead Sea was now within the grasp of the EEF, and the possibility of being able to use boats to carry supplies helped lessen the burden on the stretched EEF, which was still struggling due to the poor conditions of the roads. The next stage of Allenby's plan was for XX Corps to advance on a twenty six mile front, from west of the River Jordan to seven miles west of the Jerusalem to Nablus Road, and the right flank of XXI Corps was to advance in touch with the former. The main part of the advance was carried out by 60th Division, which secured the high ground north of the Wadi Aujah, which commanded the Jordan Valley; the 1st Australian Light Horse Brigade supported their attack, while the 53rd Division held a right angled front, with the 74th Division, now astride the Nablus Road, tasked with the capture of Sinjil.

On the night of 1 March the men of the 24th Welsh laid down their picks and shovels, and marched towards Ain Yebrud, where they had been tasked with capturing the Turkish positions holding the village and Hill M11. On 3 March B and D Companys launched the attack on the Turks, with C Company in reserve, the 24th RWF on the right, and 160 Brigade on the left flank. The positions were captured with little opposition, but Private John Henry Davies (320802), the son of Thomas and Charlotte Davies, of Briton Ferry, was killed. He is buried in Jerusalem War Cemetery. The battalion also lost a Lewis gun, presumably manned by Davies, to the Turks before they withdrew, and the Welsh consolidated their positions gained.

With future undertakings planned against the Hedjaz Railway and the Turks east of the

Jordan, Sir Edmund Allenby planned to deprive the enemy of the use of important roads leading into the lower Jordan Valley. As he later wrote in his despatches:

'It was essential, in the first place, to cross the Wadi Aujah and secure the high ground on the north bank covering the approaches to the Jordan Valley by the Beisan - Jericho Road (this road runs straight down the Jordan Valley, from where the railway from Haifa crosses the Jordan), and secondly, by advancing sufficiently far northwards on either side of the Jerusalem-Nablus Road, to deny to the enemy the use of all tracks and roads leading to the lower Jordan Valley. This accomplished, any troops we might determine to transfer from the west to the east bank of the Jordan would have to make a considerable detour to the north. I therefore ordered the XXth Corps to secure Kh el Beiyudat and Abu Tellul, in the Jordan Valley, north of the Wadi Aujah, and farther to the west the line Kefr Malik - Kh Abu Felah, the high ground south of Sinjil, and the ridge north of the Wadi el Jib, running through Kh Aliuta-Jiljilia thence to Deir es Sudan and Nebi Saleh.'

The 24th Welsh were, unknown to them, about to take part in their final operation in Palestine. On 5 March a reconnaissance aircraft belonging to the Royal Flying Corps reported that the Turks had retired from the line Attara – Sudan – Arura – Abwein – Sinjil – Mezrah – esh Sherkiyeb. Spence-Jones sent an officers patrol from B Company out to check the Turkish lines and which found them deserted. He sent a patrol from C Company to check a hill at N 6 d, and ordered the officers that if that position was not held, to push on to Yebrud and Selwad. The enemy was, however, found to be holding positions at the hill, north of Yebrud, and they opened fire on the patrol, which luckily escaped without harm. The only casualties suffered were several men with twisted and sprained ankles, due to the precipitous nature of the ground they were moving across.

A desolate road north of Jerusalem.

On the night of 6 March, the 24th Welsh marched forward to take the hill, now named Raspberry Hill, but found that the Turks had again withdrawn. Kh Kefrana was also occupied by the 24th Welsh during the early hours of 7 March, again with no opposition, the men finding the bodies of two dead Turks to be the sole occupiers. Later that day the Turks attacked Raspberry Hill, but after over two hours of fighting gave up, and retired, with no casualties suffered by the 24th Welsh, apart from one man who was hit through the shoulder by a spent bullet.

Private Ernest Idris Cumpstone (320756) was born on 7 March 1898, the son of Ernest Edward and Elizabeth Cumpstone (née Ballard), of Llantrisant. He worked as a collier before enlisting into the Glamorgan Yeomanry on 18 September 1914. The young soldier was celebrating his twentieth birthday, having survived over three years of war, and would in later life write his memoirs of the war:

'The light began to fade and then it came just as I began to feel safe, the bullet entered my shoulder and I sank to my knees. There was a cry for a stretcher – I felt faint but held on and was quickly whisked to safety under a rock. During the darkness most of my pals were able to come to see me and give me the water they had had issued to them. My breathing by now was particularly bad, I was coughing blood, and I was aware that there was no exit to the bullet. With all the water gone I now had to await being picked up by the R.A.M.C. from the advanced field dressing station. Toward midnight I could see a light approaching my shelter and to this day I cannot understand why these three R.A.M.C. men carried this lamp. If the Turks could not see the reflection from that lamp then why did the whiz-bangs keep following us? I was put on to a stretcher in a sitting up position in order to breathe and spit blood. This meant being left totally exposed when the lads, on hearing a shell coming, dived into shelter.

It was a nightmare of a journey which took hours, winding in and out of those hills. It was daybreak when we arrived at the Dressing Station and I was immediately given the anti-tetanus injection and then continued my journey by mule-cart into Jerusalem.'

The bullet was found to have lodged near his heart, and Cumpstone endured several weeks in hospital in Alexandria before being evacuated to England aboard the Hospital Ship SS *Dunluce Castle*. The bullet was never removed, but it did not prove to be fatal, as Cumpstone had a full life, living until 1994!

The diarist, Private Ernest Idris Cumpstone, 24th Welsh.

The battalion began consolidation of its newly gained positions. At 6.30 pm on 8 March, Spence-Jones received orders from the commander of the 74th Division, Major General Girdwood, relating to an attack on 9 March. In his orders General Girdwood expressed the hope of the Higher Command that the advance would be so rapid that: 'the enemy will be driven off the line Turmus-Aya-Sinjil-Jiljilia before he has time to recover from the first blow, and it is hoped that this may also result in the capture of the enemy's artillery grouped round Selwad and Attara. The operation will therefore be completed in two days.'

Captain David Lloyd Popkin Morgan, MC.

According to Dudley Ward, the 53rd Division, on the right of the 74th, had been given the objective of Kh Abu Felah to Mezrah to esh Sherkiyeh. The 10th Division, on the left, attacked in two groups: the right on the objective Attara to Hill 2791, and the left away to Nebi Saleh. The 74th Division, in the centre, would get firmly astride the Nablus Road, with 231 Brigade on the right, driving for positions on the line Mezrah-esh Sherkiyeb-Sheikh Saleh-Burj el Lisaneh, and 230 Brigade would attack a hill 1,000 yards south of Aliuta. At midnight on 8 March the 24th Welsh moved up to support the 10th KSLI, which was tasked with the capture of Selwad. With that position gained, the KSLI would then attack Burj el Lisaneh, while the 25th RWF were to attack Sheikh Saleh and Mezrah. Early in the morning of 9 March the attack was launched. The 25th RWF came under enfilade fire from two hills, and two companies of the 24th Welsh were detailed to clear the enemy from them. In the fighting which followed, Selwad was captured, but the 24th Welsh suffered its last casualties in Palestine. Captain David Lloyd Popkin Morgan MC, and three other ranks were killed, and a dozen men of the battalion were wounded.

David Lloyd Popkin Morgan was the son of David Henry and Jane Sybil Morgan, of 98 Bryn Road, Swansea. He had been a keen sportsman prior to the war, and was well known in sailing circles in Mumbles. He was working in Peru as a metallurgist before the war, but returned to Wales to enlist into the Pembroke Yeomanry. He was awarded his Military Cross for the period leading up to the capture of Jerusalem. The citation was published in the *London Gazette* of 2 July 1918, and reads:

'For conspicuous gallantry and devotion to duty. When a gap occurred in the line after the capture of an enemy position he made repeated journeys over a fire-swept zone carrying information and keeping in close touch with the situation. By his initiative and coolness he was largely responsible for driving back an enemy counter-attack.'

He is buried in Jerusalem War Cemetery, alongside the three other men killed during the attack: Sergeant William Evans (320117) of Llandeilo; Private John Henry Meade (59987) of White Luckington, Somerset; and Private David Gwilym (52896) of Llanelli, who died the following day. Private Gwilym was the last casualty suffered by the 24th Welsh in Palestine, although a former officer of the Glamorgan Yeomanry, Major Richard Gerald Mansell Prichard, who was attached to the 38th King George's Own Central India Horse, was killed later in the campaign, on 7 June 1918, and is buried in Jerusalem War

Major Richard Gerald Mansell Prichard, a former officer of the Glamorgan Yeomanry. Died of wounds suffered while serving with the 38th King George's Own Central India Horse, at Jerusalem on 7 June 1918.

The grave of Major Richard Gerald Mansell Pritchard, at Jerusalem War Cemetery.

Cemetery. Prichard had fought with the Imperial Yeomanry during the Boer War, where he was mentioned in despatches, and had worked as a mines inspector in the years leading up to 1914, before volunteering for service overseas with the Yeomanry.

On 10 March Spence-Jones led the battalion to Selwad, ordering B and D Companies to support the 25th RWF. Supply of rations and water was a real problem during the day, owing to the terrain, and nothing reached the men until almost midnight. After some food and water, the remainder of the battalion moved after midnight to positions at Mezrah esh Sherkiyeh, arriving just after dawn, to support the 10th KSLI and 25th RWF, before advancing through a wadi towards Sh Selim on the 11th. Patrols were then sent out to attempt to gain contact with the enemy, and returned safely after having come under fire. While the ground being crossed by the 74th Division was treacherous, the 53rd Division were even worse off, being in many places so steep that men had to help each other over ledges and up slopes, due to the precipitous nature of the ground. After further advance by the 74th Division during 11 and 12 March, on the 14th it relieved the 53rd Division, which moved back by stages to Lydda. Two days later, the Westminster Dragoons came under the command of General Girdwood, and joined the 74th Division in its move forward to Kh. el Nejmeh, where the division remained until the first week in April, carrying out several small raids against the Turks.

The 24th Welsh had spent the last two weeks of March back at work building roads, and by 31 March had moved to Ain Siwia, where the men began disinfecting once more. From 1 to 4 April the battalion returned to construction work, on the Jerusalem to Nablus

Road, work which finished at mid-day on the 4th. In the meantime, on 3 April General Girdwood received orders to prepare the 74th Division for a move to France.

On 21 March 1918 the Germans launched a huge last ditch offensive against the British line stretching from the south of Cambrai down to St Quentin. This was known as the *Kaiserschlacht*, or *Kaiser's Battle*, and was an attempt to split the allies on the Western Front and at least capture the vital allied railhead at Amiens, forcing the Allies into surrender before the might of the American army could make its presence felt. There were four separate German attacks, codenamed Michael, Georgette, Gneisenau, and Blücher-Yorck.

The Germans launched their initial offensive against the British Fifth Army and the right wing of the British Third Army. The artillery bombardment began at 04.40hrs on 21 March 1918, hitting targets over an area of 150 square miles. This was to be the heaviest barrage of the entire war, with over 1,100,000 shells fired in just five hours.

A map showing the German Offensives in 1918.

The German armies involved were the Seventeenth Army under Otto von Bülow, the Second Army under Georg von der Marwitz and the Eighteenth Army under Oskar von Hutier, with a corps from the Seventh Army supporting Hutier's attack. Although the British had learned the approximate time and location of the offensive, the weight of the attack and the preliminary bombardment was an unpleasant surprise. The Germans were also fortunate in that the morning of the attack was foggy, allowing the elite storm-troopers leading the attack to by-pass the various British redoubts, hardly scathed.

By the end of the first day, the Germans had broken through at several points on the front of the British Fifth Army, and after two days it was in full retreat. As it fell back, many of the redoubts were left to be surrounded and overwhelmed by the following German infantry. The right wing of Third Army also retreated, to avoid being outflanked. The German breakthrough occurred just to the north of the boundary between the French and British armies, but after three days, the German advance began to falter as the infantry became exhausted and it became increasingly difficult to move artillery and supplies forward to support them. Tales of near starving German troops gorging themselves on freshly captured British supplies and French wine became widespread.

Fresh British and Australian units were moved to the vital rail centre of Amiens and the defence began to stiffen. After fruitless attempts to capture Amiens, Ludendorff called off Operation Michael on 5 April 1918. The Allies lost nearly 255,000 men (British, British Empire, French and American). They also lost 1,300 artillery pieces and 200 tanks. All of this could be replaced, either from British factories or from American manpower. German troop losses were 239,000 men, largely the specialist storm-troopers, who were irreplaceable. As a result of this, several units that were in Palestine with the EEF were withdrawn in order to move to France, and bolster the British forces there.

On 5 April Spence-Jones received orders to move, and 231 Brigade concentrated in K29, where it was inspected the following day. On 7 April the battalion began moving to Lydda with the rest of the division, and marched from its camp, reaching a place known as Turks Grave, near Balua Lake, where the men bivouacked for the night. Over the coming days the battalion marched onwards to Lydda, bivouacking each night. Sir Edmund Allenby rode past the column on the morning of the 8th, having left Jerusalem, where he had been invested as a Knight of the Order of St John of Jerusalem in the courtyard of the Tower of David by HRH the Duke of Connaught on 19 March.

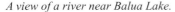

A view of a river near Balua Lake.

Allenby's Investiture on 19 March 1918.

By 11 April the battalion had arrived at Lydda. Spence-Jones kept the men busy training under company arrangements, and the men strangely were issued with sun helmets, along with box respirators, gas masks, which they would need in France. On 12 April Spence-Jones split the battalion into three parties, which separately entrained at Lydda for Qantara: the first party left at 5.51 pm; the second at 7.21 pm; and the third at 8.51, arriving at Qantara to join up with the first two parties at 12.40 am on the 13th. Qantara lies on the eastern Suez Canal, a hundred miles north-east of Cairo, and thirty miles south of Port Said. It was a busy garrison town, full of troops from all parts of the Empire: British, Australians, South Africans and Indians, and was well known to the original Yeomanry from the days when it was central to the defence of the Canal. It was also the starting point of the railway that had been constructed during the Palestine offensive, through the Sinai to Jerusalem.

By 10.30 am the 24th Welsh arrived at their camping area at Kilo 4, and over the coming days the new gas masks were fitted to the men and a draft of seven officers and 214 other ranks arrived to bring the battalion back up to strength. Companies were reorganised, and the men subscribed to a fund to erect a memorial to its fallen in Jerusalem. (It is not known if this memorial was ever erected or still exists).

At 11.30 pm on 28 April the battalion entrained at Qantara for Alexandria; the baggage was sent on by motor lorry, and the men were played to the station by the Divisional Band. By 9.00 am the train reached Gabbari Quays, and the men detrained and gathered their kit before boarding HMT *Canberra*. All of the men were aboard by 1.00 pm, and two hours later *Canberra* pulled from the quay and remained at anchor in Alexandria Docks, awaiting orders to sail. The convoy had assembled by 2.50 pm on 1 May, and *Canberra* steamed out of harbour: The 24th Welsh had lost just over a hundred men dead in Egypt and

The famous desert railroad, with rails made of Dowlais steel.

Palestine, and to the men aboard *Canberra* who had lost close friends, even relatives, in the campaign, who knows what they felt as they watched the dusty shoreline retreat into the distance. The convoy comprised of seven ships, carrying the 74th Division, escorted by Japanese destroyers and several aircraft, as it steamed through the Mediterranean. The sea was a dangerous place to be; German submarines patrolled its waters, and the British had lost many ships as a result, from battleships to transports.

Allenby had lost several formations and numerous units: The 52nd Division had left Palestine, preceding the 74th Division by a few days, and nine yeomanry regiments, twenty-four battalions of infantry, five and a half siege batteries and five machine gun companies had left for France. The loss of these troops was made good by the arrival of several Indian divisions, and Allenby continued his successful campaign in Palestine. Both Allenby and the XX Corps Commander, Philip Chetwode did, however, appreciate the good work done by the 74th Division and the latter wrote a fond farewell letter to General Girdwood:

'XXTH CORPS, JERUSALEM,
3rd April, 1918.

'MY DEAR GIRDWOOD,
'The whole of the XXth Corps, and myself in particular, suffer an irreparable loss by the transfer of your gallant Division to another theatre.

'No man has been better served than I have by them, or could wish to command finer troops. Every task set the 74th has been carried through with uniform gallantry and success, and no division in Palestine has a finer record.

'We shall watch your deeds and follow your fortunes, wherever you may find yourselves, with the most intense interest and sympathy, knowing beforehand that whatever you set your hands to you will carry through with the same gallantry and devotion that you have displayed since you were first formed into a division.

'On my own behalf and that of the whole Corps I wish you and your gallant Division God Speed and Good Fortune.

'Yours sincerely,
PHILIP CHETWODE.'

Girdwood was also sent the following letter by a grateful Sir Edmund Allenby:
'GENERAL HEADQUARTERS,
EGYPTIAN EXPEDITIONARY FORCE,
9th April, 1918.

'MY DEAR GIRDWOOD,
'I cannot let you and your Division go without writing to tell you how sorry I am to lose you.

'As you will understand, it is not advisable to issue a farewell order, but I want you to know that I am proud to have had you and the 74th Division under my command. Your work has been splendid, and I am sure that, wherever you may go, you will acquit yourselves equally well and win further distinction.

'You have my warm congratulations and thanks, and my hearty good wishes.

'Yours sincerely,
EDMUND H. H. ALLENBY.'

Viscount and Lady Allenby.

Chapter 9

The Western Front – Flanders

After a mercifully uneventful voyage, the 24th Welsh arrived at Marseille at 9.00 am on 7 May. The battalion disembarked at 2.00 pm, and at 4.30 pm was assembled before marching to Mousso Camp. The young private from Laugharne, John James John, was now walking in the path his elder brother David had walked in 1916, when the 1st Australian Division moved to France from Egypt.

The harbour at Marseille.

The Germans launched offensive: against the British; on the Lys on 9 April, Operation Georgette. Big gains were made over the next weeks, including all the ground so painfully won during the Third Battle of Ypres. The first train containing men of the 74th Division left Marseille on the night of 7 May, bound for Noyelles-sur-Mer. An officer of the Fife and Forfarshire Yeomanry wrote of the journey:

'The contrast from the East was indeed marked and delightful, and the long train journey passed quickly in our joy at seeing once more green fields and green trees, villages and farms, long fair hair and fair complexions. We could hardly have had more beautiful scenery than we had during the first day through the south of France. We kept to the branch lines, to the west of the main Rhône Valley Line, and wound in and out all day at the foot of steep hills crowned with old castles and picturesque villages, which looked so peaceful that it was hard to realise that there was a war on. The second day saw us skirting Paris by Juvisy, and gave us a good view of Versailles and the numerous airships at St Cyr. The last day our route lay chiefly through water meadows, and by 9.30 we had reached our detraining station, Noyelles, whence, after a hot breakfast, we marched ten miles to our destination, St Firmin, near the mouth of the Somme.'

While the first elements of the division were already under way, the 24th Welsh had a pleasant first day in Marseille after Stand To on the 9th. The men paraded before heading to the bath house at Mousso Camp, and made full use of them before entraining at 9.50pm that night. Noyelles was not reached by the Welsh until 11.50 am on 12 May and, after detraining, the men marched to billets in the village of Canchy, four miles north of Abbeville, by 6.50 pm. The 24th Welsh were now in a particularly beautiful part of France, near the mouth of the River Somme, where it flows into the English Channel, and by the famous battlefield of Crécy. Some of the officers had an enjoyable stroll in Abbeville, and one found it:

'strange and uncanny to be in a large town again after being so long in a wild and sparsely inhabited country as Palestine. We spent the next day in visiting the best hotels and ordering the best procurable meals... The country looked very beautiful, with its fields and woodlands - such an absolute contrast to the terrible country we had just left and had spent so many dreary months in ...'

On 13 May the battalion assembled for parade, before being inspected by the Commander in Chief, Sir Douglas Haig. The battalion remained in Canchy for several days, where the 74th Division assembled; and the men trained and were supplied with new uniforms and kit. Spence-Jones returned home on leave during this period, leaving the battalion under the command of Major J. B. H. Woodcock. An interesting note in Dudley Ward's history of the 74th Division mentions that the division was put through bayonet drill, but he remarked that: 'any one platoon of the 74th Division had probably made more use of the bayonet than any battalion in France'. Haig tended to look down at formations that had fought in other theatres: this was most notable with his judgment of units which had fought in Gallipoli.

During the morning of 23 May the 24th Welsh marched to the village of Gouy en Ternois, about twenty miles north-east of Abbeville. The men entrained there at 8.30 pm, reaching Ligny-Saint-Flochel at 2.30 the following morning, where the battalion detrained, before marching back to billets in Gouy en Ternois. On 25 May the battalion marched to Lattre-Saint-Quentin, eight miles west of Arras. It was billeted here, along with the rest of the division, and on 29 May was inspected by Major General Girdwood. During this period, the division, considered to be 'green', trained in tactical exercises of attack, defence and counter-attack. Some of the men were lucky enough to receive leave, a luxury after over two years away from home, while the battalion was reorganised; all the units in 231 Brigade were instructed that a full complement of men in a battalion would be no more than 900 other ranks. Each brigade was to lose one battalion, and on 21 June the Norfolks, the Royal Scots Fusiliers, and the 24th RWF left the division to join the 31st Division, which had held the German attack at Merville in April.

Spence-Jones returned from leave early in June, and the battalion continued on its hard training regime, along with the rest of the 74th Division, for the first three weeks of the month. By 23 June all men had returned from leave, and a draft of 101 other ranks had joined the battalion from Étaples. Two days later the battalion left its billets, and marched to Tinques, where it entrained at 11 am, before heading for Aire, which was reached by 3.30 pm. During the Battle of the Lys the Germans had penetrated the British line to a considerable depth, and although the offensive had petered out, the Allied line there was stretched. Before the German attack on the Chemins des Dames on 27 May, the 8th, 21st, 25th, and 50th British Divisions had been sent there, constituting IX Corps. During the afternoon of 25 June Spence-Jones led the battalion to billets in the village of Bourecq, about five miles south of Aire, in the St Hilaire sector.

On 26 June the whole of the 74th Division had moved to Norrent Fontes, where it was at four hours' notice for the purpose of reinforcing either XI or XIII Corps, and at twenty-four hours' notice for GHQ reserve. The men were put to work building rear defences for both Corps, and on 30 June came under orders of XI Corps.

A view across the peaceful fields that once marked the battlefield near St Floris, 11 August 2010.

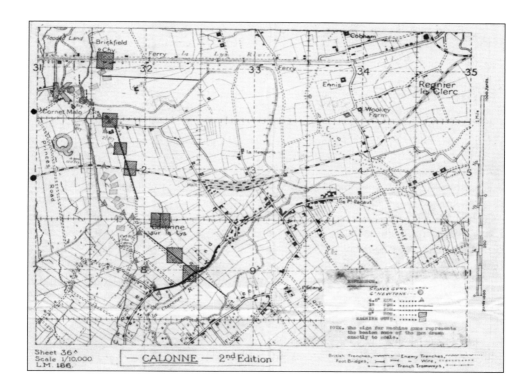

In the meantime, the 24th Welsh had been in billets at Chocques, before relieving the 36th Battalion, Canadian Infantry on 30 June. The 24th Welsh was ordered to prepare to rejoin the 74th Division at very short notice in case of emergency. The battalion remained at Chocques during the coming days, furnishing working parties, while Spence-Jones took out a party of his officers to reconnoitre the front line from Houchin – Lillers – Steenbecque. After further reconnaissance work on 8 July, on the 10th 231 Brigade received its orders to take over the line in the St Floris Sector, and moved up to relieve 183 Brigade of the 61st Division. The 24th Welsh, conforming to its part in the orders, marched from Chocques at 7.30 am, and relieved the 9th Northumberland Fusiliers, billeted in Hamet Billets, moving into Brigade Reserve. The battalion transport moved to billets in Berguette, while a party proceeded to Witternesse. The battalion remained here for the coming days, providing working parties; on the night of 14/15 July it suffered its first casualties in France when Private William John Biddle (320891), of Swansea, and Private William George Whitson (320982), of Ebbw Vale, were wounded. Whitson lived a full life for many years after the war, dying in Oxford in 1981.

On 14 July General Girdwood took command of the right sector of the Corps' front. The line occupied by the 74th Division was between the La Bassée Canal and the River Lys, with the left resting on the small village of Corbie. The town of Merville, in enemy hands, was some 3,000 yards away. On 16 July the 24th Welsh relieved the 10th KSLI at St Floris, and began its first tour of front line duty in France. The front here was on marshy ground, and as a result did not conform to the usual idea of a strongly defended trench, but rather was a series of outposts, known by the men as Islands, situated along the front, built of walls of sandbags or whatever other material was to be found, which were used to build breastworks.

The battalion war diary of 19 July explained the method used to hold the front line: One company would hold the line, with two companies in support, and the fourth in reserve. On 22 July D Company relieved C Company in the front line, which in turn moved into battalion reserve. The division then began sending out patrols from each battalion's sector, in order to maintain superiority over the enemy in No Man's Land and also to gain intelligence. On one such raid on 23 July the 24th Welsh suffered its first men killed on the Western front, although the war diary fails to mention this, reporting that no enemy were encountered.

The men were Corporal John Rupert Mills (61653), of Swansea; and Private George Llewellyn Norbury (57588), of Shotton, Flintshire. Both men are buried in Merville Communal Cemetery Extension. Another man, Private John James Parkinson (58965) was badly wounded, dying later that day at 230 Field Ambulance.

Mills was the son of George Alfred and Elizabeth Mills, of 8 Military Road, Pennar. He was a baker before the war, and lived at Hafod, Swansea. Mills enlisted at Swansea on 25 January 1915 in the Army Service Corps, and served at home before being posted to the Middle East, where he served in Gallipoli and Egypt before being transferred into the 24th Welsh on 31 January 1918. He had a brief spell back at Swansea on leave in June 1918, and married Kitty Grealey, of 47 Vivian Street, Hafod, Swansea on 15 June 1918. He rejoined the 24th Welsh in France, and was twenty six years old when he was killed on 23 July 1918.

Norbury was the son of James and Lucy Norbury, of 58 Trilby Terrace, Shotton. He enlisted at Wrexham on 22 November 1917, and was posted to the 53rd (Young Soldiers') Battalion, Welsh Regiment. On 21 June 1918 he was posted to the 24th Welsh from Étaples, and was just nineteen years old when he was killed.

Parkinson was the son of Richard and Sarah Alice Parkinson, of The Halfway House, Torrisholme, Morecambe. He worked as a hawker, selling pottery, before the war, and enlisted on 20 January 1916 into the King's Own Loyal North Lancashire Regiment, before being transferred to the Welsh Regiment at Prees Heath on 20 April 1917. He joined the 24th Welsh in Egypt, and moved to France with the battalion. Parkinson was twenty eight years old, and is buried in Berguette Churchyard.

Private John James Parkinson (58965).

On 25 July the weather turned, and it began to rain hard. The defences held by the division soon got into a poor state, but the 24th Welsh had completed its first tour of duty, and on the 28th the battalion was relieved by the 25th RWF and marched back to billets in Hamet. During the first few days of August the battalion remained in Brigade Reserve, supplying working parties for various duties, and on 4 August the brigade moved into divisional reserve, where it remained until 16 August. During this period, on the 6th a draft of officers joined the 24th Welsh: Second Lieutenants

The grave of Private John James Parkinson (58965), at Berguette Churchyard.

W. Temple; A. Lidstone; A. S. Ouzman; G. E. Jackson; and W. T. Harries. On that same day the enemy was found to have begun a withdrawal, and Girdwood advanced the divisional line in the St Floris and Robecq sectors.

On 16 August Spence-Jones moved the battalion from La Miquillerie to take over the right of the brigade front in the Robecq Sector from the 15th Battalion, Suffolk Regiment. A and D Companies took up the front line, with C in support and D in reserve. Captain and Adjutant J. F. A. Lewis left the battalion for a staff officer's course.

The Germans continued to withdraw slowly and, as a result, on 18 August the two leading companies of the 24th Welsh advanced just over 500 yards, taking over a section of trench known as Wolf's Track. During this advance, Second Lieutenant Charles William Trevor Trask was killed and eleven other ranks wounded. Trask was the son of Charles James and Evelyn E. M. Trask, of 'Broadshard', Norton-sub-Harndon, Somerset. He was just nineteen years old, and is buried in St Venant-Robecq Road British Cemetery, Robecq.

The stalemate on the Western front had been broken by this time. Marshal Foch, the Allied supreme commander, had issued the following order for the August offensive:

> The British 4th Army and the French 1st Army will advance on the 8th, under the command of Field Marshal Sir D. Haig, the former north and the latter south of

The ruins of the Hospice at Merris, after the German offensive.

the Amiens - Roye Road. The offensive, covered by the Somme, will be pushed as far as possible towards Roye. The French IIIrd Army will attack the left flank of the Montdidier Salient on the 10th inst. The French Xth Army in the Oise Valley (on left bank) will continue to advance eastwards.

On 8 August a combined British, Australian, Canadian and French offensive, centred on Villers-Bretonneux, had smashed open the German front, paving the way for a major advance by the Allies. Ludendorff, the German commander, called it 'The Black Day of the German Army'. Realising that the situation was dire, Ludendorff ordered a slow retreat back towards the safety of the Hindenburg Line. The Germans were retreating in front of the 74th Division, and on the night of 18 August great fires could be seen in their lines as they began burning supplies which they could not take with them. On the following morning the 24th Welsh had a brush with the Germans while attempting to see what was happening, and Second Lieutenant G. E. Jackson and seven other ranks were wounded.

On the morning of 20 August, Spence-Jones issued orders for the 24th Welsh to advance towards Beaupré, conforming with the battalion on its left and right flanks. The objectives were reached, but at the cost of three men killed and seven wounded. The dead were Sergeant James Cecil Biddle (320692), of Leominster; Private John Edward Bullock (59956), of Bristol; and Private Frederick William Carlisle (57525), of Seedley, Lancashire. The battalion was relieved by the 10th KSLI on the following day, and moved by route march to Quentin, where it bivouacked. Nine other ranks were injured by gas shells during the withdrawal. On 22 August the battalion moved back into the line, relieving the 1st SLI. It held the line until being relieved by the 12th SLI on the night of 24/25 August, suffering one man killed on the 23rd, nine other ranks wounded, and four men gassed. The dead man was Private James Hall (61612), of Grangetown, Cardiff.

During the 24th the battalion moved to St Venant Asylum, in divisional support. One man was killed, and five other ranks wounded by shellfire. The dead man, Private Alfred James Juliffe (60255) was from Llwynypia, and is commemorated on the Loos Memorial.

One of the wounded was Company Quartermaster Sergeant Evan Charles Evans (320161), known affectionately as Charlie. He was taken to the 39th Stationary Hospital in Aire, where he died of his wounds the following day. He was born in 1888, the son of David Hugh and Mary Evans, of 34 Bridge Street, Lampeter, and was serving with the Pembroke Yeomanry at the outbreak of war. He was 30 years old, and is buried at Aire Communal Cemetery.

Company Quartermaster Sergeant Evan Charles Evans (320161), of Lampeter. Died of wounds on 25 August 1918

The day that Charlie died, the entire 74th Division was relieved by the 59th Division on 26 August, and received orders to move to the Somme. At 6.00 am on 28 August the 24th Welsh entrained at Aire, and at 3.30 am the following day arrived at Mericourt l'Abbé. The men marched to Treux, and were billeted in empty houses.

The grave of Company Quartermaster Sergeant Evan Charles Evans (320161), at Aire Communal Cemetery

Chapter 10

The Western Front –
The Advance to Victory

The remaining battalions had entrained by the following day, and the entire 74th Division was headed for the Somme, its HQ being established at Beaucourt Château: The division was now attached to III Corps, part of the Fourth Army. By this time no less than 128,000 prisoners, 2,069 guns, and 13,783 machine guns had been captured from the Germans in the great battle that was raging.

On 30 August the 24th Welsh marched back to Mericourt l'Abbé, and embussed for Trigger Wood, south of Carnoy, the entire division assembling nearby in preparation to move up to the front line. During the following day, the 74th Division was ordered into the line, and was taken by bus to Maricourt. 229 Brigade then relieved the first line troops

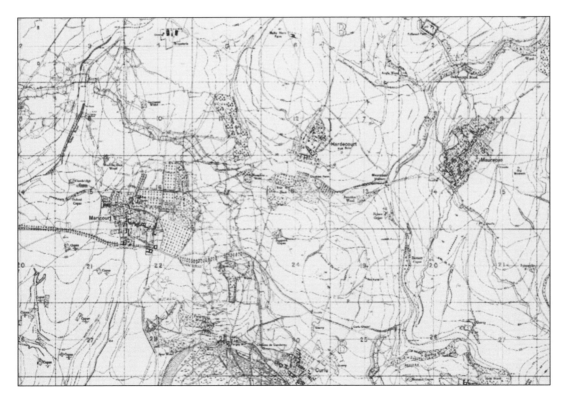

of the 58th Division about three miles to the north of Péronne. The situation on this front was described in great length by Sir Douglas Haig in his despatches:

'By the night of the 30th August the line of the IVth and the IIIrd Armies north of the Somme ran from Cléry-sur-Somme past the western edge of Marrières Wood to Combles, Lesboeufs, Bancourt, Frémicourt, and Vraucourt, and thence to the western outskirts of Écoust, Bullecourt, and Hendecourt. Any further advance would threaten the enemy's line south of Péronne along the east bank of the Somme, to which our progress north of the river had forced him to retreat.

'This latter movement had been commenced on the 26th August, on which date Roye was evacuated by the enemy, and next day had been followed by a general advance on the part of the French and British forces between the Oise and the Somme. By the night of the 29th August, allied infantry had reached the left bank of the Somme on the whole front from the neighbourhood of Nesle, occupied by the French on the 28th August, northward to Péronne. Further south the French held Noyon.'

It was becoming obvious that the Germans were intent on making a stand. Accurate and deadly artillery fire coupled with frequent counter-attacks hampered the Allied advance, but a brilliant operation carried out by the 2nd Australian Division on the night of 30th - 31st August saw the storming and capture of the strategic position of Mont St Quentin, which commanded the Somme crossings at Péronne. As a consequence of this succesful attack, on 1 September the Australians captured Péronne itself.

The 2nd Australion Division memorial at Mont St Quentin.

In support of the operations against Mont St Quentin Fourth Army, comprising the 3rd Australian, 18th, 47th and 58th Divisions), succesfully attacked and captured the villages of Bouchavesnes, Rancourt and Frégicourt, taking several hundred prisoners.

By the end of 1 September the Germans had been pushed back to the line of the River Somme and the high ground above the villages of Rocquigny and Beugny, where their intent was to hold out for as long as possible before retiring slowly back to the Hindenburg Line defences, which would allow time to further strengthen these defences, as well as allow men, munitions and material ample time to be evacuated.

The line taken over by 229 Brigade was just south-east of the newly captured village of Bouchavesnes. The divisional artillery moved to the valleys south of Maricourt, while the 24th Welsh remained in divisional reserve. Overall, the plan was for III Corps to attack, with the 74th Division on the right, the 47th in the centre, the 18th on the left: The 2nd Australian Division, on the right of the 74th, was to co-operate, and the objectives were the spurs west and south-west of Nurlu.

The attacking troops had a tough task. The Germans on their immediate front held a strong position west of Moislains, covering the Canal du Nord, a steep sided canal, which was ideally situated for defence. The length of the Canal du Nord, which stretched from

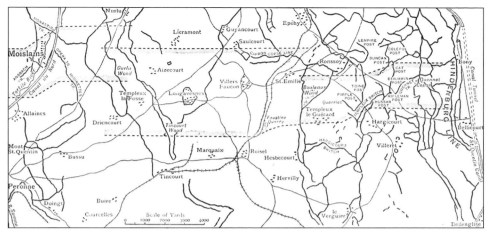

Map showing the advance of the 74th Division during the Battle of Epehy. The divisional sector was within the dotted lines, heading left to right (west to east), with the objective being the mighty Hindenburg Line.

Péronne northwards past Étricourt-Manancourt and enters a long tunnel, before emerging again three miles further north, above Ruyalcourt, was all heavily defended, and was an important part of the outer defences for the Hindenburg Line. The attack of 229 Brigade was launched at 5.30 am on 2 September, the infantry following behind a creeping barrage. A slight error in distance meant that the barrage missed the German front line, and the first wave, the Somersets, were forced to deal with these Germans, causing a delay to their attack, which meant that the artillery barrage moved on too far, making the advance even harder going. The attacking troops of 229 Brigade managed, however, to cross the Canal du Nord, east of Moislaines, gaining their objectives. On the same day 231 Brigade moved closer to the front, following the advance. The 24th Welsh lost one man killed: Private Philip Martin (10658), from Lambeth, during the move. He is buried in Hem Farm Cemetery, Hem-Monacu.

While the advance was taking place, 231 Brigade followed behind in reserve, and on the night of 6 September received orders to carry the advance on the following day. At 8.00 am on 7 September the 24th Welsh moved through the 16th Suffolks, taking over the right front of the advance, with the 10th KSLI on the left. After some heavy fighting, the battalions of 231 Brigade attained the objective of Villers-Faucon, and the town was occupied with little resistance by 3.00 pm. The brigade had in fact outpaced the 58th Division, which was on its left, and the 3rd Australian Division on the right, and so the 25th RWF and the Suffolks were called upon to form flanks.

The 24th Welsh had suffered heavy casualties during the taking of Villers-Faucon on 8 September: Lieutenant Wakeford and eleven other ranks were killed; five officers and seventy other ranks had been wounded. Charles Herbert Stanley Wakeford was the son of Herbert

Captain Charles Herbert Stanley Wakeford. Killed on 7 September 1918.

The graves of Lieutenant Charles Herbert Stanley Wakeford and Private John O'Shea, at Tincourt New British Cemetery.

Steele and Mary Wakeford, of Meadow View, Clive Crescent, Penarth. He had been commissioned on 27 October 1915 into the Glamorgan Yeomanry, and sailed for Egypt with the Yeomanry in 1916. He was 28 years old when he was killed, and is buried in Tincourt New British Cemetery, along with seven other men killed alongside him on 7 September.

On the following morning 231 Brigade, with the 25th RWF in the lead, made an attempt on the trenches north-east of Hargicourt, but the 58th Division was still struggling to take Épehy and, as a result, when the Welshmen moved forward, they were enfiladed by heavy machine gun fire from Épehy and the high ground south-east of the town, suffering heavy casualties. The Australians also did not advance during the day, so the brigade fell back to its original line, and was relieved during the night by 229 Brigade. The 24th Welsh had suffered one man killed, Private John O'Shea (61620), of Haverfordwest, and one officer and twenty other ranks gassed. Spence-Jones took temporary command of 229 Brigade for its assault, leaving Captain E. J. C. David in command of the 24th Welsh.

While the 24th Welsh moved into reserve, Major Woodcock rejoined the battalion on 14 September, assuming command of the battalion: the 58th Division attempted to capture Épehy and 229 Brigade attacked the Horse Shoe Trench system, but the Germans put up a stout defence, and both attacks failed. Haig did not want to risk the loss of too many casualties during the push on the Hindenburg Line; realising that limited attacks would be of no use against a determined enemy, ordered plans to be drawn up for a full scale attack: the Battle of Épehy.

The overall picture of progress during the advance prior to the Battle of Épehy must be appreciated to understand the reasoning behind it: the Canadian Corps, of First Army, and the left of Third Army had made great progress between the Sensée and Scarpe Rivers, and on 2 September the Drocourt-Quéant Line Hindenburg Line was broken by the Canadians. This was followed by a general withdrawal, a rapid falling back of the enemy on the whole of Third Army front, and on the right of the First Army, astride the Scarpe, on the line of the Canal du Nord. Near Havrincourt the Hindenburg Line left the Canal du Nord and ran south-east across the Beauchamp and la Vacquerie and Bonavis Ridges, to the Scheldt Canal at Bantouzelle, and along the canal to St Quentin. In front of the Hindenburg Line there were formidable positions at Havrincourt and Épehy, which had to be taken before a final attack on the main line could be launched. On 12 September IV and VI Corps, Third Army, on the left of Fourth Army and the front where the 74th Division was engaged, attacked and captured the villages of Trescault and Havrincourt, the area where the Hindenburg Line was broken in November 1917, at the Battle of Cambrai.

The date fixed for the Battle of Épehy was 18 September, and the plan was for the Third and Fourth Armies to attack on a front of seventeen miles, in conjunction with the 1st French Army on their right. The British attack was from Holnon to the southern edge of Havrincourt Wood, and was a preliminary to the attack by the First and Third Armies on the Canal du Nord, which was to take place on 27 September. General Girdwood drew up his plans for the 74th Division's part in the attack: He would attack on the 18th on a two brigade front; 231 on the left, 230 on the right. Girdwood was struggling with troop numbers though; on the 16th the division had suffered 350 casualties from gas in the two attacking brigades, although the 24th Welsh had been lucky and had suffered just four men dead since the attack of 7 September.

Girdwood's orders are quoted in the divisional history;

'The IIIrd Corps is continuing the attack in conjunction with Corps and Armies on either flank, with a view to securing a position affording good observation of the Hindenburg Line.

'The 38th Division, with 96th, 95th, 94th Infantry Regiments from right to left, is believed to be holding the line from Templeux to Ronssoy.

'230th Brigade will be the right attacking unit, 231st the left. To each brigade one battalion of the 229th Brigade will be attached - 16th Devons to 231st, 12th Somersets to 230th...

'Both brigades will attack the first objective with two battalions, and will leap-frog two battalions through for the attack upon the second objective.

'230th will, on Y/Z night, move its right battalion south of the Cologne River, and will be allotted ground by the 1st Australian Division... 230th will attack Templeux and the Quarries east of it, with the battalion south of the river, moving in a north-east direction in close co-operation with the left of the 1st Australian Division, which will attack Bolsover Switch simultaneously with the 230th attack upon the Quarries. The left battalion, 230th Brigade, will attack Templeux and the Quarries from the north-west. Special parties will be detailed for mopping up Templeux and the Quarries.'

An elaborately detailed plan for the supporting artillery and machine-gun barrage was also laid out in Girdwood's plan, detailing how the barrage would open 200 yards in front of the infantry, whose attack would be covered by a combination of a creeping field artillery barrage, a heavy artillery barrage and a machine-gun barrage.

The creeping barrage was intended to force the German defenders to remain down in their bunkers and was planned to start at zero hour, with no preceding fire to warn the Germans of the impending attack, timed to lift 100 yards every three minutes, a rate deemed suitable for the attacking infantry to be able to keep up. The heavy barrage would deal with any counter-artillery fire behind the German front line, while the machine-gun barrage, perfected by the Australians on the Somme in 1916, would rain down on the German lines. This latter barrage was also well planned, timed to fall 250 yards in front of the artillery fire.

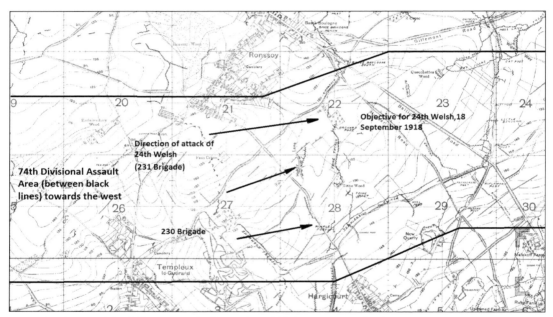

Attack area of the 74th Division 18 September 1918 (Map 62cNE2 Épehy).

Three objectives were given to the division known, as the Green, Red, and Blue Lines, and trench maps were issued to officers with these objectives clearly marked. At 5.20 am on 18 September the infantry of the 24th Welsh formed up in heavy rain, with A and D Companies in the front, and began their attack towards the battalion's allotted objective, at map reference F22.d.1.3, a former British strongpoint named Orchard Post, just east of the village of Ronssoy. The men advanced through the rain under heavy German artillery fire, making conditions extremely difficult, with visibility down to no more than a dozen yards, and the leading battalions found it difficult to keep touch and direction. The conditions, however, favoured the British, as the Germans could not see them coming until the Welshmen were on top of them. 230 Brigade attacked with the Suffolks supported by the

Buffs on the right, and the Sussex, supported by the Somersets, on the left. The Suffolks, attacking from the Australian area, swept through Templeux and over the Quarries. This flank attack took the enemy completely by surprise, and the whole of the objectives on 230 Brigade's front were taken by 7.15 am. After a short pause the assault on the Red Line commenced: The Buffs went through the Suffolks and secured their objective, one company reaching the Blue Line, which was the outpost of the Hindenburg System, but was unable to maintain this position, and fell back after suffering heavy casualties.

The 24th Welsh in 231 Brigade had met with fierce opposition, though. Attacking with the Devons on the right and the Welsh on the left, the first objective was taken without much trouble, but when the KSLI and RWF passed through to carry on the assault, they found the second objective was strongly held and defended. On the left of the Divisional front, a strong point, known as the Quadrilateral, which should have been captured by the 18th Division, was untouched, and had turned all its guns onto 231 Brigade, holding up the advance.

Spence-Jones noted in the war diary that the 24th Welsh had captured their objectives by 8.30 am, but overall, the division's attack was now struggling. Girdwood ordered the divisional artillery to bombard the Red Line at 3.50 pm, and the KSLI, who had crawled into No Man's Land ready to attack, rushed the line. The RWF were, however, in difficulties against a strongly defended position, and failed, setting up a defensive flank along the Bellicourt Road. Heavy fighting continued throughout the day. The 18th Division had failed to advance beyond their first objective, but the Australians had taken their second objective. At 6.00 pm the Germans counter-attacked the 74th Division, but after some fierce fighting, the division remained in control of the Red Line. Although the final objective had not been taken, the division had done well, with over eighteen German officers and 873 other ranks captured, as well as ten 77 mm guns, three 4" howitzers, and about eighty machine guns.

Sir Douglas Haig's Despatch about the battle noted that:

'In this operation our troops penetrated to a depth of three miles through the deep, continuous, and well-organised defensive belt formed by the old British and German lines. On practically the whole front our objectives were gained successfully; the 1st, 17th, 21st, and 74th Divisions and the 1st and 4th Australian Divisions distinguished themselves by the vigour and success of their attack. On the extreme right, and in the left centre about Épehy, the enemy's resistance was very determined, and in these sectors troops of the 6th, 12th, 18th, and 58th Divisions had severe fighting.'

The 24th Welsh dug into the newly gained positions during the night, but had suffered heavily: one officer, Second Lieutenant William Dillwyn Griffiths, and twelve other ranks had been killed during the attack; four officers and sixty one other ranks were wounded, four of whom died in the following days. During the next two days the division remained in the newly won positions, consolidating them and awaiting the 18th Division to get ready to attack again on the left, but sporadic gunfire accounted for another five men of the 24th in the meantime.

The next phase of the offensive saw much heavier fighting. At 5.40 am on 21 September a creeping barrage began, and the attacking troops of the 74th Division rose from their trenches again. The object was to capture the Blue Line, but between the objective and the division was the strongly defended Gillemont Farm, a veritable fortress. 230 Brigade attacked on the right, and under heavy fire the attacking battalions, the Buffs and Sussex, headed for the Blue Line, but finding their way blocked by thick barbed wire entanglements were forced to take cover in shell holes. Confused fighting followed, with the Sussex pushing on around Quennet Copse, where ninety prisoners of the 26th and 60th Infantry Regiments of the 121st Division were taken. The battalion pushed on, but the copse had not been cleared, and the men found they were being shot at from behind.

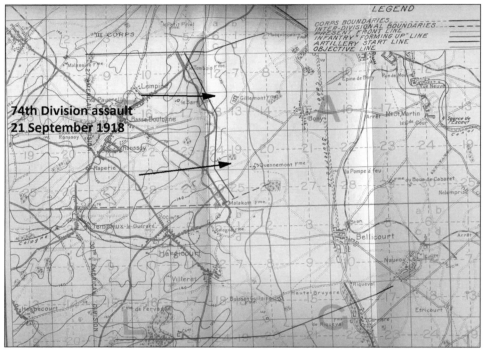

The attack of the 74th Division on 21 September 1918, advancing into the killing fields before Gillemont Farm.

While 230 Brigade were struggling due to heavy casualties and a strong willed German defence, 231 Brigade, on the left, had to change direction. The plan was for the 25th RWF, with four tanks, to advance on, and to pass through, the Quadrilateral, followed by the 24th Welsh, with the objective of Gillemont Farm. The barrage was to halt for fifteen minutes 200 yards east of this objective. Then the Welsh Regiment was to capture Gillemont Farm, and the RWF would capture and consolidate the Blue Line. The Shropshires, advancing in the rear, were to mop up the dugouts and shafts of the Quadrilateral. Unfortunately the tanks failed even to reach the starting point for the attack, so were of no use. Confusion now reigned; the RWF had passed over the Quadrilateral before continuing eastwards, but the 24th Welsh had lost direction and, instead of attacking Gillemont Farm, were following behind the RWF, while the 18th Division was again held up. The left flank was now up in

118

the air, and the Germans took advantage of the situation, pouring reinforcements into the fray through the Quadrilateral. The Germans then began pouring fire into the rear of the RWF and 24th Welsh who attempted, without success, to bomb the Germans out. By the time that darkness had descended, 231 Brigade had been forced to withdraw to Benjamin Trench, its original line, and was relieved by 230 Brigade during the night. The division had suffered heavily during the day. In total, during September the division lost: thirty four officers and 436 other ranks killed; 143 officers and 2,712 other ranks wounded; eight officers and 188 other ranks missing, most of whom were killed.

Lieutenant William Woolf.

Private John James John.

Private David John Dawson (320494), of Swansea. Killed on 21 September 1918.

The 24th Welsh lost two officers, Lieutenants William Woolf and David Louis Clemetson, and twelve other ranks killed; four officers and ninety two other ranks wounded; and one officer and twenty three other ranks missing. At least ten of the missing had been killed, making a total of twenty two other ranks during the day. Among the other rank casualties was Private John James John (320374), the son of William and Eliza John, of Halfpenny Furze, Laugharne. John was twenty five years old and was buried along with thirteen other men in an isolated battlefield grave. During battlefield clearances in the area in August 1919 his grave was exhumed, and he was reburied in Unicorn Cemetery, Vendhuile, just thirty miles away from where his elder brother David had been killed two years earlier.

Private Edward Rockingham (320155), a farm worker at Abergwili prior to the war. Edward has only recently been commemorated by the CWGC after ninety years 'out in the cold'.

Another of the dead was Private David John Dawson (320494), the twenty nine year old son of David John Dawson and Mary Lane Dawson, of Swansea. He has no known grave and is commemorated on the Vis-en-Artois Memorial.

Among the missing was Private Edward Rockingham (320155), a farm labourer from Abergwili. Edward mysteriously remained un-commemorated by the Commonwealth War Graves Commission for ninety one years: He was born at Norwood, Surrey, but was orphaned at an early age, and came to Abergwili, where he worked for Mrs. Rees, at Penybont. He enlisted at Carmarthen into the Pembroke Yeomanry, Army Number 2237, and moved to Egypt with the Yeomanry in 1916. Rockingham has only recently been accepted for commemoration by the CWGC, after evidence of his omission was presented to them by the author, and his name will be added to the Vis-en-Artois Memorial.

Lieutenant David Louis Clemetson was a Jamaican who was being educated at Clifton College when war broke out. He enlisted into the Sportsmen's Battalion of the Royal Fusiliers, and served in Salonika before being commissioned into the Pembroke Yeomanry. He is buried in Unicorn Cemetery.

Lieutenant David Louis Clemetson, of Jamaica. Possibly the first black officer in the British Army.

Altogether, fourteen of the men of the battalion killed that day are commemorated on the Vis-en-Artois Memorial. Some of these men may lie in some of the eighty or so graves of unknown men, which are inscribed to 'A Soldier of the Great War', who are buried in Unicorn Cemetery, which lies about 4,000 yards north-west of Gillemont Farm, the objective of these men. The farm eventually fell to American and Australian troops on 29 September.

Due to the heavy casualties that were incurred by the 74th Division, it was decided not to use it again: However, the Germans were still holding the Quadrilateral, and an attack was arranged, using just the 10th KSLI in conjunction with the 18th Division, at 3.00 am

Unicorn Cemetery in about 1920, soon after the battlefield clearances began and which gathered up the graves of Lieutenant David Louis Clemetson (the battalion's only known mixed race officer), Sergeant Francis Charles Taylor, and Privates David Barnacle, Hugh Evans, Hubert Thomas George, John James John and Edward Thomas, for concentration there.

on the following day. This was the last action by the 74th Division in this sector. That day the 24th Welsh moved into support along the Bellicourt Road, and began the slow move back towards Villers-Bretonneux, the division being relieved on 24 September, and bivouacked for the night near Péronne.

During the week following the 24th Welsh attack in the Battle of Épehy, nine of the wounded men died, all apart from one being buried locally in France. Among the men to die of wounds suffered at Épehy in the following days were: Private John Clarke Harries (320401), the son of James and Hannah Harries, of Riverside House, Cynwyl Elfed, near Carmarthen, wounded at Gillemont Farm and evacuated to Colchester Hospital, where he died of his wounds on 3 October 1918. He is buried in Rhydargeau (Horeb) Baptist Chapelyard. He had returned home from Canada to enlist into the Pembroke Yeomanry in September 1915.

Private Ivor Morris (25427), of Aberdare. Died of wounds on 23 September 1918.

Private Ivor Morris (25427), had fought in France with the 40th (Bantam) Division, before being wounded. He was transferred to the 24th Welsh after recovering from his wounds, and had fought at Jerusalem. He was 38 years old when he died on 23 September and is buried in Ste. Emilie Valley Cemetery, Villers-Faucon.

On the night of 24/25 September the 74th Division was relieved by the 27th American Division, which in turn suffered heavy casualties during the next attempts to take Gillemont Farm and the Hindenburg Line at nearby Bony. On 27 September the First and Third Armies attacked the Hindenburg System on the Canal du Nord and broke through. On 28 September the Belgian Army and the British Second Army attacked in Belgium, and from the coast down to Ypres, began driving into the German lines. In between these two great advances lay the Fifth Army.

During the morning of 25 September the Division entrained from Tincourt and Péronne, and left for Villers-Bretonneux. The 24th Welsh entrained at Péronne at 3.00 pm and arrived at Villers-Brettoneaux at 9.00 pm, being billeted in the ruined town overnight. Spence-Jones rejoined the battalion on the following day, and the battalion marched to Corbie on 27 September, prior to entraining with the remainder of the division for Chocques, in the Fifth Army area,

Private John Clarke Harries (320401), of Cynwyl Elfed. Died of wounds on 3 October 1918.

and arrived at Norrent Fontes on the 28th. The 24th Welsh took up billets in Chocques village, and Spence-Jones left again to take temporary command of 230 Brigade. On 1 October the Division relieved the 19th Division in the line at Locon, the 24th Welsh relieving the 10th Battalion, Royal Warwickshire Regiment.

Due to the situation facing them now, the Germans also began to withdraw on the front facing the Fifth Army. There were no plans for the Fifth to attack, however, merely to follow up the German withdrawal. As a result, General Girdwood issued the following order:

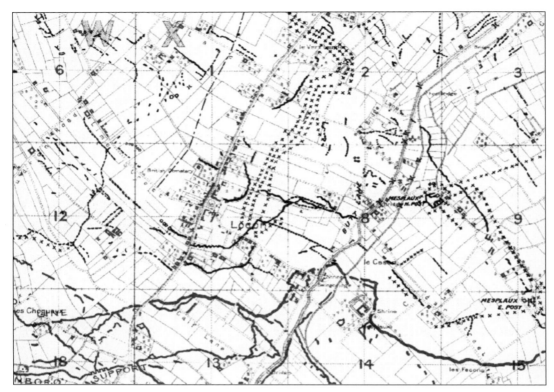

A section of trench map showing the location of Locon (36SW1–Aubers).

'29th September 1918. The successful offensives being conducted by the allied armies may cause the enemy opposite the front of the Vth Army to continue his withdrawal to the line of the Douai - Lille Canal and the Lille defences.

'In order to test the strength of the enemy forces opposite to the XIth Corps, minor operations are being carried out by three divisions tomorrow morning.

'On taking over the front of the 19th Division, it is of great importance that the Division should be prepared to act promptly as soon as indications are obtained that the enemy intends to withdraw, or is in process of retiring...'

Girdwood did not intend for the 74th Division to attack and force the Germans to withdraw, but instead wanted it to be ready to follow up any withdrawal that might occur, thus limiting the number of casualties among his men. There was no real need for heroics at this stage of the war; the Germans were on the retreat, but the men were told to be ready to act quickly if such a withdrawal took place, and to seek out opportunities to cut off and capture any isolated posts that may then occur in order to gain intelligence from their garrisons about the enemy's dispositions.

The division was alloted the Halpegarde to Herles road for traffic and signal communications, and both brigade and divisional headquarters would be located as near as possible to the road.

At 11.00 am on 2 October it was noticed that the Germans had vacated the trenches in front of the division, so Girdwood ordered his battalions forward. After just a day in the reserve trenches at Locon, 231 Brigade was sent up: the 24th Welsh marched to relieve the 9th Battalion, South Staffordshire Regiment, in the front line at Aubers Ridge, with Battalion HQ setting up in map reference N 26 c 8.3, and the 10th KSLI on the right. As had occurred during the German withdrawal to the Hindenburg Line in March 1917, their withdrawal here was also well executed: cross roads and bridges were blown up; culverts were destroyed; booby traps of all types were left; and wire obstacles were erected. Girdwood ordered the division to advance to the line La Bassée-Aubers-Fromelles, and it was dark before the trenches were reached.

On the following day, 3 October, the advance continued; no opposition was encountered, and 231 Brigade consolidated their new positions during the night, along the line Basse Rue, Fournes, Petite Hate, Bourdin, le Marais, Hockon, and Sainghin. Again, on the following morning the advance continued, but this time the Germans slowed the brigade with artillery fire, causing four casualties in the 24th Welsh. One of the men wounded died that same day in hospital in Béthune. Private Alan Morgan (60219) was the son of Jane Morgan, of Pwllswyddog, Tregaron. He was

Private Alun Morgan (60219), of Tregaron. Died of wounds at Béthune on 4 October 1918

A section of trench map showing Aubers Ridge (Map 36SW1 Aubers).

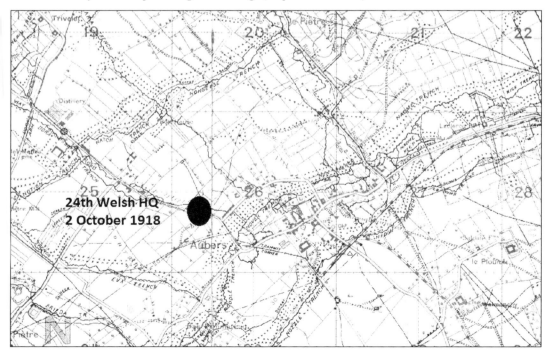

A British soldier manning a hastily erected roadblock during the period of the German offensive on the Lys.

twenty years old and is buried in Béthune Town Cemetery. The division reached a line east of Wavrin and Lattres, along the railway to la Haie, by nightfall, and patrols found the Germans holding positions in force directly in front of the divisional line. The situation remained unchanged here for the coming days, with several casualties being suffered by the 24th Welsh due to sporadic artillery fire and sniping.

On 7 October half of the battalion moved into reserve; A and C Companies were relieved by the 10th KSLI, and B and D Companies side-stepped, taking over the line held by A Company of the 23rd Battalion, London Regiment. On 8 October command of the sector held by the 55th and 74th Divisions passed from XI Corps to III Corps. Conditions by now must have been poor, as many of the casualties suffered during this period were succumbing to sickness, probably victims of the Spanish Flu outbreak, a pandemic which lasted from January 1918 until December 1920, killing over fifty million people. On the 9th the Germans raided the trenches held by the 10th KSLI, and on the following night the battalion retaliated, killing over twenty Germans and bringing in a live prisoner for interrogation. The 24th Welsh were relieved on the following morning by the 12th SLI, and withdrew to La Cliqueterie Farm, where it assembled for inspection on 12 October.

The front remained static while the 24th Welsh was in reserve, but on the 15th patrols from 230 Brigade once more found the German trenches at la Haie deserted, so the division moved on again, until machine-gun fire halted the advance of 230 Brigade in front of the canal near Mangre. On 16 October the 24th Welsh moved to Herlies, and on the following day moved into brigade reserve at Faches. On the following morning the Germans were found to have disappeared again, having covered their withdrawal by machine-gun fire from the canal until 4.30 am. Patrols were sent out, but did not contact the enemy, and reports came in that the Germans had evacuated Lille.

The war was drawing to a close, and the 74th Division was lucky not to be involved in any set piece battles. Further south, there was heavy fighting around Cambrai and north of Le Cateau during the Battle of the Selle, in which the 38th (Welsh) Division was caught up.

Sir Douglas Haig wrote of this time in his despatches:

'Our advance on the north of the Lys had brought our troops far to the east of the Lille defences on the northern side, while our progress on the le Cateau front had turned the Lille defences from the south. The German forces between the Sensée and the Lys were once more compelled to withdraw, closely followed by our troops, who constantly drove in their rear-guards and took a number of prisoners. The enemy was given no opportunity to complete the removal of his stores and the destruction of roads and bridges, or to evacuate the civil population.

'The movement began on the 15th October, when, in spite of considerable opposition, our troops crossed the Haute Deûle Canal on a wide front north of Pont-à-Vendin. By the evening of the 17th October the 8th Division, of General Sir A. Hunter Weston's VIIIth Corps, had entered Douai, and the 57th and 59th Divisions, of Lt. - General Sir R. C. B. Haking's XIth Corps, were on the outskirts of Lille. At 5.50 am, on the 18th October, our troops had encircled Lille, which was clear of the enemy...'

The 74th Division kept up the pursuit, suffering fewer casualties by now as German resistance wilted on this sector. 230 Brigade crossed the canal and moved forwards to the line Wattignies - l'Arbrisseau on 17 October. The bridges had been partially destroyed, but that only slightly slowed the advance, the division entering Habourdin that day, before setting up a forward line along the railway east of Ronchin. The advance was slower on the 18th, being held up by a fog. The 231st Brigade had taken over the right and found the enemy rearguard, mostly machine guns covered by a battery of field guns, at Sainghin. The village was cleared without difficulty, and an outpost line taken up on the River la

Marcq. The 229th Brigade encountered the enemy on that day at Ascq, but retired before the patrols, and was found to be holding the east bank of the river. An outpost line was established on the line of the railway, west of the river.

The advance continued on 19 October, with 231 Brigade reaching Camphin and 229 Brigade reaching Baisseur. The 24th Welsh moved into billets at Lamain on the following day, its lucky run on casualties coming to an end with one man killed and one wounded. The dead man was Company Quartermaster Sergeant John Jenkin Davies (320157), the forty two year old son of John and Anne Davies, of Frondeg Farm, Llanfarian, and the husband of Elizabeth Davies, of 32 Bridge Street, Aberystwyth. He is buried in Lamain Communal Cemetery.

The battalion remained in Lamain until 30

CQMS John Jenkin Davies.

125

General Birdwood's triumphal entry into Lille.

October, resting and carrying out battalion drill, as well as supplying working parties. On the 30th the battalion relieved the 16th Battalion, Royal Sussex Regiment in the front line opposite Tournai. The nearby village of Orcq was strongly held by the Germans, and was attacked by the 12th SLI that day, but only small footholds were made on the village.

Apart from the Battle of the Sambre, which took place on 4 November, the last of the great battles had now been fought, and only isolated actions now took place. The Germans opposite the 74th Division seemed content behind strongly fortified positions, which were defended by belts of barbed wire, but the only action seen by the division was a series of patrols and melees on their front, while the great advances to the north and south were still pushing the Germans back. On 2 November the 24th Welsh and 10th KSLI pushed strong patrols forward, behind a creeping artillery barrage, to test German strength, but came under heavy machine-gun fire and withdrew. Second Lieutenant W. T. Harries and one other rank were wounded.

The division stayed put over the coming days, the 24th Welsh being kept busy consolidating the line, and the only noteworthy event was an attempted trench raid by the Germans on the 24th Welsh on the night of 4 November, which was beaten off with just one casualty. There is no mention in the battalion war diary of Private Thomas Thomas (320981) the twenty three year old son of John and Mary Thomas, of Tredegar, being killed on the 3rd. He has no known grave and is the only man of the battalion commemorated on the Ploegsteert Memorial.

The battalion did not move for the next two days, losing three men on 6 November: Private Owen Davies (59941), of Beddgelert, was killed; Private Albert Heath (61697), of Cardiff, died of wounds; and Private Hubert George Smith (320057), of Tenby, died of sickness.

Private Thomas Thomas's name on the Ploegsteert Memorial, the only member of the 24th Welsh commemorated on it.

During the morning of 8 November, patrols of the RWF entered Tournai, and a Belgian lady came into the outpost line to report that the Germans had evacuated the town at 3.00 am. General Girdwood then sent patrols of the 24th Welsh into it. Tournai is split by the River l'Escaut, and the patrols found that the Germans had blown up all of the bridges and lined the opposite bank with machine guns. After the patrols had reported the situation, the battalion was relieved by the 10th KSLI, and moved into support along the Froyennes to Tournai Road. It had suffered its last man killed in action during the war during the patrol, when Private David John Davies (73690), of Maesteg, was shot by a sniper. He was 25 years old and is buried in Tournai Communal Cemetery Allied Extension.

The divisional engineers bridged the river during the morning, and the 10th KSLI crossed to the east bank, the 25th RWF close behind in support. The Germans were now forced into retreat and the division advanced to the line Beclers - Thimougies. Thimougies was entered that evening, and was found to have been evacuated by the Germans. The 24th Welsh formed pickets on the eastern exits of Tournai on the 9th, and that night moved into billets at Havinnes. On the following day the battalion moved to billets in Herquegies, while the division advanced to the railway line north of Grundmetz, finding the road to be mined, but no sign of any Germans, who had failed to detonate the mines.

At 8.30 am on 11 November 1918, the leading element of the 74th Division, 231 Brigade, entered Ath, and at 8.45 am General Girdwood sent the following message to his brigades:

'Hostilities cease 11.00 today, after which hour no further easterly movement will take place. Outposts will be put out, and all military precautions taken. Contact with the enemy will be avoided. Troops at present in movement will halt at 11.00 and occupy best available billets, or return to last night's billets if no facilities exist.'

The 24th Welsh moved to billets in Oeudeghien, remaining there until the 16th, when it moved to billets in Moustir, en route to Beclers. On the following day the battalion reached Velaines, where it was billeted for the night, and on 17 November reached Beclers, furnishing working parties, which were utilised in road repairing and repairing the embankment of the Tournai to Ath Railway.

As December dawned, coalminers began being demobilised and returned home. The battalion remained at Beclers until 4 December, and moved to Velaines the following day, undergoing two days of training before parading on the 7th along the Leuze to Tournai Road for inspection by His Majesty King George V. The battalion remained here for a further week before moving to Moustir on 15 December, en

King George V during a presentation ceremony in France.

128

route for Grammont, which was reached on 18 December. The battalion were billeted in Overboulaere, a part of Grammont, which is a town inside Belgium, roughly ten miles north of Ath. Major J. B. H. Woodcock assumed command of the now depleted battalion on 22 December, while Spence-Jones assumed command of 231 Brigade. The battalion's first and last Christmas in France was celebrated here, in a most pleasant part of Belgium. The main problem suffered now, after four years of war, was boredom, which breeds discontent, so the battalion took part in various organised pastimes: it re-assumed its early prowess as a fine rugby playing battalion, and a member of the battalion even triumphed in an army boxing tournament in Lille. Educational training was undertaken, preparing men for a return to civilian life, as well as relieving boredom.

Over 120 men were demobilised during the first week of January, so it must have been a strange feeling for the men left behind in France, especially when more batches of men were demobilised as the month drew on; during the month almost half of the remaining battalion, 248 men, had returned home. During February demobilisation continued, with an officer and sixteen men leaving on the 5th; one officer and twenty three men on the 6th; and on 7 February, after the demobilisation of forty nine more men, a motion was carried to form an Old Comrades Association. The battalion was now down to one company.

During the 13th and 14th, the Assistant Director of Armaments inspected the battalions weapons, and on 16 February five officers and a hundred other ranks were detailed to join the Army of Occupation in Germany, leaving the battalion the following month. Educational classes and gymnasium work carried on regardless throughout February, and a party of officers and men received three days leave to visit Brussels. On 8 March Major Woodcock tallied up the battalion's casualties during its time in France:

Killed	Officers	6	Other Ranks	55
Wounded	Officers	9	Other Ranks	385
Missing	Officers	-	Other Ranks	24
Wounded & Missing	Officers	1	Other Ranks	1
Injured	Officers	1	Other Ranks	1
Died of Wounds	Officers	-	Other Ranks	42

After the death of David John Davies on 8 November, only eight more men from the battalion are known to have died as a result of the war: Four more men from the battalion died of wounds prior to the Armistice, and four more are recorded of dying of sickness after the war.

Several more awards to men of the battalion were also noted: The Meritorious Service Medal to QMS J. L. Jones; the Military Medal to Private Wareham (320342); and the Distinguished Conduct Medal and Belgian Croix de Guerre to Sergeant T. Lougher (320523). Details of these awards, and more, are to be found in the Appendix 'Awards to the 24th Welsh'.

News also reached Major Woodcock on 26 March that Company Sergeant Major Edwin Jenkins (320011), of Haverfordwest, who was reported as missing, had died in German hands on 26 September 1918. He is buried in Honnechy British Cemetery.

Sergeant Thomas Lougher, DCM, of Tregaff, Llancarfan, near Cowbridge.

*The grave of C.S.M.
Edwin Jenkins at
Honnechy British
Cemetery.*

The last days of the battalion are very sketchy. The battalion War Diary for April 1918 holds little clue to the goings on of the few men left. Twenty men left the battalion on 20 April by motor lorry to join the 6th Battalion, South Wales Borderers, at Gislenghien. A week later the last three mules owned by the battalion were despatched to Corcolo, and on 26 April the diary noted that Second Lieutenant O. Olive had been promoted to lieutenant. The last diary entry notes the total number of men demobilised during the month to have been seven officers and fourteen other ranks, although ten other ranks had re-enlisted.

On Tuesday 24 June 1919 the cadre of the 24th Welsh landed at Dover, after over three years overseas. The cadre consisted of two officers (Major J. B. H. Woodcock, DSO, and Lieut. T. L. Curtis) and eighteen men, who arrived at Carmarthen on the following day, after having caught the 5.20 am train from Dover. No one in the town knew that the battalion was returning, and so there was no civic reception. This was hastily arranged for Thursday 3 July, and notices were put in all of the local newspapers to advertise the ceremony, and also appealing for former members of the battalion to attend.

At 3.30 pm on 3 July 1919 the cadre of the 24th Welsh paraded at Carmarthen Barracks, prior to marching through the town to St Peter's Church, where Major Woodcock presented the battalion colour, which was erected alongside that of the 15th Welsh. Sadly the battalion was never reformed, but in its short life it had won several famous and hard fought, battle honours: 'Egypt, 1916-17', 'Gaza', 'Jerusalem', 'Jericho', 'Téll Asur', 'Palestine, 1917– 18', 'Somme, 1918', 'Bapaume, 1918', 'Hindenburg Line', 'Epehy', 'Pursuit to Mons' and 'France and Flanders, 1918'

Some 224 men from the battalion were killed during its time at war, admittedly a low number compared to most of the other battalions of the Welsh Regiment, especially compared to the 9th Welsh, for example, who lost almost 800 men died, or the 2nd Welsh, who lost almost 1,400 men; but many other men had been wounded or invalided home suffering from illness and disease contracted during the tough campaign in Palestine. The second line battalions of the Pembroke and Glamorgan Yeomanry, on the other hand, had supplied a constant stream of well trained recruits to units in other theatres of war, at least 104 of them killed or died of wounds.

When the Territorial Force was reformed in 1920, all but the first fourteen of the fifty-three regiments of Yeomanry were converted to other roles. The Pembroke Yeomanry became the 102nd Field Brigade, Royal Artillery, recruiting in Pembrokeshire and Cardiganshire. It consisted of four batteries, two in each county, and saw service with the Eighth Army in the Middle East during World War Two; and also fighting in Italy before taking part in the Battle of Normandy.

Appendix I

Honours and Awards to the 24th Welsh

An accurate picture of the various medallic awards to the 24th Welsh is not known, but on the following pages, compiled from information from various sources, are details of the known awards to the Battalion, and also known awards to officers and men of the Pembroke and Glamorgan Yeomanry who did not serve with the 24th Welsh. The Carmarthen Journal of 4 July 1919 did, however, note that:

'A splendid share of honours and awards was won by the battalion. Lieutenant Colonel Spence-Jones, the commanding officer, was made CMG (appointed to the Order of St Michael and St George) and was awarded the DSO; Major J. B. H. Woodcock won the DSO; ten officers secured the MC and one gained the Bar to MC; whilst among the other ranks, two won the MSM, thirteen the DCM; and nineteen the MM. Seven officers and seven other ranks were mentioned in despatches.'

Victoria Cross

Major Stewart Loudon Shand VC. He had served with the Pembroke Yeomanry during the Boer War. During the First World War, he served with the 10th Battalion, Yorkshire Regiment, and commanded the battalion on the opening day of the Battle of the Somme. His award of the Victoria Cross was published in the *London Gazette* of 8 September 1916:

'For most conspicuous bravery. When his company attempted to climb over the parapet to attack the enemy's trenches, they were met by very fierce machine gun fire, which temporarily stopped their progress. Maj. Loudoun-Shand immediately leapt on the parapet, helped the men over it, and encouraged them in every way until he fell mortally wounded. Even then he insisted on being propped up in the trench, and went on encouraging the non-commissioned officers and men until he died.'

Companion of the Order of St Michael and St George (C.M.G.)

Lieutenant Colonel Cecil John Herbert Spence-Jones. His notification of the investiture of the C.M.G. was published in the *London Gazette* of 3 June 1919. He was also awarded the Distinguished Service Order.

Lieutenant Colonel Edward Miller. He commanded one of the reserve battalions of the Pembroke Yeomanry.

Gerald Trevor Bruce DSO. His notification of the investiture of the C.M.G. was published in the *London Gazette* of 3 June 1919. He had served with the Glamorgan Yeomanry before being given command of a battalion of the Lincolnshire Regiment.

Order of the British Empire (OBE)

Wing Commander James Bevan Bowen. He had served with the Pembroke Yeomanry before transferring to the Royal Air Force, becoming a Wing Commander.

The Distinguished Service Order

Lieutenant Colonel Gerald Trevor Bruce. His award of the Distinguished Service Order was published in the *London Gazette* of 3 June 1918. There was no citation, as the award was made in the King's Birthday Honours List.

Lieutenant Colonel Delmé William Campbell Davies-Evans. He was a member of the Pembroke Yeomanry, but commanded the 2/8th Battalion, Worcestershire Regiment. His award of the Distinguished Service Order was published in the *London Gazette* of 3 June 1919. There was no citation, as the award was made in the King's Birthday Honours List, but the award was for: 'his fine leadership at Verchain during the Battle of the Selle in October 1918.'

Lieutenant Colonel Ernest Helme DSO and Bar. Helme was a member of the Glamorgan Yeomanry before becoming second in command of the 15th Welsh. He won the DSO twice. The citation for his first DSO, dated 2 December, 1918 reads:

'For conspicuous gallantry and ability. He organised and carried out the crossing of a river by his battalion with great foresight and skill, and during the subsequent advance and operations lasting several days, his example of personal courage, and his powers of organisation and command enabled his men successfully to accomplish all the tasks they were called on to perform.'

Helme was awarded a bar to his DSO soon afterwards. The citation in the *Gazette*, dated 30 July 1919 read:

'For gallant and skilful leading of his battalion near Villers Outreaux on October 8th, 1918. Owing to another brigade having been checked in their attack on the front enemy trenches his battalion had to delay their advance for some time while suffering heavily from artillery barrage. By his personal efforts, skill and determination the battalion, which had been thrown into some confusion, was rallied and assembled for the further advance, eventually reaching a further final objective. It was almost entirely due to his gallant leading that the advance was enabled to continue after the check experienced.'

Lieutenant Colonel Edward Darley Miller. He had commanded one of the reserve battalions of the Pembroke Yeomanry. His award of the Distinguished Service Order was published in the *London Gazette* of 3 June 1919. There was no citation, as the award was made in the King's Birthday Honours List.

Major Llewellyn Partridge. His award of the Distinguished Service Order was published in the *London Gazette* of 26 March 1917, and reads:

'For conspicuous gallantry and devotion to duty. He displayed great judgment and skill in the leadership of his three light patrols, and showed inexhaustible resource in overcoming the most serious physical obstacles. Later, in action he proved himself a dashing and competent leader.'

Lieutenant Colonel Cecil John Herbert Spence-Jones. His award of the Distinguished Service Order was published in the *London Gazette* of 2 July 1918, and reads:

'For conspicuous gallantry and devotion to duty during an enemy counter-attack. He went forward into the firing line and remained with his men, and by his presence and example under heavy fire encouraged them to hold on to a very difficult and exposed position.'

Lieutenant Colonel Odo Richard Vivian DSO MVO TD. His award of the Distinguished Service Order was made while he was in command of the 6th Welsh in France. The citation was published in the *London Gazette* of 7 March 1918, and reads:

'For conspicuous gallantry and devotion to duty when commanding his Battalion. At a most critical period of an attack he rallied his men and led an advance on an enemy strong point which was taken and held. He organised the defence of the ground gained, exposing himself under heavy fire for some hours, with an utter disregard of personal safety. Had it not been for his initiative at a difficult time no ground would have been gained at this point.'

Major John Burrell Holme Woodcock. His award of the Distinguished Service Order was published in the *London Gazette* of 30 May 1919. There was no citation, as the award was made in the King's Birthday Honours List.

The Military Cross

Lieutenant Cecil Mein Probyn Coxwell-Rogers. His award of the Military Cross was for a period when he had been attached to the 74th Battalion, Machine Gun Corps. The citation was published in the *London Gazette* of 29 July 1919, and reads:

'East of Templeux le Guérard, September 21st, 1918, this officer advanced with his guns as a link between the attacking brigades of the division, and by skilful disposition of his guns inflicted heavy casualties on the enemy and broke up a determined counter-attack. During the day, although his section suffered 16 casualties [i.e. two-thirds of its strength], he managed to keep two guns in action, and by his cool courage and unfailing cheerfulness under fire encouraged the survivors. His resource and initiative throughout the recent operations have been of the highest order.'

Second Lieutenant Evan John Carne David. His award of the Military Cross was published in the *London Gazette* of 4 February 1918, and reads:

'For conspicuous gallantry and devotion to duty. When part of the line was being heavily shelled and a large number of casualties were caused, with total disregard of danger he steadied his men and maintained his position. Later, he led his company with great success in an attack.'

Lieutenant Daniel John Davies. His award of the Military Cross was published in the *London Gazette* of 29 July 1919, and reads:

'For conspicuous gallantry and devotion to duty in bringing up rations and ammunition under 'heavy shell and machine-gun fire when transport officer. Though wounded, he remained at duty and never failed under any circumstances to bring his transport up to the front line. His calmness under shell fire and quiet and confident bearing were an example to all.'

Lieutenant David Morris Davies. His award of the Military Cross was for his service at Bourlon Wood, while he was attached to the 17th Welsh. The citation was published in the *London Gazette* of 4 February 1918, and reads:

'For conspicuous gallantry and devotion to duty. When two parties of the enemy had been passed over by the attack and opened fire in rear of the assaulting troops, he quickly grasped the situation and rushed the enemy, killing several and capturing 16 prisoners. By his prompt action he saved what might have proved a very dangerous situation.'

Lieutenant (Acting Captain) Vincent Griffiths. His award of the Military Cross was published in the *London Gazette* of 15 February 1919, and reads:

'For conspicuous gallantry and leadership. On September 18th. 1918, during operations east of Ronssoy, he led his company with exceptional determination and skill, and the capture of Orchard Post, on the first objective, was entirely due to him. On September 21st he led his company with marked ability in the advance on Gillemont Farm, gained his objective, and consolidated his position. Later, under heavy counter-attack, he withdrew his command successfully, showing great coolness and ability.'

Lieutenant Percival Hay. His first award of the Military Cross was published in the *London Gazette* of 4 February 1918, and reads:

'For conspicuous gallantry and devotion to duty throughout two days' operations. On two occasions he endeavoured to reach a party of men who had been cut off by the enemy, and only desisted when most of his men were put out of action. He also did good work.'

He was also awarded a Bar to his Military Cross; the citation, which was published in the *London Gazette* of 14 February 1919, reads:

'For most conspicuous gallantry and initiative. During the operations east of Ronssoy on September 19th, 1918, while his battalion was advancing on Orchard Post, he, with only one other rank, forced an enemy post containing two machine guns which had been harassing the left flank of the battalion to surrender, thereby greatly assisting the advance. Later, he and the same man again captured an enemy post containing two machine guns. During these operations he and the man captured four machine guns and over fifty prisoners. These splendid acts of courage were invaluable.'

Lieutenant Richard Fleetwood Jenkins. He was commissioned into the Pembroke Yeomanry, but was attached to the 1/4th Cheshires. His award of the Military Cross was published in the *London Gazette* of 4 October 1919, and reads:

'On 16th October, 1918, he led a patrol party of eight men, who crossed the Lys Canal on a temporary raft, which only two men at a time could occupy, under heavy machine-gun and rifle fire. He maintained himself in face of machine-gun and minenwerfer fire on the enemy's bank until reinforced by a company of another regiment. He showed marked gallantry and dash.'

Second Lieutenant James Henry Lewis. He was commissioned into the Pembroke Yeomanry, but was attached to the 1/7th Cheshires. His award of the Military Cross was published in the *London Gazette* of 3 October 1919, and reads:

'In the operations near Menin, on 14th October, 1918, he led his platoon with great gallantry. Before reaching our barrage he captured a pill-box with one machine gun and fifteen prisoners, and later, in the second phase, rushed two more enemy machine guns and captured their crews. Throughout he inspired his men with confidence by his splendid example and untiring energy and fearlessness under heavy fire.'

Lieutenant John Frederick Allen Lewis. His award of the Military Cross was published in the *London Gazette* of 30 May 1919. The award was in the King's Birthday Honours List, and had no citation.

Lieutenant David Lloyd Popkin Morgan. His award of the Military Cross was published in the *London Gazette* of 2 July 1918, and reads:

'For conspicuous gallantry and devotion to duty. When a gap occurred in the line after the capture of an enemy position he made repeated journeys over a fire-swept zone carrying information and keeping in close touch with the situation. By his initiative and coolness he was largely responsible for driving back an enemy counter-attack.'

Reverend Hugh Rees. He was serving as chaplain to the 24th Welsh when he won his award of the Military Cross. The award was mentioned in the battalion war diary on 16 December 1917, and was in the New Year's Honours List.

Reverend Abraham Rees-Morgan. He was serving as chaplain to the 24th Welsh when he won his award of the Military Cross. The award was published in the *London Gazette* of 2 July 1918, and reads:

'For conspicuous gallantry and devotion to duty. He rendered the greatest service to the battalion by his organisation of stretcher bearers and dressing stations during an engagement. He showed complete contempt of danger.'

Lieutenant (Quartermaster) George Matthew Rumball. His award of the Military Cross was published in the *London Gazette* of 2 July 1918, and reads:

'For conspicuous gallantry and devotion to duty. When ammunition was urgently needed and the position was inaccessible to transport, he personally carried 900 rounds to the firing line under heavy shell and machine-gun fire.'

Lieutenant George Alfred Sheridan Shedden. His award of the Military Cross was for a period when he was attached to the 74th Battalion, Machine Gun Corps. The citation was published in the *London Gazette* of 29 July 1919, and reads:

'For conspicuous gallantry east of Ronssoy, September 21st, 1918, when in charge of a section of machine guns. During the advance his section and the infantry with him suffered heavy casualties from hostile shelling, and he found himself separated from neighbouring troops by a wide valley. He was fired at by small bodies of the enemy, whom he ordered to surrender, disarmed, and sent to the rear. When his advance was held up he dug in under heavy machine-gun fire from three sides and subsequently broke up a hostile counterattack directed between his guns and the infantry. Throughout the operation he set a fine example of courage and devotion to duty.'

Lieutenant Howell Cyril Watkins. His award of the Military Cross was published in the *London Gazette* of 15 February 1919, and reads:

'For gallantry, good leading and initiative near Ronssoy. When his company commander was killed during the attack on September 7th, 1918, he immediately took command of the company, which he steadied by his personal example and powers of command, and led with great dash throughout the rest of the day's operations. On September 18th and 21st he again showed great gallantry and dash, fighting his company with conspicuous ability and in spite of a wound, with which he was later evacuated.'

Captain James Hamilton Langdon Yorke. His award of the Military Cross was published in the *London Gazette* of 2 July 1918, and reads:

'For conspicuous gallantry and devotion to duty. When part of the line was driven back by the enemy he rapidly reorganised the situation with great skill under very heavy shell and machine-gun fire. He showed splendid leadership and initiative.'

He was killed during the action on 27 December 1917 and is buried at Jerusalem War Cemetery.

The Distinguished Conduct Medal

The Distinguished Conduct Medal, or DCM, was the highest award for gallantry, apart from the Victoria Cross, that could be awarded to other ranks. The following men of the 24th Welsh gained the award of the DCM during the Battalion's short time at war:

Sergeant Bertie Averill, 320926. (Brynmenin). His award was published in the *London Gazette* of 10 January 1920. The citation read:

'For conspicuous gallantry, initiative and good leadership. During the operations east of Ronssoy on 21st September 1918, when his company commander and company serjeant-major became casualties, he reorganised the company and led it in the advance. Later he led a Lewis gun detachment with great dash to a position on the exposed flank and silenced two enemy machine guns. He was later sent with a handful of men to an exposed flank, where, owing to his fine example and leadership, his party succeeded in beating off a counter-attack.'

Private John Davies, 320156. (Carmarthen). His award was published in the *London Gazette* of 10 January 1920. The citation reads:

'For conspicuous gallantry in the advance on Orchard Post on 18th September 1918. With total disregard of personal safety he advanced and captured an enemy post, consisting of an officer and thirty men, who with three machine guns were holding up the advance. By his splendid action the line was materially aided in moving forward to its objective.'

Sergeant David L. Evans, 320159. (Ammanford). His award was published in the *London Gazette* of 28 March 1918. The citation reads:

'For conspicuous gallantry and devotion to duty. When the whole of a Lewis gun team became casualties, he fetched in the gun and spare parts under heavy fire organised a team, and got the gun into action again with great success. He showed splendid initiative and determination.

Acting Company Sergeant Major John Hancocks, 320016. (Camrose, Pembroke). His award was published in the *London Gazette* of 11 March 1920. The citation reads:

'For conspicuous devotion to duty, ability and leadership as platoon commander. He has on various occasions led his platoon, setting an excellent example to all ranks.'

Sergeant David James Hinds, 320049. (Tenby) His award was published in the *London Gazette* of 1 May 1918. The citation reads:

'For conspicuous gallantry and devotion to duty when in charge of the battalion advance report station during an attack. In the final stages of the attack he occupied a most exposed position under shell and machine-gun fire, and continued to send back messages until the enemy's position was captured. He showed splendid courage and resource.'

Corporal Llewellyn Hopkins, 288185. (Laverock). His award was published in the *London Gazette* of 2 December 1919. The citation reads:

'During operations near Ronssoy, 18th/21st September 1918, he was placed in charge of a section and did excellent work. During the most trying hours of the advance he led and cheered the men under him, and by his cool and fearless manner gave them confidence. On the morning of the 21st September, he again did good work while leading and organising his two platoons. His judgement and excellent capabilities greatly encouraged the men, and undoubtedly helped the company in an awkward situation.'

Private Alfred H. Jones, 320297. (Pontycymmer). His award was published in the *London Gazette* of 10 January 1920. The citation reads:

'For conspicuous gallantry and initiative during the advance E of Ronssoy on September 21st 1918. This man, noticing that an enemy post was delaying the advance of his company, single-handed advanced on the post, killing two of the garrison: the remainder, six in number, then surrendered to him. This splendid act materially assisted in the advance and saved many casualties.'

Sergeant Thomas Lougher. (Llancarfan). His award was published in the *London Gazette* of 12 March 1919. The citation reads:

'For conspicuous gallantry and initiative. On 21st September 1918, when all the officers of his company had become casualties during the advance on Gillemont Farm, he took charge of the company and elements of other battalions in South

Gillemont Trench. When counter-attacked on three sides and forced to withdraw, he displayed considerable tactical skill in disposing his command so that the withdrawal was successfully carried out, frequently exposing himself to heavy artillery and machine-gun fire with absolute disregard of his personal safety.'

Private Thomas J. Morgan, 61656. (Port Talbot). His award was published in the *London Gazette* of 10 January 1920. The citation reads:

'For conspicuous gallantry in the advance on Orchard Post on 18th September 1918. This man, in company with two others, with total disregard of personal safety, advanced on and captured an enemy post consisting of an officer and thirty men, who, with three machine guns, were holding up the advance. By this splendid act of courage the line was materially aided in moving forward to its objective.'

Private John O. Nicholas, 320252. (Coughton, near Ross). His award was published in the *London Gazette* of 2 December 1919. The citation reads:

'For most conspicuous courage and initiative during the operations east of Ronssoy on 18th September 1918. Together with an officer he forced an enemy post with two machine guns, which were harassing his battalion's left flank, to surrender. Later, he again, with the same officer, succeeded in capturing another post with two machine guns. During these two operations the total captures made by this officer and himself were four machine guns and over 50 prisoners. These acts undoubtedly saved many casualties. He did magnificent work.'

Sergeant Simon Rees, 320408. (Kidwelly). His award was published in the *London Gazette* of 11 March 1920. The citation reads:

'On 19th September 1918, near Ronssoy, he collected all available men, and, by repeated journeys, kept up the supply of ammunition, thereby enabling the guns to put out of action an enemy machine gun which was holding up the advance. Two days later, in charge of a section, he got his guns into position under heavy shell fire.'

Private James W. Thomas, 22256. (Aberbargoed). His award was published in the *London Gazette* of 10 January 1920. The citation reads:

'For conspicuous gallantry in the advance on Orchard Post on 18th September 1918. This man, in company with two others, with total disregard of personal safety, advanced on and captured an enemy past consisting of an officer and thirty men, who with three machine guns were holding up the advance. By his splendid act of courage the line was materially aided in moving forward to its objective.'

Acting Company Sergeant Major Rhys Thomas, 320160. (Lampeter). His award was published in the *London Gazette* of 1 May 1918. The citation reads:

'For conspicuous gallantry and devotion to duty. He was on several occasions instrumental in establishing his portion of the line when driven back by superior numbers of the enemy, who were counterattacking. During the third counterattack, after his company commander had become a casualty, he led the line most gallantly, reorganised the defence of two companies, and held his ground, personally accounting for seven of the enemy with the bayonet. His gallantry and disregard of danger proved a fine incentive to the men.'

Acting Sergeant John Williams, 320166. (Nr. Corwen). His award was published in the *London Gazette* of 18 February 1918. The citation reads:

'For conspicuous gallantry and devotion to duty. He rendered very valuable service on light armoured car patrols, and set a splendid example to the men under him.'

Sergeant William Williams, 320121. (Nantgaredig). His award was published in the *London Gazette* of 11 March 1920. The citation reads:

'For gallant and able leadership on 7th September 1918, during the advance from Templeux la Fosse. When his company suffered heavy casualties from enemy barrage he reorganised two platoons, pushed on and obtained his objective. But for his initiative the line would have been held up.'

The Military Medal

Benjamin, Henry	Private	26532	Merthyr	
Beynon, William	Private	320256	Whitland	19/03/1918
Campbell, John	Private	57533	Liverpool	14/05/1919
Davies, Rhys T.	Private	320556	Bridgend	14/05/1919
Davies, William R.	Private	320384	Cardigan	19/03/1918
Hindle, Fred	Sergeant	320216	Lechlade	19/03/1918
Hunt, Albert James	Private	18648	Newport	14/05/1919
Jones, John Lewis	Q.M. Sgt	320108	Llandeilo	18/01/1919
Jones, Thomas	Private	320869	Bridgend	14/05/1919
Llewellyn, Evan D.	Corporal	203575	Letterston	13/09/1918
Llewellyn, William E.	Sergeant	320527	Broadway	10/04/1918
Lougher, Thomas	Serjeant	320523	Llancarfan	12/03/1919
Marks, William J.	Private	320932	Porth	19/03/1918
Maton, Eric William	Private	320500	Cardiff	19/03/1918
Miles, Edwin Albert	Private	57122	Bridgend	29/08/1918
Miller, Charles Frank	Corporal	525		
Morgan, Benjamin	Private	320351	Boncath	19/03/1918
Nott, Daniel G.L.	Sergeant	320801	Maynalls	10/04/1918
Phillips, David Lewis	Private	320071	Begelley	13/03/1919
Radcliffe, Tudor	Corporal	320572	Bridgend	14/05/1919
Redler, George Henry	Private	320563	Bristol	25/04/1918

Small, William	Corporal	320682	Porthcawl	14/05/1919
Thomas, Niah	Private	320489	Frousgawen	19/03/1918
Wareham, Edwin	Private	320342	Manchester	20/08/1919
Williams, John	Sergeant	320166	Bala	14/01/1918
Williams, William R.	Corporal	320529	Port Eynon	14/05/1919

The Meritorious Service Medal

Cole, Victor James	L/Corporal	WR/178798	Llanelli	14/06/1918
Jones, David Thomas	C.S.M.	320539	Glamorgan	03/06/1919
Jones, John Lewis	Q.M. Sergeant	320108	Llandeilo	18/01/1919

Mention in Despatches

Allen, John	Sergeant	320514	18/03/1917
Barnes, C. G. S.	Captain		05/07/1919
Basset, W.H.	Corporal	320755	28/12/1918
Bruce, G. T.	Lt Colonel		18/03/1917
Bruce, G. T.	Lt Colonel		05/07/1919
Collis, R. H.	Major		
Cotes, Henry J.	Sergeant1	1242	09/07/1919
Croucher, Ernest	Captain		05/07/1919
Edwards, R. G.	Sergeant	320554	18/03/1917
Fisher, Oakden	Captain		05/07/1919
Helme, E.	Major		05/07/1919
Helme, E.	Major		20/12/1918
Izzard, John	Sergeant	320005	09/07/1919
Langford, Francis	Sergeant	320381	09/07/1919
Lougher, Thomas	Sergeant	320523	09/07/1919
Miers, R. H.P.	Captain		18/03/1917
Miller, E.D.	Lt Colonel		05/07/1919
Partridge, Llewellyn	Major		18/03/1917
Phillips, W. A.	Lieutenant		20/12/1918
Pope, A.L.	Captain		05/07/1919
Richards, John L.	Lieutenant		14/06/1918
Roberts, Arthur T.	Sergeant	320533	18/03/1917
Roberts, Arthur T.	C.S.M.	320533	28/12/1918
Rosser, Brinley R	Private	320892	09/07/1919
Spence-Jones, C. J. H.	Lt Colonel		05/07/1919
Venables, J. C.	Sergeant	320579	18/03/1917
Williams, C. H.	Second Lieutenant		18/03/1917
Williams, Jonathan T	Private	320931	09/07/1919
Woodcock, J. B. H.	Major		20/12/1918
Woodcock, J. B. H.	Major		05/07/1919

Foreign Decorations

Serbian Order of the White Eagle, 4th Class.
Lieutenant Colonel Gerald Trevor Bruce. The award was published in the *London Gazette* of 15 February 1917.

Italian Bronze Medal for Valour
Corporal John Williams, 320166. The award was published in the *London Gazette* of 31 August 1917.

Croix de Chevalier
Major Llewellyn Partridge. The award was mentioned in the battalion war diary entry on 4 April 1917.

Romanian Croix de Virtute Militaire 2nd Class
Sergeant Thomas Lougher, 320523. The award was published in the *London Gazette* of 20 September 1919.

French Croix-de-Guerre
Captain Oakden Fisher. The award was published in the *London Gazette* of 12 December 1919.

In addition to these gallantry awards, there were also 257 awards of the Territorial Force War Medal to men of the battalion, including 127 to the Glamorgan Yeomanry and 125 to the Pembroke Yeomanry, plus thirty seven awards of the Territorial Force Efficiency Medal to men of the battalion. Details of these awards have been kindly supplied to the author by Mark Collins, but there is insufficient space to publish all of the details.

Officers of the 24th Welsh

Geoffrey William Pepperall Abraham, Captain, Glamorgan Yeomanry. Abraham was born at Christ Church Vicarage, Lichfield, Staffordshire on 6 September 1895, the son of the Right Reverend Charles Thomas Abraham, the Vicar of Bakewell and Bishop of Derby, and of Mary Theresa Abraham. He was educated at Cheltenham College, and was later in business with E and A Robinson, Redcliffe, Bristol. Abraham joined the Glamorgan Yeomanry as a trooper on 5 August 1914, and was commissioned within months, rapidly rising to captain. He served in Egypt from January 1916 with the Glamorgan Yeomanry and after its merger with the Pembroke Yeomanry joined the 24th Welsh. Abraham was lightly wounded on 31 September 1917 at the attack on Beersheba, but was more seriously wounded in the attack on Sheria on 6 November 1917, dying as a result in hospital at Port Said on 19 November 1917. He was 22 years old, and was buried at Port Said War Memorial Cemetery, Egypt. Abraham is commemorated on the Bakewell War Memorial, Derbyshire.

Alexander Gifford Ludford Astley, Captain. Astley was born on 18 February 1882, the son of Reverend Benjamin Ludford Astley and Maria Astley, of Cadeby, Leicestershire. He married Maria Christobel Young (née Arbuthnot), of 8 Sloane Terrace Mansions, SW1, on 3 June 1914. He had been commissioned into the Royal Fusiliers and transferred to the 14th Hussars on 28 October 1908, being promoted Captain on 24 December 1912. Astley was the Adjutant to the Glamorgan Yeomanry during their summer camp of 1914, but at the outbreak of war rejoined his old regiment, the 14th Hussars. Astley served in Egypt with his regiment before it took part in the advance into Mesopotamia in 1917. He was killed in action near Larjj on 5 March 1917, aged thirty five. He is commemorated on the Basra Memorial.

Capel Lisle Aylett-Branfill, Captain, Glamorgan Yeomanry. Branfill was born at Morro Velho, Brazil on 24 August 1884, the son of Capel Aylett Branfill and Gwladys Gwendoline Branfill (née Miers), of The Plas, Crickhowell, Breconshire. He was educated at Harrow, where he became a member of its Officer Training Corps, and played in the cricket and football First XIs. Branfill was commissioned into the Glamorgan Yeomanry in 1907, and had been promoted Captain by the time the Glamorgan Yeomanry moved to Egypt in 1916. He became ill with pneumonia and died in Egypt on 11 May 1916. He was buried at Cairo War Memorial Cemetery, Egypt. His Commanding Officer wrote: 'His death is a great loss, as he was one of the best officers in the regiment. His loss will be much felt by the regiment. He was everybody's friend and nobody's enemy. He was beloved by his men.' Branfill married Susannah Hamilton at Napleton Church, Worcester on 26 March 1913, and the couple had a young daughter, Gwendoline Hamilton Aylett, born 14 September 1914. Tragically Susannah and Gwendoline died on 24 January 1915.

Geoffrey Douglas Aylett-Branfill, Lieutenant. Branfill was born on 9 May 1895, the son of Capel Aylett Branfill and Gwladys Gwendoline Branfill (née Miers), of The Plas, Crickhowell, Breconshire. He was commissioned into the Glamorgan Yeomanry, and later transferred into the 10th Hussars. By the end of the war Branfill was attached to the 3rd Machine Gun Squadron. He was awarded the British War and Victory Medals for his service, which were sent to him in Nyasaland, where he had taken up a post as superintendent of police. Branfill died at Pembroke in 1967, aged 72.

Arthur William Back, Lieutenant. Back was commissioned into the Pembroke Yeomanry from the Inns of Court OTC on 20 November 1914. He embarked for Egypt with the Pembroke Yeomanry, and was then attached to the Somaliland Camel Corps. He was awarded the British War and Victory Medals for his wartime service.

Herbert Jodrell Barclay, Lieutenant. Barclay was born at Manorbier in 1881, the son of Henry Ferguson Barclay and Agnes Hermione Barclay (née Jennings). He qualified as a solicitor prior to the war and married Amy Beatrice Burnes Holland on 22 December 1913. Barclay was commissioned into the Pembroke Yeomanry from the Inns of Court OTC on 20 November 1914. He served with the 2/1st Pembroke Yeomanry before being posted to the 2nd Welsh, and served with them during the final offensive in France, from October 1918, in the rank of captain. Barclay survived the war, being awarded the British War and Victory Medals for his service, which were sent to him at Albion Chase, Broad Street, Bristol. He was also awarded the Territorial Force War Medal. Barclay died at Weston-Super-Mare in 1968, aged 86.

Richard Charles Edward Barclay, Major. Barclay was born at Manorbier in 1879, the son of Henry Ferguson Barclay and Agnes Hermione Barclay (née Jennings). He was commissioned into the Pembroke Yeomanry on 3 October 1912. On 17 May 1917 Barclay moved to France with the Royal Field Artillery. He survived the war, and was awarded the British War and Victory Medals for his services, which were sent to him at Croft House, Manorbier. He was also awarded the Territorial Force Efficiency Medal. Barclay married Nesta Lloyd of Glangwili in 1925, and died at Pembroke in 1957, aged 79.

Cyril Gwynne Sedley Barnes, MID, Captain. Barnes was born in 1883, the son of Robert and Alice Maria Barnes, of Harley Street, London. He was commissioned into the Pembroke Yeomanry on 1 September 1910. At the outbreak of war he was working as a chauffeur at Cilgwyn, Myddfai, and was mobilised with the Yeomanry, embarking for Egypt in 1916. Barnes was promoted captain on 10 August 1916, and served with the 24th Welsh until the battalion returned home in 1919. He survived the war, and was awarded the British War and Victory Medals for his services, which were sent to him at Abbey Wells, Woolton Hill, Newbury. Barnes married Ellen Seymour Methuen on 1 November 1924. He died at Chard on 2 December 1954, aged 71.

Alfred Stephen Barrett, Quartermaster, Captain. Barrett was born in 1868, and was an old soldier, having served with the 7th (Queen's Own) Hussars in India. He married his wife Catherine Cole in India in 1895. By 1911 he was a sergeant major with the Glamorgan Yeomanry, and on 1 November 1913 was commissioned into the regiment. He served during the war as Quartermaster and captain with the Glamorgan Yeomanry, embarking for Egypt with the Yeomanry in 1916. Barrett survived the war, being awarded the British War and Victory Medals for his services. He was also awarded the Territorial Force War Medal. He probably died at Tonbridge, Kent, in 1948.

John Walton Bishop, Major. Bishop was born in 1881 in Llandeilo, the son of Lewis and Ramona Bishop. He practised as a solicitor at Ammanford and at Burry Port. He was promoted captain on 26 November 1914, and embarked for Egypt with the yeomanry in 1916. He was promoted major on 24 February 1917, with precedence from 8 November 1916. Major John Walton Bishop TD, relinquished his commission on 13 May 1920, retaining the rank of major. He was awarded the British War and Victory Medals for his wartime services, as well as the Territorial Force War Medal, which were sent to him at Brynilltyd, Pembrey. He died in Carmarthen in 1962, aged 81.

Henry James Bladon, Second Lieutenant. Bladon was born on 29 April 1890, the son of James and Mary Jane Bladon of 8, Glenroy Street, Roath Park, Cardiff. He worked in London as a clerk, prior to attesting on 13 November 1915 into the 7th Welsh (T.F.), with the service number 11623. After almost two years on home service with the Territorial Force, where he was attached to the Glamorgan Yeomanry, Bladon joined the Inns of Court Yeomanry on 9 July 1917, and was discharged to a commission in the 4th Welsh (T.F.) on 25 June 1918. In the meantime, he had married Grace Lewis at St Martin's Parish Church, Cardiff on 18 October 1917. Bladon was posted to France in the summer of 1918, and joined the 15th Welsh around the time of the launch of the great advance in August. He was mortally wounded during the Battle of Morval, and died of his wounds on 1 September 1918. Bladon was 28 years old, and is buried at Morval British Cemetery, France in grave B. 22. His medals, the British War and Victory Medals, and the Memorial Plaque and scroll, were sent to his widow, who had by then remarried a Lieutenant Oliver.

John Alexander Bonnyman MBE, Captain. Bonnyman was born in South Shields, Durham on 27 November 1887, the son of James Smith. He was educated at University College, and served an engineering apprenticeship with Smith's Docks. In 1911 he was described as a mechanical engineer and ship repairer for the same company, and living in South Shields. By the outbreak of the war he had qualified as a draughtsman and marine surveyor, and was a university lecturer in Engineering. He was also assistant manager at Smiths Docks, of Teeside and Tyneside. He was now living in Llandaff, Cardiff, where the company had an office. Bonnyman travelled back from Cardiff to Newcastle to enlist as a private in the 9th Battalion, Northumberland Fusiliers, on 5 September 1914. On 21 December 1914, he was discharged from the Fusiliers as 'not likely to become an efficient soldier', but had already received a commission into the 4th Welsh. He served in Gallipoli with the 4th Welsh, and in 1917 was posted to the 24th Welsh, joining them in Palestine on 30 June 1917, in time to take part in the Third Battle of Gaza. On 26 December 1917

Bonnyman was wounded during an attack on Hill 1910. He was recorded as having received gunshot wounds to face, and bomb wounds to head and face on 27 December. He was hospitalised and subsequently graded B1 on 21 March 1918. Because of his engineering background, he was then seconded to the RAF Engine Repair facility in Egypt as an acting captain on administrative duties. On 30 May 1919 he was transferred to the unemployed list. On 12 September, Bonnyman relinquished his R.A.F. commission on re appointment to the Territorial Force, and was permitted to retain the rank of lieutenant. He served with 3rd Northamptonshire Brigade, RFA as a lieutenant, with precedence from 1 July 1917, and was promoted to Captain with 74th Northampton Brigade, RFA on 28 July 1920. After demobilisation he returned to his old position with Smith's Docks, and lived at 2 Belgrave Terrace, South Shields. Bonnyman eventually returned to South Wales, living at Wood Cottage, Sketty, Swansea. His business address was 104, Bute Street, Cardiff. In 1929 he patented a design for 'an improved cargo hatch cover'. During his time at war, Bonnyman had been awarded the M.B.E., which was gazetted on 3 June 1919. He was also awarded the Territorial Force War Medal, as well as receiving the British War and Victory Medals for his wartime service. Bonnyman attained the age limit and relinquished his commission, retaining his rank, on 11 December 1937. He died in Cardiff in 1957.

James Bevan Bowen, OBE, Wing Commander. Bowen, known to his family and friends as 'Van' Bowen, was born on 20 March 1883 at Llwyngwair, near Newport, Pembrokeshire, and was educated at Winchester and Trinity College, Cambridge. He was commissioned into the Pembroke Yeomanry in 1910, but as a trained wireless operator was accepted into the Royal Flying Corps in 1916, and became lieutenant colonel in 1917, wing commander in 1918, group captain in 1928, and air commodore in 1932, in which rank he retired in 1937. He was re-employed as a group captain at the outbreak of the Second World War. Bowen took an active role in Pembrokeshire life, being appointed a Justice of the Peace in 1907, a deputy lieutenant in 1932, vice-lieutenant in 1952 and some two years later became Lord Lieutenant of Pembrokeshire, an appointment he held until he resigned in 1958. He was appointed OBE in 1919, and in 1937 advanced to CBE. He married twice; first on 30 January 1915, Noel, elder daughter of Leonard Marshall of Nepicar House, Wratham, Kent, by whom he had six children. She died in 1951. Seven years later he married Muriel Ethelwyn Thomson of Monkton Old Hall, Pembroke, where he died in August 1969, at age of 86. For his services during the Great War Bowen was awarded the British War and Victory Medals. He was also the holder of the Territorial Force War Medal.

Arthur Patrick Bray, Lieutenant. Arthur was born in Harwich in 1882, the son of Arthur and Eliza Bray. He was commissioned into the 19th Welsh and served in France with them from 24 April 1917, but then returned home and was transferred to the 2/1st Pembroke Yeomanry. He survived the war, and was awarded the British War and Victory Medals for his services, which were sent to him at 35 Tewkesbury Terrace, Bounds Green Road, New Southgate. He married twice after the war, firstly to Norah Davey, who died in 1933, and then to Margaret Gertrude Cockman. Arthur died at Watford on 10 November 1958, aged 76.

Edmund Brewer, Second Lieutenant. Brewer was the son of Henry Gould and Rhoda Brewer, of 10, Norman Street, Caerleon, Monmouth. He was mobilised with the Royal Gloucester Hussars in August 1914, and landed in Egypt on 15 November 1915 with the regiment, after marrying Gwendoline Ireland at Gloucester. Brewer was commissioned into the Glamorgan Yeomanry on 8 December 1916. He was then attached to the 12th Battalion, South Wales Borderers, and was promoted captain. He was wounded at Bourlon Wood, and died of wounds on 12 January 1918, aged 33. Brewer is buried at Achiet-le-Grand Communal Cemetery Extension, France. For his services during the war, he was awarded the 1914/15 Star, British War and Victory Medals, which were sent to his widow at 17, Corporation Road, Newport, Monmouth.

Sir Gerald Trevor Bruce, DSO MID, Lieutenant Colonel. Bruce was born near Swansea in 1871, the son of Lewis Knight and Emelia Caroline Bruce (née Sullivan). He was a well renowned solicitor, and was commissioned into the Glamorgan Yeomanry on 20 August 1901. Gerald was promoted lieutenant on 4 October 1902, and major by 1908. Gerald embarked for Egypt with the Yeomanry in 1916, and served with the 24th Welsh during the Palestinian campaign. He was promoted to lieutenant-colonel in the North Staffordshire Regiment during the war, and was given command of a battalion of the Lincolnshire Regiment. He survived the war, returning to South Wales, where he became a very well known barrister. Bruce was awarded the British War and Victory Medals for his services during the war, which were sent to him at Lanelay, Pontyclun. He was also awarded the Territorial Force War Medal and the Distinguished Service Order, as well as being Mentioned in Despatches. Bruce died at Bridgend on 7 July 1953, aged 82.

John Clarence Napier Bruce, Second Lieutenant. Bruce was the son of Henry Campbell Bruce, Lord Aberdare, and Lady Constance Mary. He was commissioned into the Glamorgan Yeomanry on 21 September 1914. He was promoted Lieutenant on 30 December 1916 upon transferring to the Reserve Regiment of the Second Life Guards, and on 30 December 1916 transferred to the Guards Machine Gun Regiment. He later became an aide de camp on the army staff on 23 December 1917, and relinquished his commission on 14 June 1918. Bruce was awarded the British War and Victory Medals for his wartime service, which were sent to him at 1, Lowndes Square, S.W.1. He later became third Baron Aberdare, and died on 4 October 1957, aged 72.

John Geoffrey Bruce, Captain. Bruce was born at Pentyrch on 4 December 1897, the son of Gerald Trevor and Lilian Isabel Bruce (née Booker). He followed his father into the Glamorgan Yeomanry, being commissioned in 1914. Bruce served with the Yeomanry in Egypt and with the 24th Welsh in Palestine, before transferring to the Indian Army in 1917, where he was attached to the 6 Ghurkha Rifles. He was a member of the Mount Everest expeditions of 1922 and 1924. John married Marjorie Isabel Coney in 1932, before becoming an Instructor at the Staff College, Camberley. He then commanded the 2nd Battalion, 6th Ghurkha Rifles on the North West Frontier expedition, before returning to Britain. He served as a brigadier general on the General Staff during the Norwegian Expeditionary and France campaigns of 1940, and then commanded an infantry brigade in India before becoming Deputy Director of Military Operations, India, until 1942; major general in charge of the British Military Mission to China 1942; District Commander, India 1942-1944; Deputy Chief of General Staff, India 1944-1946; General Officer Commanding, Lahore District, India 1946-1948; retired 1948; Commandant, Civil Defence Staff College 1952-1956. He died at Bridport, Dorset in 1972, aged 74.

Honourable John Hamilton Bruce, Lieutenant. Bruce was born on 14 June 1868, the son of Henry Campbell Bruce, Second Baron Aberdare and Constance Mary Beckett. He served with the Glamorgan Yeomanry prior to the war. Bruce did not serve overseas, and his application for service medals was rejected. His address at the end of the war was Ross Bridge House, Cowrie. He died on 8 April 1964.

Sir Geoffrey Robert Sidney Byass, Captain. Byass was born at Craigafon, Port Talbot on 30 September 1895, the son of Sir Sidney Hutchinson Byass. He was educated at Winchester before going into his father's steel and tinplate business. Byass was commissioned into the Glamorgan Yeomanry, becoming a lieutenant on 5 April 1915. He was then attached to the Royal Field Artillery, being promoted captain on 6 February 1917. Byass survived the war, and was awarded the British War and Victory Medals for his wartime services, which were sent to him at Craig-y-Parcau, Bridgend. He returned to work in his father's business, and on 20 September 1919 married Marian Bruce, the daughter of Sir Gerald Trevor Bruce, becoming the second and last baronet after the death of his father in 1929. He died at Tilford, Surrey on 4 November 1976, aged 81.

Frank Herbert Byfield, MID, Lieutenant. Byfield was born at Cirencester in 1875, the son of Henry and Victoria Byfield. By 1911 he was living at The Parsonage, Carmarthen, with his wife Alice Maria (née Western), giving his occupation as Cavalry of the Line. He was commissioned from the 1st Dragoon Guards into the Welsh Regiment on 25 March 1917, and served with the 24th Welsh for the remainder of the war, being promoted lieutenant on 25 September 1918. Byfield survived the war, and was awarded the British War and Victory Medals for his service, which were sent to him at Bennett's House, Stawley, Wellington, Somerset. He was also Mentioned in Despatches during the war and died at Totnes, Devon in 1933, aged 58.

Herbert Reginald Chapman, Captain. Herbert was born in Cardiff in 1891, the son of William and Ellen Chapman. He had served with the 4th Welsh Brigade, Royal Field Artillery from 1901 onwards, before being commissioned into the Glamorgan Yeomanry after the outbreak of war. On 21 December 1914 he was gazetted as Second Lieutenant into the 13th Welsh, and served in France with the battalion from 2 December 1915. He survived the war, being awarded the 1914/15 Star, British War and Victory Medals for his services, which were sent to him at Lynwood, Windsor Esplanade, Cardiff.

Hugh Archibald Christy, Captain. Christy was born at Highfield in Bramhall, Cheshire, the son of Stephen Christy JP, hat manufacturer, and Blanche (née Chichester). He was educated at Harrow and Christ Church, Oxford. He was commissioned into the Glamorgan Yeomanry on 21 September 1914 and was promoted lieutenant on 20 October 1916, and Captain on 30 June 1917, serving with the 17th Welsh, before being attached to the Royal

Naval Division. He was awarded the British War and Victory Medals for his wartime service, which were sent to him at Llangoed Hall, Radnorshire. He died on 4 April 1946, aged 68. His brother, Stephen Christy, was killed on the Marne in 1914.

David Louis Clemetson, Lieutenant. Clemetson was born in Jamaica, the son of David R. and Mary E. Clemetson, of Frontier, Port Maria, St Mary, Jamaica. On 25 September 1912 he arrived in Britain, where he had been sent for education at Clifton College by his parents. Clemetson originally enlisted into the Sportsmen's Battalion, Royal Fusiliers, before being commissioned into the Welsh Regiment. He joined the 24th Welsh in France, and was killed near Gillemont Farm on 21 September 1918, aged 24. He is buried at Unicorn Cemetery, Vendhuile, France. Clemetson was awarded the British War and Victory Medals for his services during the war, which were sent to his mother at Frontier, Port Maria.

Robert Henry Collis, CMG, DSO, MID, Lieutenant Colonel. Collis was born in Ireland on 13 January 1875, the son of Robert Henry and Mary Anna Collis (née Phillips). He was commissioned into the 3rd Battalion, Leicester Regiment on 3 May 1892. He had retired as a captain in the army by 1908, and was gazetted major in the Pembroke Yeomanry on 1 April 1908. He continued to serve with the Pembroke Yeomanry during the war, attached to the Army Remounts Depot. He was Mentioned in Despatches twice during the war, and was awarded the 1914/15 Star, British War and Victory Medals for his services, which were sent to him at Kirklington Hall, Bedale, Yorkshire. Collis died at Poona, India on 9 November 1930, aged 55.

Lord William Cope, Major. Cope was born in Roath, Cardiff on 18 August 1870, the son of Matthew Cope and Margaret Harrison. He was educated at Repton School before attending Clare College, Cambridge in 1888. Cope was awarded his BA in 1891 and in 1895 collected his MA. He was a noted rugby player who played for Cambridge University while a student, and in 1891 played in the Varsity Match against Oxford, gaining a Blue. From 1891 through to 1895 Cope turned out for Cardiff, and after leaving university represented Blackheath. He was also capped for the Barbarians and for Wales. After leaving Cambridge he entered the legal profession and was admitted to the Inner Temple, he was called to the Bar in 1894. On 5 September 1900 he married Helen Shuldham, and they had two children: Helen Margaret Latita and William Shuldham. With the outbreak of war in 1914, Cope joined the Glamorgan Yeomanry, rising to the rank of major. Upon returning to Britain in 1918, he ran for Parliament, standing for the seat of Llandaff and Barry. In 1923 he became a Junior Lord of the Treasury, a post he held until 1928. On leaving the Treasury he was given the role of Comptroller of the Royal Household, a role he undertook for just a year, when he left government in 1929. Created a baronet, he held several offices in his home county of Glamorgan. He was a Justice of the Peace, and a Deputy Lieutenant and in 1932 was made High Sheriff of Glamorgan. In 1933 he was invested as a King's Council and was elevated to the peerage as Baron Cope of St Mellons in July 1945.He died on 15 July 1946.

Walter Frank Corbett, Major. Corbett was born in Richmond, Surrey in 1863, the son of Frank and Elizabeth Corbett. He transferred into the South Staffordshire Regiment from the South Wales Borderers on 28 February 1885. He was promoted into the Pembroke Yeomanry as a temporary major on 9 November 1914. Walter served as a staff officer in France for two years. He was awarded the British War and Victory Medals for his services during the war, which were sent to him at Glandofan, Rhoshill, Pembrokeshire. He died at Radnor on 28 May 1936, aged 73.

Cecil Mein Probyn Coxwell-Rogers MC, Lieutenant. Coxwell-Rogers was born on 29 May 1893, the son of Francis and Marion Dighton. He was commissioned into the Pembroke Yeomanry on 18 June 1915. On 25 September 1915 he took the name of Coxwell-Rogers by deed poll, due to the terms of the will of his good friend Richard Hugh Coxwell-Rogers, who was killed in Gallipoli on 21 August 1915. He embarked for Egypt with the Yeomanry, and served with the 24th Welsh until being attached to the 74th Battalion, Machine Gun Corps. He died at Dowdeswell on 6 March 1953, aged 59.

Hamilton Walker Crawford, Lieutenant. Hamilton was born in Wrexham in 1882, the son of James Stewart Crawford and Elizabeth Crawford (née Bagnall). His mother was from Carmarthen, and the family had moved to The Arlais, Kidwelly, prior to the war. Hamilton was a qualified solicitor. He was commissioned into the Pembroke Yeomanry, and served with the 2/1st Pembroke Yeomanry throughout the war. He married Martha Hector Eccles, eldest daughter of Mr and Mrs Herbert Eccles, of Broadway, Laugharne, on 4 June 1917. Hamilton was awarded just the British War Medal for his services during the war, which was sent to him at The Ridge, Longlands Bay, near Swansea. He died in 1943, aged 60.

Robert Bagnall Crawford, Lieutenant. Robert was born in Wolverhampton in 1888, the son of James Stewart Crawford and Elizabeth Crawford (née Bagnall). His mother was from Carmarthen, and the family had moved to The Arlais, Kidwelly, prior to the war. Robert was educated at Llandovery College, before becoming a qualified solicitor. He was commissioned into the Northumberland Fusiliers, and served in Salonika from 5 November 1916, before returning home. He was then posted as Captain with the 2/1st Pembroke Yeomanry, and served with them for the duration of the war. He was awarded the British War and Victory Medals for his services during the war, which was sent to him at The Ridge, Bishopsmead, Bristol. He probably died in 1954, aged 66.

Francis Gwilym Crawshay, Captain. Crawshay was born at Treforest on 27 March 1875, the son of Francis Richard and Isabella Crawshay (née Vignoles). He was commissioned into the Glamorgan Yeomanry on 29 October 1914. He served throughout the war with the Pembroke Yeomanry, being awarded the British War and Victory Medals for his services, which were sent to him at Llanblethian, Cowbridge. He died at Weymouth in December 1971, aged 96.

Ernest Croucher MID, Captain. Croucher was born at Frensham, Surrey in 1877, the son of John and Elizabeth Croucher. On 17 March 1917 he was commissioned as quartermaster and lieutenant with the Pembroke Yeomanry, and posted to the 3/1st Battalion. He was promoted captain on 17 March 1919, and transferred to the 4th Welsh on 22 March 1920. His medal card shows that he served in France from 24 March 1917, probably while on temporary attachment to a battalion of the South Lancashire Regiment. He died in Devon in 1970.

Thomas Luke Curtis, Lieutenant. Curtis originally served with the Shropshire Yeomanry, and was commissioned on 8 December 1917. His name does not appear in any of the records of the 24th Welsh, but he was among the members of the Cadre of the battalion who returned to Wales in 1919.

Evan John Corne David MC TD, Captain. David was born on 22 June 1888, the son of Evan Edgar David and Mabel Gwladys David (née Nicholl-Corne), of Nash Manor, Cowbridge. He was commissioned into the Glamorgan Yeomanry on 1 March 1911. He was mobilised at the outbreak of war, promoted lieutenant on 26 August 1914 and embarked with the Yeomanry for Egypt. On 20 June 1916 he was promoted captain, and remained with the 24th Welsh for the duration of the war, being awarded the Military Cross on 16 December 1917, and taking temporary command of the battalion on 9 September 1918. David served with the Royal Field Artillery after the war, being awarded the British War and Victory Medals for his services, which were sent to him at 81st Welsh Brigade, R.F.A. Headquarters, Swansea. David was also awarded the Territorial Force War Medal. He was promoted major on 22 July 1920, and served again during WW2. David relinquished his commission on 4 November 1942, having attained the upper age limit. He died on 23 March 1982, aged 93.

Daniel John Davies MC, Lieutenant. Davies was commissioned into the Pembroke Yeomanry. He was attached to the 24th Welsh when he was awarded the Military Cross. (See the Honours and Awards Section).

David Morris Davies, MC, Lieutenant. Davies was possibly from Taff's Well, Cardiff. He was commissioned into the Pembroke Yeomanry from the Inns of Court OTC on 20 November 1914. He was later posted to the 17th Welsh in France, and was awarded the Military Cross for services during the fighting at Bourlon Wood. He was promoted temporary lieutenant on 20 October 1918.

John Bowen Davies, Captain. Davies was promoted to temporary lieutenant in the Pembroke Yeomanry on 9 November 1914. He was later promoted captain on 13 August 1918, while serving in France with a Labour Company of the Labour Corps. He was seconded for service as Court Martial Officer on 26 April 1918. Davies survived the war, earning the British War and Victory Medals for his services, which were sent to him at Derlwyn, Llanpumsaint.

Delmé William Campbell Davies-Evans DSO TD, Lieutenant Colonel. Davies-Evans was born at Llanwenog, Cardiganshire on 25 April 1873, the son of Herbert Davies-Evans and Mary Eleanor Geraldine Lilla Jones. He was commissioned in to the 1st (Pembrokeshire) Volunteer Battalion, Welch Regiment on 14 November 1900, and on 29 May 1901 transferred to the Pembroke Imperial Yeomanry. On 29 April 1903 he married

Gwladys Maud Kathleen Morris at Carmarthen. Davies-Evans was a banker and farmer, and lived with his wife at Penylan, Golden Grove, Carmarthenshire. He was promoted to major on 1 April 1910, and embarked for Egypt with the Yeomanry in 1916. He was promoted to command the 5th Battalion, Lincolnshire Regiment as acting lieutenant colonel from 28 January 1917, and from 25 August 1918 commanded the 2/8th Battalion, Worcestershire Regiment. He returned to Britain on 14 April 1919. Davies-Evans was awarded the DSO and the Territorial Decoration (TD). On 3 July 1920 he was promoted to lieutenant colonel, commanding the 4th Welsh. He stood as the Conservative candidate for Carmarthen in the 1931 elections, but lost. He died at Carmarthen in 1953, aged 80. His wife died in 1968.

Aleth Thomas Septimus Leguen de Lacroix, Second Lieutenant. De Lacroix was commissioned into the Glamorgan Yeomanry from the Royal Flying Corps on 29 January 1916. He rejoined the Royal Flying Corps, and was promoted flying officer (Observer) on 18 April 1917, with seniority from 5 March 1917, and lieutenant with the Glamorgan Yeomanry on 29 July 1917 while seconded to the RFC. He was awarded the British War and Victory Medals for his wartime services, which were sent to him at Cheddiston Grange, Halesworth, Suffolk. He remained in the Royal Air Force after the war, being promoted flight lieutenant on 1 July 1925. He married Mollie Constance Mullens in 1927, and died in Ipswich in 1967, aged 73.

Baron Alan Frederick James De Rutzen, Lieutenant. De Rutzen was born in 1876, the son of Sir Albert de Rutzen, a famous Metropolitan Magistrate at Bow Street. He was educated at Eton and became a member of the Stock Exchange. He married, in 1908, Eleanor Etna Audley, the only child of Captain Pelham Thursby Pelham, of Abermarlais Park, Carmarthenshire, and Ridgeway, Pembrokeshire. De Rutzen succeeded his uncle as Baron de Rutzen in 1915. At the outbreak of the war he joined the Pembroke Yeomanry, being gazetted in August 1914, and went with them to Egypt in March 1916. Whilst there he volunteered for the Imperial Camel Corps, with which he was serving at the time of his death. He fell leading a company of the Camel Corps against the Turks near Katia. The following extract, testifying to his great ability as an officer and leader of men, is from a letter of an officer of the Camel Corps to the Colonel of the Pembroke Yeomanry: "You will probably have heard, before this reaches you, that Baron de Rutzen was killed yesterday. He was in command of this company and the amount of confidence he put into his men helped considerably towards holding a very tight corner. A brave man and a real topper in the field and out of it. His men simply adored him, as did all his brother officers." Baron De Rutzen had travelled extensively. He was greatly interested in horses, hunting and agriculture, and was a keen fisherman.

William Armine Edwards, Second Lieutenant. Edwards was born on 3 May 1892, the son of William Henry and Margaret Hannah Edwards (née Williams), of The Hill, Sketty. He was educated at Harrow, and became a well known cricketer, playing for Glamorgan County prior to the war. William married Aerona Sails in 1914. He was serving with the Glamorgan Yeomanry when war broke out, and was commissioned into the regiment on 20 December 1915, before embarking with the Yeomanry for Egypt in 1916. Edwards was mortally wounded while leading his platoon in the attack on the Beersheba position on 1 November 1917, and died a few hours later. He was 25 years old and is buried at Beersheba War Cemetery, Israel. For his services during the war Edwards was awarded the British War and Victory Medals and the Territorial Force War Medal, which were sent to his widow at Porteynon, Gower. His medals were sold at Christies in 1982.

Joseph Patrick Fehily, Captain. Fehily was the son of Patrick and Margaret Fehily, of Ballineen, Co. Cork. He was a surgeon prior to the war, and on 31 December 1915 was commissioned as a surgeon in the Royal Navy. On 4 December 1916 he was promoted temporary captain in the Royal Army Medical Corps. He landed in Egypt on 24 January 1917, and on 12 July 1917 was taken on strength by the 24th Welsh. Fehily survived the war, being awarded the British War and Victory Medals for his service, which were sent to him at Ballineen, Cork. He was in Hong Kong when its garrison surrendered to the Japanese in December 1941, but was released the following year. He returned to Hong Kong as Director of Medicine after the war, relinquishing his commission as lieutenant colonel, and was granted the honorary rank of colonel on 24 June 1946. His brother, Thomas Joseph Fehily, was killed at Merville on 13 April 1918, while Medical Officer with the 2nd Royal Fusiliers.

Oakden Fisher Croix de Guerre MID, Major. Fisher was born in 1885, the son of Henry Oakden and Helen Agnes Fisher of Ty Gwyn, Radyr, Cardiff. He was a solicitor at Heathfield, Sussex prior to being commissioned into the Glamorgan Yeomanry on 21 October 1908. He was mobilised in August 1914, and sailed with the Yeomanry for Egypt in 1916, and was with the regiment when it merged with the Pembroke Yeomanry to form the 24th Welsh. Fisher survived the war, being wounded on 27 December 1917, and was awarded the British War and Victory Medals for his services, which were sent to him at Ty Gwyn, Abergavenny. He was awarded the Croix de Guerre by the French Government, and was Mentioned in Despatches, as well as being awarded the Territorial Force War Medal. He died at Pontypool on 3 August 1965, aged 79. His brother, Lieutenant Colonel Harry Bruges Fisher, was killed in France while in command of the 12th Battalion, York and Lancaster Regiment on 3 October 1916; and another brother, Lieutenant Colonel Herbert George Fisher DSO and Bar, and died on 29 July 1919 as a result of wounds received during the war.

Philip Fisher, Captain. Fisher was the son of Henry Oakden and Helen Agnes Fisher of Ty Gwyn, Radyr, Cardiff. He was commissioned into the Glamorgan Yeomanry on 1 January 1912, and was promoted lieutenant on 13 April 1915. Fisher sailed for Egypt with the Yeomanry in 1916, and was with the regiment when it merged with the Pembroke Yeomanry to form the 24th Welsh. He served with a battalion of the King's Yorkshire Light Infantry towards the end of the war. Fisher was awarded the British War and Victory Medals for his service during the war, which were sent to him at Ty Gwyn, Abergavenny, and was also awarded the Territorial Force War Medal for his service. He died at Crickhowell in 1968, aged 80.

William James Foster MC, Major. Foster was born on 5 April 1885, the son of William Foster, of 51, the Parade, Cardiff. He attended St Mary's Hall School, Cardiff. Foster enlisted in the Glamorgan Yeomanry on 9 March 1909, at the age of twenty-nine, and attended camp in that year at Llandovery, then in 1910 at Porthcawl. In 1911 he was promoted lance corporal, and attended camp at Builth Wells. Forster was promoted Corporal in 1913 and attended camp at Llandeilo, he then attended camp at Porthcawl in May 1914, and was embodied for overseas service on 5 August 1915 in the machine gun section Glamorgan Yeomanry after having attended a machine gun course at Bisley in May 1915. On 30 May 1915, while a lance sergeant in the Glamorgan Yeomanry at Aylsham in Norfolk, he applied for a commission in the 16th Welsh, expressing a preference to join the machine gun section, his next of kin being given as Mr William Foster, 42, Park Place Cardiff. His application for a commission was accompanied by a certificate of moral character by Charles E. Dovey JP, Cardiff, in which he states 'an exemplary young man'. Foster was subsequently commissioned second lieutenant in the 16th Welsh on 9 June 1915, and moved to France with them in December that year. He was wounded several times; on 14 May 1916, 14 September 1916, 31 July 1917 and 5 September 1918. His worst injury appears to have been a deep gunshot wound and shell fragment injury to the right thigh which became septic, at Ypres on 14 September 1916. Forster had been promoted to captain whilst commanding a Company on 7 August 1916, and joined the 15th Welsh as acting major early in 1917, when the 16th Welsh was broken up. William was awarded the Military Cross for his actions during the fighting at Pilckem Ridge (see Appendices: Awards to the Battalion). As well as his Military Cross, Foster was awarded the 1914/15 Star, British War and Victory Medals, which were sent to him at 'Maindy House', North Road, Cardiff. He served in the Second War with the Home Guard, having worked for some years as a valued member of the Regimental Benevolent Fund Committee. Foster died on 4 December 1965 in Cardiff.

Edgar Richard Bastin French, Lieutenant. French was born at Northleach, Gloucestershire in 1891, the son of Samuel and Anne French, and had moved to Swansea prior to the war to work as a coachman. He was commissioned into the Pembroke Yeomanry on 5 July 1917. He was awarded the British War and Victory Medals for his wartime service, which were sent to him at 34, Terrace Road, Swansea. French served again during the Second World War with the Duke of Wellingtons, after being commissioned on 25 November 1942. He died in Swansea in the summer of 1962, aged 72.

William Henry Gabbett, Captain. Gabbett was serving with the Pembroke Yeomanry at the outbreak of war. He was commissioned lieutenant on 26 August 1914 and remained on home service with the 2/1st Pembroke Yeomanry, being promoted captain before being forced to retire from the army due to ill health on 27 May 1916 at the age of 47. His home address was given as Mount Rivers, Newport, Limerick.

Frederick William Alfred Herbert Gillett, Major. Gillett was born on 21 March 1872, the son of Alfred and Ceciley Gillett. He was educated at Cambridge, and inherited the title of Lord of the Manor of Headington from his father in 1895, but soon sold it. His mother was from Haverfordwest and, with his ties to the county, Frederick was commissioned in the Pembroke Yeomanry. He was promoted temporary major in the Pembroke Yeomanry on 9 November 1914. On 29 November 1915 he was appointed a staff captain. He does not seem to have served overseas, and relinquished his commission on 10 June 1916. He embarked for Jamaica with his family on 26 November 1923, and nothing further is known of him.

Edgar Rees Griffiths, Lieutenant. Griffiths was the son of John and Martha Griffiths, of 139, Elkington Road, Burry Port. He was commissioned into the Pembroke Yeomanry on 10 August 1915. He was promoted lieutenant on 23 August 1917, probably remaining on home service. He died in 1957, aged 66.

Vincent Griffiths MC, Lieutenant. Griffiths was born in 1892. He was raised by his uncle, Thomas Griffiths, in Burry Port, and was commissioned into the Pembroke Yeomanry on 10 August 1915. He embarked for Egypt with the Yeomanry in 1916, and was promoted lieutenant on 1 June 1916. He was wounded in Palestine on 31 September 1917, and promoted captain on 19 July 1918. He was awarded the Military Cross for his service at Épehy. (See the Honours and Awards appendix). He was awarded the British War and Victory Medals for his wartime service, which were sent to him at Glanmor, Burry Port. He died at Llanelli in 1943, aged 51.

William Dillwyn Griffiths, Second Lieutenant. Griffiths was the son of William and Sarah Anne Griffiths, of West Cottage, Treforest. He was commissioned into the 4th Welsh in May 1918, and posted to the 24th Welsh. He was killed in action at Épehy on 18 September 1918, aged 24, and is buried in Ronssoy Communal Cemetery.

Sir John Charles Harford, Major. Harford resided at Falcondale, Lampeter. He was promoted captain on 6 December 1916, and granted the temporary rank of major, serving in France with a regular battalion from 13 June 1917. He relinquished his commission on 2 December 1918. He was awarded the British War and Victory Medals for his wartime services, which were sent to him at Falcondale. His son, John Henry Harford, was killed on the Somme in 1916. Harford died on 16 July 1934, aged 74.

William Thomas Harries, Lieutenant. Harries was commissioned from the Artists' Rifles into the 3rd Welsh. He joined the 24th Welsh in France on 6 August 1918, and was wounded on 2 November 1918. He resigned his commission on 1 April 1920, retaining the rank of lieutenant. He was awarded the British War and Victory Medals for his wartime services, which were sent to him at 46, Chestnut Avenue, Stockton Lane, Yorkshire.

John Julian Boyd Harvey, Lieutenant. Harvey was born in Carle Ignigue, Chile in 1892, the son of John Boyd Harvey and Jualieta Grenadino. He returned to England with his parents before the turn of the century and they moved back to the family home at Llangynwyd. Harvey was serving with the Glamorgan Yeomanry prior to the war but transferred to the Welsh Horse Yeomanry. He served in Gallipoli and Egypt before transferring to the Royal Flying Corps. He survived the war, being awarded the 1914/15 Star, British War and Victory Medals, which were sent to him at 19 Bridgend Road, Llangynwyd.

Percival Hay MC, Lieutenant. Hay was the son of George and Lottie Hay, of Swansea. He was commissioned into the 1/6th Welsh from the Army Cyclist Corps on 27 August

1917. He served in Egypt with the 53rd (Welsh) Division, before being posted to the 24th Welsh. He was awarded the Military Cross and Bar, the bar being for his action at Épehy, while attached to the 24th Welsh. (See the Honours and Awards appendix). Hay was awarded the British War and Victory Medals for his wartime service, and also the Territorial Force War Medal, which were all sent to him at 41, Finsbury Terrace, Swansea. He died in Dorset on 16 June 1964, aged 69.

Ernest Helme DSO and Bar, Lieutenant Colonel. Helme was the son of Richard Mashiter, of Gower and Prince's Gate, London, and of Louisa Helme. He was commissioned second lieutenant with the Glamorgan Yeomanry in 1904, serving as lieutenant at the outbreak of the Great War, and on 30 April 1915 was promoted to captain, embarking for Egypt with them in April 1916. Helme was attached to the II Anzac Corps in Egypt, before returning to France to take up a posting as second in command of the 15th Welsh on 8 May 1917. He survived a direct hit on his bunker during the Battle of Pilckem in August 1917, and went on to share the command of the battalion with Lieutenant Colonel Parkinson until the end of the war, earning himself two Mentions in Despatches and the Distinguished Service Order twice (see Appendices: Awards to the Battalion). For his services during the war, Helme was also awarded the British War and Victory Medals, and the Territorial Force War Medal, which were sent to him at 'Llanganydd', Reynoldston, Glamorgan. He died in Westminster, London in 1949.

John Arthur Higgon, Major. Higgon was born on 12 November 1873, the son of John Donald George Higgon of Scolton Manor. He married Lurline May Moses, daughter of Hon. Henry Moses, on 27 July 1900 in Hong Kong while serving with the Royal Welsh Fusiliers, and rose to the rank of captain in the service of them. He became a major with the Pembroke Yeomanry before the outbreak of war, and was posted to the Australian Imperial Force, which was stationed in Egypt, where it doubled in strength after the evacuation from Gallipoli. He joined the AIF at Alexandria, and then embarked on HMAT *Transylvania*, bound for Marseilles, arriving on 23 June 1916. Higgon then travelled to northern France, where he took command of A Company, 32nd Battalion, Australian Imperial Force, which was then based in the Fromelles sector. He was with his new unit for less than a month before it was sent into action at Fromelles on 19 July 1916. Higgon was killed while leading his men out of the trenches on 20 July 1916. He is reported to have been standing on the parapet, shouting, 'Come on, boys!', when a German bullet hit him between the eyes, and he fell dead, aged 42. His body was one of the few to be recovered from the battlefield at the time, and he is buried in Ration Farm Military Cemetery. His brother Archibald also fell.

Reginald Arthur Hoare, Captain. Hoare was born on 13 July 1878, the son of Charles Arthur Richard Hoare and Margaret Short. He married Una Mildred Williams, daughter of Thomas C. Williams, on 23 February 1909. Hoare was commissioned in the Pembroke Yeomanry prior to the war, and was restored to the establishment on 6 April 1916. He was promoted captain on 8 November 1916, and was posted to France on 22 April 1918, where he was attached to the 1st Battalion, King's Shropshire Light Infantry. The battalion was attached to 16 Brigade, 6th Division. Hoare joined the battalion at Ypres, and saw his first action during the desperate fighting around Messines. At the end of August the Division was ordered south, to take part in the offensive on the Aisne. On 13 September the Division took up positions near Holnon Wood, which they were tasked with attacking on 18 September. Hoare was killed in action here on 19 September 1918, aged 40. He is buried in Chappelle British Cemetery, Holnon.

Herbert Charles Richards Homfray, Lieutenant. Homfray was born on 22 July 1890. He was commissioned from Sherborne School's Officer Training Corps into the Glamorgan Yeomanry on 12 September 1914. He never served overseas and relinquished his commission on account of ill health on 11 March 1917, being granted the honorary rank of Lieutenant. He was Master of the Glamorgan Foxhounds, and died at Penllyn Castle, Cowbridge on 10 July 1960, aged 70. His son, Captain John Charles Richards Homfray, of the Welsh Guards, was killed in Normandy in 1944.

John Hamilton Howell, Captain. Howell was born in Solva, Pembrokeshire on 27 September 1879. He was commissioned into the Pembroke Yeomanry on 29 March 1910, and promoted lieutenant on 10 August 1916, after being promoted temporary captain on 27 May 1916. He relinquished his temporary rank of lieutenant on alteration of his posting on 27 January 1917. He does not seem to have served overseas. Howell died in Pembrokeshire in 1970, aged 91.

Arthur William Hunt, Lieutenant. Hunt was commissioned into the Pembroke Yeomanry on 1 September 1915. He was promoted lieutenant on 1 July 1917, and served with the 24th Welsh in Palestine from 12 December 1917. He was awarded the British War and Victory Medals for his wartime services, which were sent to C. J. Hunt, Esq., 45/46 St Paul's Churchyard, E.C.4.

James Laurie McKie Hutchinson, Captain. Hutchinson was born on 19 July 1879, the son of J. W. Hutchinson, of Laurieston Hall, Castle Douglas, Dumfries and Galloway. He was educated at Harrow and was commissioned on 9 March 1898 into the 3rd Battalion, King's Own Scottish Borderers (Militia). He joined the 2nd Dragoons in 1899 and served in South Africa from October 1900 to May 1902. He served with his regiment in France as Lieutenant from 14 November 1914 to 15 March 1915. In March 1916 he was appointed Adjutant of the Pembroke Yeomanry and served with the Egyptian Expeditionary Force until February 1917, when he was appointed to the Staff, firstly as Staff Captain G.H.Q. 3rd Echelon, and from October 1917, as D.A.A.G. G.H.Q. 3rd Echelon, E.E.F., until October 1918. He was mentioned in despatches on three occasions; 14 June 1918, 22 January and 5 June 1919 and was also awarded the OBE. His medals, The Order of the British Empire, Queen's South Africa, with three clasps, King's South Africa, 1914 Star, British War and Victory Medals, were sold at auction in 2005. He died on 31 December 1923.

George Edward Jackson, Lieutenant. Jackson joined the 24th Welsh in France from the 3rd Welsh on 6 August 1918. He was wounded at Épehy on 19 August 1918 and was promoted lieutenant on 27 September 1919. He resigned his commission on 1 April 1920, retaining the rank of lieutenant. He was awarded the British War and Victory Medals for his wartime services, which were sent to him at 90, Chapman Street, Grimsby.

Richard Fleetwood Jenkins MC, Lieutenant. Jenkins was born in Uzmaston, near Haverfordwest, in 1886, the son of Thomas and Sarah Jane Jenkins. He embarked with the Pembroke Yeomanry for Egypt in 1916, and was commissioned on 19 January 1917, before being posted to France, joining the 1/4th Battalion, Cheshire Regiment. He was promoted lieutenant on 19 July 1918. He was awarded the British War and Victory Medals for his wartime services, which were sent to him at Cashfield, near Haverfordwest. Jenkins was awarded the Military Cross in France (see the Honours and Awards appendix). He died at Narberth in 1958, aged 71.

Brettle Evans Jollands, Lieutenant. Jollands was brought up by his mother's (Mary Ann Evans') family in Haverfordwest after the death of his father William in 1905. He was commissioned from No. 2 Supernumerary Company, 1st Battalion, The Herefordshire Regiment, to be second lieutenant in the Pembroke Yeomanry on 5 July 1915. He embarked for Egypt with the Yeomanry in 1916, and was granted the temporary rank of Lieutenant on 22 June 1916, after he was made Adjutant to the Pembroke Yeomanry. He was transferred to the 1st Lovats Scouts on 1 February 1917, and promoted lieutenant on 16 May 1919. He relinquished his commission on 11 February 1919, retaining the rank of lieutenant. He was awarded the British War and Victory Medals for his wartime services, which were sent to him at 72, Fore Street, Hertford. He died in Hampshire in 1923, aged 51.

E.G. Jones, Lieutenant. Jones was commissioned into the Pembroke Yeomanry on 26 May 1903. He was promoted Lieutenant on 7 February 1906.

Karl Meredith Jones, Lieutenant. Jones was born on 4 June 1892, the son of Arthur and Margaret Jones, of Oystermouth. He was commissioned into the Glamorgan Yeomanry on 15 April 1915, and embarked with the yeomanry for Egypt in 1916. He was promoted lieutenant on 1 June 1916 and served with the 24th Welsh before being attached to the staff on 21 October 1917. He was awarded the British War and Victory Medals for his wartime services, as well as the Territorial Force War Medal, which were sent to him at Rotherslade House, Mumbles. He served again during the Second World War, remaining in the Territorial Force after the war, and died in Swansea in 1981, aged 89.

Richard Charles Jones, Lieutenant. Jones was attached to the 24th Welsh from the 5th Welsh in Egypt. He was promoted lieutenant on 1 July 1917, but was forced to relinquish his commission due to ill health on 17 July 1917. He was awarded the British War and Victory Medals for his wartime services, which were sent to him at 1, Land's End, Holyhead.

William Reginald Karslake, Major. Karslake was born in 1867, the son of William and Annie Karslake, of Westcott, Surrey. He had served in France with the BEF in 1914, and was commissioned into the Pembroke Yeomanry from the British Red Cross on 23 August 1915, and immediately promoted temporary captain, and later temporary major. He died on 29 December 1917, aged 50, and is buried in Paignton Cemetery. He was awarded the 1914 Star, British War and Victory Medals for his wartime services, which were sent to his widow, Laura Maynard Karslake, at 11, Montpelier Square, S.W.7.

Sidney Hausell Kirby, Lieutenant. Kirby was commissioned into the Glamorgan Yeomanry on 15 April 1915. He embarked for Egypt with the Yeomanry in 1916, and was promoted lieutenant on 1 June 1916. He was promoted captain in the 24th Welsh on 29 April 1917, and posted to 231 Brigade Stokes Mortar Battery on 15 May 1917. He was awarded the British War and Victory Medals for his wartime services, as well as the Territorial Force War Medal, which were sent to him at Trewelyn, Cardiff Road, Dinas Powis. He died in Bath in 1924, aged 38.

Edward Lambton, Captain. Lambton was born on 5 February 1877, the son of Lieutenant Colonel Francis William Lambton, of Brownslade, Pembrokeshire, late Scots Guards, and Lady Victoria Alexandrina Elizabeth, eldest daughter of John Frederick Campbell, second Earl of Cawdor. He was educated at Wellington College and Cooper's Hill, prior to taking up a post as Director of Public Works for the Egyptian Government in Cairo. Edward trained with an Egyptian Cavalry regiment prior to the war, having been commissioned into the Pembroke Yeomanry on 16 August 1909, and returned to England, where he became a Captain with the Pembroke Yeomanry. He embarked with the yeomanry for Egypt in 1916. Edward became ill soon after arriving back in Cairo, and died there on 28 March 1916. He was 39 years old, and is buried at Cairo War Memorial Cemetery. He was awarded the British War and Victory Medals for his wartime services, which were sent to his brother George at Brownslade.

James Henry Lewis, MC, Second Lieutenant. Lewis resided at 1, Prendergast Hill, Haverfordwest. He was commissioned into the Welsh Regiment from the Pembroke Yeomanry, probably serving in Egypt before being posted to France, where he joined the 1/7th Battalion Cheshire Regiment, which left the 53rd (Welsh) Division on 31 May 1918 to embark for France. He was awarded the Military Cross in France. (See the Honours and Awards Appendix). He was also awarded the British War and Victory Medals for his wartime services.

John Frederick Allen Lewis MC, Captain. Lewis was born in 1891, the son of John and Gwendoline Lewis, of St David's, Pembrokeshire. He was commissioned into the Pembroke Yeomanry from the Inns of Court OTC on 20 November 1914. He was promoted to lieutenant on 26 July 1917, with precedence as from 12 August 1916. On 3 August 1917 he was appointed Adjutant of the 24th Welsh and promoted to temporary captain. On 16 August 1918 Lewis was attached to 230 Brigade HQ. He was awarded the Military Cross for his services in France. (see the Honours and Awards Appendix). He was also awarded the British War and Victory Medals for his wartime services, which were sent to him at The Rectory, South Normanton, Derbyshire.

Rupert Wyndham Lewis MID, Captain. Lewis was born in Devon in 1882, but was raised in Cardiff by his parents, Henry and Rose Lewis. He was commissioned into the

Glamorgan Yeomanry on 12 September 1908, and promoted lieutenant on 8 October 1911. He later transferred to the Welsh Guards on 2 April 1915, at its formation, and was wounded at Loos. He was given the rank of temporary captain while commanding No. 4 Company on 21 July 1916, after the battalion had suffered heavy casualties on the Somme. He relinquished his temporary rank on 1 February 1917. He was awarded the 1914/15 Star, British War and Victory Medals for his wartime services, which were sent to him at the 1st Battalion, Welsh Guards HQ, Wellington Barracks, S.W.1. His horse riding skills and personality were legendary in the Welsh Guards:

'The feature of our lot was Rupert [Lewis] who went slowly round on an old pony, knocking everything flat; but he was very clever to get round at all... Lewis's glasses had got fogged and dirty, it was pitch dark, and he had fallen into a trench and bruised his head. He had been promptly jumped on by some cavalrymen who occupied the trench and thought he was a German. However, when he had recovered his wind and senses, he explained who he was and was allowed to go.... Rupert Lewis had a wonderful mackintosh cape, not issued by the Ordnance but bought somewhere in Cardiff, and with this thing covering two or three overcoats, his little figure bent nearly double under the weight, gum-boots reaching up to his waist, a shapeless cap, large, black-rimmed glasses, and large fingerless gloves, he looked like a little old witch. His physique was against him, but he resisted the conditions gallantly...'

He died in 1951, aged 69.

Sir Wilfred Hubert Poyer Lewis OBE MID, Captain. Lewis was born in London on 9 February 1881, the son of Arthur Griffith Poyer, barrister-at-law, of Henllan, near Narberth, Pembrokeshire, and of Annie Wilhelmine Lewis. He was the grandson of Richard Lewis, Bishop of Llandaff. He was educated at Eton and University College, Oxford , where he graduated in History in 1903. He was called to the Bar by the Inner Temple in 1908 and served in the South Wales Circuit until 1914. He was promoted temporary lieutenant in the Glamorgan Yeomanry on 24 September 1914, having originally been commissioned into the Eton Rifle College Volunteers, and promoted captain on 1 June 1916. During the war he was twice mentioned in despatches and awarded the OBE while serving as a staff officer in France, relinquishing his appointment as ADC on 26 January 1919 (see the Honours and Awards Appendix). After the war he settled in London, where he became a successful barrister, specialising in ecclesiastical law and was chancellor of the dioceses of Llandaff, 1914-35, Monmouth, 1921-35, Manchester and Blackburn, 1929-35, and Worcester, 1930-35. In 1930, he became a junior counsel to the Treasury, and was in July 1935 appointed judge in the King's Bench division and knighted. On his first circuit in Wales he heard the case of the burning of the aerodrome in Llŷn at Caernarfon, when the jury failed to agree on a verdict. He served as J.P., chairman of Quarter Sessions, and Deputy Lieutenant of Pembrokeshire. He was awarded the British War and Victory Medals for his wartime services, which were sent to him at 3, Hare Court, Temple, E.C. He died on 15 March 1950, aged 69.

Albert Lidstone, Second Lieutenant. Lidstone was born in Swansea in 1886, the son of Alfred and Annie Lidstone. He was a clerk at a provisions merchant in Brixton prior to the war, and married Edith Alice Jenkins there on 6 September 1913. Lidstone originally served with the King's Royal Rifle Corps, with the service number R/25454. He was commissioned into the Welsh Regiment in March 1918, and joined the 24th Welsh in France on 6 August 1918. Lidstone was awarded the British War and Victory Medals for his services during the war, which were sent to him at 10, Winterwell Road, Brixton Hill, S.W.2. He died in Essex in 1933, aged 46.

Sir Charles Leyshon Dillwyn Venables Llewellyn, Lieutenant Colonel. Llewellyn was born on 29 June 1870, the son of John Talbot Dillwyn, 1st Baronet, and Caroline Julia Llewellyn (née Hicks-Beach). His father was High Sheriff of Glamorgan, Mayor of Swansea and MP for Swansea. He was elected Conservative MP for Radnorshire in January 1910 during the hung parliament of that year, but lost the seat in the election in December. He was Lieutenant Colonel commanding the Glamorgan Yeomanry at the outbreak of war, but instead served with the Royal Welsh Fusiliers and the Labour Corps. He retired on completion of the tenure of his command on 2 April 1919, retaining the rank of lieutenant colonel. He was awarded the British War and Victory Medals for his wartime services, which were sent to him at Llysdinam, Newbridge-on-Wye, Radnorshire. He inherited the baronetcy on the death of his father in 1927. He was Lord Lieutenant of Radnorshire from 1929 to 1949 and High Sheriff of Radnorshire in 1924. He died on 24 June 1951, aged 80.

Griffith Robert Poyntz Llewellyn, Captain. Llewellyn was born on 26 February 1886, the son of Robert William and Harriet Llewellyn, of Baglan Hall. He was educated at Oxford University. He married Emily Constance Elwes on 29 April 1911. He embarked for Egypt with the Yeomanry but transferred to the Light Car Patrols, an early forerunner of the Long Range Desert Group. He later transferred to the Royal Air Force Volunteer Reserve, and served during the Second World War. Llewellyn died in 1972.

Edmond Long-Price, Lieutenant. Long-Price was born on 31 March 1874, the son of David and Susannah Long-Price, of Talley, Carmarthenshire. He was commissioned into the 1st (Pembrokeshire) Volunteer Battalion, Welch Regiment on 26 September 1903. He was promoted to temporary lieutenant in the Pembroke Yeomanry on 9 November 1914, and full lieutenant on 13 February 1917. He was transferred to the Labour Corps, with the rank of temporary captain, on 16 March 1917, presumably after the formation of the 24th Welsh. He died on 30 May 1962, aged 88 and is buried in Talley.

Herbert Overton Long-Price, Captain. Long-Price was born in Talley, Carmarthenshire, on 13 September 1875. He served in the Boer War with the 35th and 39th Imperial Yeomanry and later retired from the army with the rank of lieutenant. He was reappointed lieutenant with the Pembroke Yeomanry on 27 September 1914, and was posted to France in March 1917 to command the 8th North Hampshire Labour Company. However, his active service at the front was short lived, and he re-embarked for England on 25 April, suffering from debility, exhaustion and neurasthenia. With his medical problems persisting, he remained in England for the remainder of the war, attaining the rank of captain on 27 December 1917. He is listed in the nominal roll of the officers of 24th Welsh, which notes that he was 'Ordered Out' on 24 October 1918. Long-Price was permitted to resign his commission and retain the rank of captain in May 1919. He died on 14 May 1927. For his service during the Great War, in addition to his Queen's South Africa Medal, which he had won during the Boer War, he was awarded the British War and Victory Medals, which were sent to him at Bosemeade, Ulting, Maldon, Essex.

Edward Ralph Marten, Lieutenant. Marten was promoted temporary lieutenant in the Glamorgan Yeomanry on 12 September 1914, gaining the full rank on 22 June 1917, with seniority as from 1 June 1916. On 20 September 1917 he was promoted temporary captain with the 3rd Battalion, Tank Corps, and posted to the Tank Corps School as an instructor on 24 October 1917. On 18 September 1918 he was appointed acting major while acting as Chief Instructor with the Tank Corps. He relinquished the rank of major after ceasing to be Chief Instructor on 12 December 1919, and was restored to the Territorial Force on 12 November 1920. He was awarded the British War and Victory Medals for his wartime services, which were sent to him at Henstaff Court, Pontyclun, Glamorgan. He died in Dorset in 1949, aged 66.

Charles David Mathias, Lieutenant. Mathias was born at Neyland in 1877, the son of Charles and Maria Mathias. He ran his own medical practice at Tenby prior to the war and was originally commissioned as Medical Officer into the Pembroke Yeomanry on 29 May 1907 (Royal Army Medical Corps attached). He was promoted lieutenant on 5 August 1914, and embarked with the Yeomanry for Egypt in 1916. He continued to serve as MO with the 24th Welsh during the early stages of the Palestinian campaign, but was invalided home, and on 13 July 1917 he was struck off the strength of the 24th Welsh. He was awarded the British War and Victory Medals for his wartime services. He returned home to 2, Rock Houses, Tenby after the war. He remained on the General List, and was promoted major on 1 March 1924, with precedence as from 29 May 1919. Mathias retired from the Territorial Army, having attained the age limit on 9 October 1926. He died in Tenby in 1954, aged 78.

Richard Henry Probyn Miers MID, Captain. Miers was born at Swansea on 12 June 1873, the son of Henry and Lydia Miers. He was raised in Tenby; he married Vera Enid Brydges Todd at Kensington on 2 June 1906. Miers had been commissioned into the Glamorgan Yeomanry on 24 February 1912. He embarked for Egypt with the Yeomanry in 1916. Miers was promoted temporary major on 3 March 1916, and relinquished the rank on 22 June 1917, becoming a captain in the 24th Welsh. He was Mentioned in Despatches on 28 August 1917, having transferred to the Royal Flying Corps, and returned home to join the 31st Training Squadron, RFC. Miers was killed in an accident while flying in DH 6 A9744 on 12 December 1917. He was 38 years old, and is buried at Wyton (St Margaret and All Saints) Churchyard. Miers was awarded the British War and Victory Medals for his services during the war, which were sent to his widow at 14, Ebbisham Road, Dorking Road, Epsom.

Edward Darley Miller CMG DSO CBE MID, Lieutenant Colonel. Miller was born on 11 February 1865, the son of Edward and Fanny Miller, of Hartsfield, Betchworth. He was educated at Harrow and Trinity College, Cambridge, and was gazetted to the 17th Lancers in October 1886, becoming captain on 26 October 1892, in which year he retired, and entered the Reserve of Officers. He served in the South African War as captain in the Lancashire Hussars, Imperial Yeomanry, and as brigade major, Imperial Yeomanry. He was mentioned in Despatches (*London Gazette*, 10 September 1901); received the Queen's Medal with three clasps, and was created a Companion of the Distinguished Service Order (*London Gazette*, 27 September 1901): 'Edward Darley Miller, Captain, Brigade Major, Imperial Yeomanry. In recognition of services during the operations in South Africa.' He was honorary lieutenant colonel, Pembrokeshire Yeomanry. He served throughout the Great War, being mentioned in Despatches for services in France in 1914, and was created a CBE in 1919, having commanded the 2/1st Pembroke Yeomanry. He married Irene Langtry, daughter of Colonel Langtry of the 8th Hussars, on 25 April 1899, and they had two sons, Gordon and Desmond, born 1900 and 1903 respectively. He was a famous polo player, and was Captain of his Rugby XV for 25 years. He also played in the winning team of the 17th Lancers in Inter-Regimental Polo Tournaments in India, 1888 and 1889, and was in the winning team of the Championship Cup at Hurlingham on five occasions. He formerly managed at different times the Hurlingham, Ranelagh, Roehampton, Rugby, Ostend, Cannes and Le Touquet Polo Clubs. He wrote a book called, *Modern Polo and Horse Management in the Field*. For his services during the Boer and Great Wars he was awarded the CBE, DSO, QSA with three clasps, 1914 Star and Bar, British War and Victory Medals, which were sent to him at The Farm, Spring Hill, Rugby. He died in 1930, and is buried in Clifton Road Cemetery, Rugby, Warwickshire. His widow survived him by thirty nine years.

Joseph Gwyn Moore-Gwyn TD, Major. Moore-Gwyn was born on 15 May 1879. He was commissioned into the Glamorgan Yeomanry on 21 November 1903. He embarked for Egypt with the Yeomanry in 1916, and on 26 July 1916 he was promoted temporary lieutenant colonel, in command of the 5th Battalion, Worcester Regiment. He relinquished his commission due to ill health on 14 February 1919, retaining the rank of major, and was awarded the Territorial Decoration on 11 November 1918. He was awarded the British War and Victory Medals for his wartime services, as well as the Territorial Force War Medal, which were sent to him at Gunfort, Tenby. He had played cricket for Glamorgan for one season, he died on 17 February 1937, aged 57.

Reverend Abraham Rees Morgan MC, Army Chaplains Department. Morgan was born in Llangyfelach in 1886, the son of William and Mary Morgan. He studied for the Ministry at Bangor University. He was gazetted as Chaplain 4th Class in the Army Chaplain's Department on 7 March 1916. He joined the Yeomanry in Egypt in January 1917, becoming Chaplain to the 24th Welsh upon its formation. He was awarded the Military Cross during the war (see the Honours and Awards Appendix). He was awarded the British War and Victory Medals for his wartime services, which were sent to him at 50, Cambria Street, Holyhead.

Abraham Rees Morgan, Captain. He was promoted captain in the Pembroke Yeomanry on 19 September 1918. Nothing further is currently known of him.

David Lloyd Popkin Morgan MC, Captain. Morgan was born in 1887, the son of David Henry and Jane Sybil Morgan, of 11, Langland Road, Mumbles. He was educated at Llandovery College from 1900 until 1903, and was a popular sportsman in the Swansea area, and well known at Mumbles as a keen yachtsman. Morgan was a metallurgist and assayer by profession and had worked as such in Peru. He was commissioned on 1 October 1915 into the Pembroke Yeomanry and embarked for Egypt with them in 1916. Morgan was awarded the Military Cross in November 1917, for his part in the attack on Beersheba. In February 1918 his Company was given the honour of guarding the Holy Sepulchre at Jerusalem. Sadly, Morgan was killed soon after, when his Battalion was ordered into a night attack on a hill at Selwad. The action took place in thick fog, and it was here that he was killed in action when his platoon came under heavy fire on 9 March 1918. He was 30 years old, and is buried at Jerusalem War Cemetery, Israel. Morgan was awarded the British War and Victory Medals for his services during the war, which were sent to his father at 98, Bryn Road, Swansea.

Frank Stanley Morgan, Captain. Morgan was born in Oystermouth on 10 January 1893. He was commissioned into the Pembroke Yeomanry on 1 March 1914. He transferred to the Imperial Camel Corps. He served with the HQ of the Imperial Camel Corps and later rose to the rank of Colonel with the Royal Signals Corps. Morgan died in Swansea in 1992, aged 99.

Frank Hall Morris, Captain. Morris was born in Bridgend on 16 July 1869, the son of Lewis and Emily Morris, of Neath. He was commissioned into the Glamorgan Yeomanry on 29 October 1914, and promoted lieutenant on 22 June 1917, with seniority from 1 June 1916. On 12 December 1917 he was promoted captain, while seconded to another unit. He played cricket for Glamorgan prior to the war, as well as for Malvern College, Swansea and Tenby. He died at Tonbridge on 21 October 1954, aged 85.

James Morris, Lieutenant. Morris was the son of David John Morris and Anne Morris, of Sea View, Birchgrove, Swansea. He was commissioned from the 3/1st Glamorgan Yeomanry into the Denbigh Yeomanry in Egypt, serving in the 74th (Yeomanry) Division. He was killed in action on 27 December 1917, aged 25, and is buried in Jerusalem War Cemetery. He was awarded the British War and Victory Medals for his wartime services, which were sent to his mother at Sea View, Birchgrove, Swansea.

John Illtyd Dillwyn Nicholl, Major. Nicholl was born at Merthyr Mawr on 1 May 1861, the son of J.C. Nicholl. He had played cricket for Marylebone Cricket Club and for Glamorgan prior to the war. His son, Second Lieutenant John William Harford Nicholl was killed with the 2nd Welsh in 1914. He became High Sheriff of Glamorgan and died on 20 September 1935.

Rev. H. S. Nicholl, Chaplain 4th Class, Army Chaplains Department. Reverend Nicholl was commissioned as Chaplain to the Glamorgan Yeomanry on 5 March 1911, and was still the Regimental Chaplain at the outbreak of war. Nothing further is presently known of him.

Gilbert Stradling Nicholl-Carne, JP, Captain. Nicholl-Carne was born on 1 March 1882, the son of John and Alice Nicholl-Carne, of St Donats, Glamorgan. He was commissioned into the Glamorgan Yeomanry on 1 February 1908, and promoted lieutenant on 8 March 1910. He embarked with the Yeomanry for Egypt in 1916, and transferred to the Army Service Corps, in the rank of lieutenant on 11 June 1916. He relinquished his commission on account of ill health on 28 May 1919, and was granted the rank of captain. He was awarded the British War and Victory Medals for his wartime services, which were sent to him at Llanmaes House, Llantwit Major, Glamorgan.

John William Nicholls, Lieutenant. Nicholls was commissioned into the Glamorgan Yeomanry on 27 October 1915. He embarked for Egypt with the yeomanry in 1916, and was taken on strength of the 24th Welsh when it was formed in 1917. He was promoted lieutenant on 1 July 1917. He was awarded the British War and Victory Medals for his wartime services, which were sent to him at the National and Provincial Bank of England, Milsom Street, Bath.

Oswald Olive, Second Lieutenant. Olive was born at Carmarthen in 1885, the son of John Samuel Olive and Saffina Olive, of the Boar's Head Hotel. He served with the City of London Yeomanry, and was commissioned into the Welsh Regiment from an Officer Cadet Unit on 1 August 1917. He joined the 24th Welsh in November 1917 and was promoted Lieutenant on 1 February 1919, while the battalion was still in France. Olive was awarded the British War and Victory Medals for his services during the war, which were sent to him at 70, Waldeman Avenue, Colehill Lane, Fulham, SW6. He died at Cardigan in 1949, aged 63. His brother, George, was commissioned into the Welsh Horse.

Alexander Stuart Ouzman, Second Lieutenant. Ouzman was born at Lambeth in 1881, the son of William and Emily Ouzman. He had served in France since 14 November 1915, and was commissioned from the Public Schools Battalion, Royal Fusiliers, into the Welsh Regiment on 26 February 1918. He joined the 24th Welsh on 6 August 1918. Ouzman relinquished his commission on completion of service on 10 November 1920, retaining the rank of second lieutenant. He was awarded the 1914/15 Star, British War and Victory Medals for his services during the war, which were sent to him at 51, Deronda Road, Herne Hill, London SE4. He died at Portsmouth in 1949, aged 68.

Sackville Herbert Edward Gregg Owen, Lieutenant. Owen was born at Slebech in 1880 and was a Solicitor. He was commissioned into the Pembroke Yeomanry on 26 August 1914. Owen embarked for Egypt with the Yeomanry and was seconded from the Yeomanry for service with the Imperial Camel Corps on 12 August 1916. He relinquished his commission due to wounds on 4 April 1918 and was granted the rank of Honorary Lieutenant and returned home to Hill House, Narberth, becoming High Sheriff for Pembrokeshire. He was awarded the British War and Victory Medals for his services, which were sent to him at Picton Castle. Owen unveiled the Tenby War Memorial in 1921. He married Dorothy Constance St. Foyre Fair in 1925 and died on 7 January 1960.

Llewellyn Partridge DSO MID, Major. Partridge was born at Winshill, Derbyshire in 1878, the son of Henry and Laura Partridge. He had served during the Boer War as a lieutenant with the 12th Lancers, having originally been commissioned into the 4th Battalion, Middlesex Regiment. Llewellyn married Mary Ciceley Onslow Cuthbert in 1903. He resigned from the 3rd Dragoon Guards on 26 February 1908, and joined the Pembroke Yeomanry as a captain. Llewellyn was promoted major on 26 November 1914. He embarked for Egypt with the Yeomanry in 1916, and was awarded the Distinguished Service Order, and French Croix de Guerre, and the Order of the Nile 4th Class just before the 24th Welsh was formed. He served for the rest of the war with the battalion, being promoted temporary lieutenant colonel on 8 September 1917. Llewellyn survived the war and was awarded the British War and Victory Medals for his services, which were sent to him at Pant-y-Beiliau, Gilwern, Monmouthshire. After the war Llewellyn became an Aide de Camp to three kings: George V, Edward VIII and George VI. He died at Stroud in 1945, aged 67.

Charles Pearce, Second Lieutenant. Pearce was commissioned into the Glamorgan Yeomanry from the Bristol University OTC on 8 March 1915. On 22 June 1917 he was promoted Lieutenant, with precedence from 1 June 1916. He seems to have remained on home service with the Labour Corps, and relinquished the acting rank of captain when ceasing to be employed by the Corps on 2 May 1919. He was restored to the establishment on 3 May 1919 and on 16 July 1919 he was promoted captain in the Territorial Force.

Charles Lewis William Penn, Captain. Penn was born on 30 September 1887, the son of Richard Poyer Lewis Penn and Edith Mary Penn (née Allen), of Camrose, Pembrokeshire. He married Mary Georgina Hoare at St Andrew's, Well Street, London on 9 March 1915. He was serving with the Pembroke Yeomanry at the outbreak of war, and on 4 April 1917 he was promoted lieutenant, with precedence from 28 March 1916. He was transferred to the Machine Gun Corps on 13 August 1918 as captain, with seniority from 23 January 1918. He was restored to the establishment on 21 January 1919 after ceasing to be employed by the Machine Gun Corps. He was awarded the British War and Victory Medals for his wartime services. Penn died on 14 July 1962, aged 74.

Sir Ivor Philipps, Major General. Philipps was born on 9 September 1861 at the vicarage in Warminster, the second of six sons of James Erasmus Philipps, twelfth baronet, vicar of Warminster, and his wife, Mary Margaret, eldest daughter of Samuel Best, rector of Abbots Ann, Hampshire. His family was one of the great landowning families of west Wales, with an ancestral seat at Picton Castle in Pembrokeshire John W. Philipps, first Viscount St Davids, was Ivor's elder brother. Philipps was educated at Felsted School and served in the Wiltshire militia from 1881 until 1883, when he was commissioned into the Manchester Regiment. He served in India, joining the Bengal Staff Corps of the Indian army in 1884 and two years later joined the 1st Battalion, the 5th Gurkha Regiment. He was promoted captain in 1894 and major in 1901, and was attached to the Burma military police in the years immediately following the absorption of Burma into India in 1886, seeing active service on the north-west frontier. He was appointed to the staff of the commander-in-chief, India, in 1900 and was awarded the DSO later that year. On retiring from the regular army in 1903 he joined the Pembroke Yeomanry, which he commanded from 1908 to 1912. On 9 September 1891 he married Marian Isobel Mirrlees, of Redlands, Glasgow. Philipps became Liberal MP for Southampton in 1906 and held the seat until 1922. On the outbreak of war in 1914 he was called to the War Office for staff duties and in November was given command of a brigade of the newly formed Welsh Division. He later became major general in command of the 38th (Welsh) Division, taking it to France. He was removed from his post after the first attack on Mametz Wood failed. In 1917 he was appointed KCB for services during the war. He was awarded the 1914/15 Star, British War and Victory Medals for his wartime services, which were sent to him at Cosheston Hall, Pembroke. He settled back into life at Cosheston Hall, Pembroke after the war, and busied himself with the restoration of Pembroke Castle, until his death in the Empire Nursing Home, Vincent Square, Westminster, on 15 August 1940, aged 78.

Walter Alfred Phillips MID, Lieutenant. Phillips was born on 18 August 1888, the son of Richard and Emma Phillips, of Cardiff. He embarked with the Glamorgan Yeomanry for Egypt in 1916 as a second lieutenant. He was promoted lieutenant on 1 July 1917 while attached to the 24th Welsh. He was awarded the British War and Victory Medals for his wartime services, which were sent to him at 164, Llandaff Road, Cardiff. He died in Cardiff in 1972, aged 83.

Albert Legh Pope MID, Captain. Pope was born in 1891, the son of Arthur and Isobel Legh Pope, of Caerleon. He was commissioned from the Monmouthshire Regiment into the Glamorgan Yeomanry on 15 November 1915, and joined the regiment in Egypt in December 1916. On 13 September 1918 he was promoted to acting captain, while commanding a Trench Mortar Battery, and relinquished the rank on 11 April 1919, reverting to lieutenant. He was awarded the British War and Victory Medals for his wartime services, which were sent to him at New Road, Slades, St Austell, Cornwall. He died in 1950, aged 59. His brother, Ernest Legh Pope, was awarded the Military Cross while attached to the 7th Battalion, Royal Fusiliers:

'On 27th September, 1918, near Bourlon Wood, he reorganised the men around him in conjunction with Lt. Driscoll, M.C., and under guidance of the C.O. led his command into action in a very gallant manner, thereby materially assisting the troops engaged in gaining their objective. The work done by him was most creditable.'

James Henry Richard Downes-Powell, Lieutenant Colonel. Downes-Powell was born in Oystermouth in 1874, the son of James and Margaret Powell. He married Evangeline Rhoda Bevan in 1908, whilst living in London. He was promoted lieutenant in the Glamorgan Yeomanry on 17 September 1914, having served in the Imperial Yeomanry, and was seconded to the Royal Welsh Fusiliers on 1 July 1915. On 8 May 1916 he was transferred to France, and was promoted acting major on 3 October 1916 while second in command of a battalion of the Royal Welsh Fusiliers, before becoming temporary lieutenant colonel while commanding a battalion. He later worked as a staff officer for the Ministry of Labour, being attached and promoted temporary lieutenant colonel on 17 September 1918. He relinquished his commission due to ill health contracted on active service on 17 July 1919, retaining the rank of lieutenant colonel. He was awarded the British War and Victory Medals for his wartime services, which were sent to him at 27, Principality Buildings, Queen Street, Cardiff. He died in Cheltenham on 10 February 1958, aged 84.

Hubert Cecil Prichard CBE MID, Major. Prichard was born in Stapleton, Gloucestershire on 6 February 1865, the son of Charles John Collins Prichard and Mary Anna Prichard (née Thomas). He was educated at Clifton College and at Magdalene College, Cambridge, before being commissioned into the 3rd Battalion, East Yorkshire Regiment in 1888. By 1896 he had been promoted captain, and retired from the army the following year, moving to Colwinstone, Glamorgan, to succeed his mother at Pwllywrach Manor in 1903. He became a captain in the Glamorgan Yeomanry on 25 September 1901. He became a J.P. for Glamorgan, and played cricket for Gloucestershire and Glamorgan. He married Nora Diana Piers on 16 October 1910. He was promoted temporary major in the Glamorgan Yeomanry on 10 September 1914, and seems to have remained on home service during the war as commandant of a Prisoner of War Camp. He was created CBE in 1919 and was mentioned in despatches twice for valuable services. He died on 12 November 1942, at Pwllywrach, Cowbridge, aged 77.

Richard Gerald Mansell Prichard, Major. Prichard was born in 1878, the third son of Richard Knight and Bridget Prichard (née Cooper), of Bryntirion, Bridgend. He was educated at Sherborne School (Wilson's House) and Camborne Mining College, and took a position in the south Wales coal field. At the outbreak of war he held an appointment at the Home Office as inspector of mines. A keen sportsman, he had served with the Glamorgan Yeomanry in the South African War, in which he earned the Queen's Medal with three clasps and was mentioned in dispatches. Prichard served again with the Glamorgan Yeomanry during the Great War, before volunteering for service with the Indian Cavalry, and saw considerable fighting in France, being once wounded, before the regiment was transferred to Palestine. He was killed in action in Palestine on 7 June 1918 and is buried at Jerusalem War Cemetery, Israel. Prichard left a widow and three young children. He was awarded the British War and Victory Medals for his wartime services, which were sent to his widow, Evelyne Bertha Prichard, at Braemount, Drake's Avenue, Exmouth.

David Garrick Protheroe, Major. Protheroe was born in Woolwich in 1868, the son of Edward Schaw and Ellen Augusta Celina Protheroe. By 1891 the family had returned to Ellen's native Llanboidy, and Protheroe was raised there. He was commissioned into the 4th Brigade, Welsh Division, Militia on 22 September 1888. He was promoted temporary major in the Pembroke Yeomanry on 9 November 1914. On 26 July 1917 he was promoted major, with precedence from 9 November 1914. He seems to have remained on home service throughout the war. He died in Carmarthenshire in 1954, aged 86. His brother, Godfrey Evan Schaw Protheroe-Beynon, also served with the Pembroke Yeomanry.

Godfrey Evan Schaw Protheroe-Beynon, Major. Protheroe Beynon was born at Harwich in 1872, the son of Edward Schaw and Ellen Augusta Cecilia Protheroe (née Beynon). During 1906 he inherited Trewern Mansion at Llanddewi Velfrey, and the following year was appointed High Sheriff of Carmarthenshire, assuming the name of Protheroe-Beynon. He was serving as captain with the Pembroke Yeomanry during 1908, when the Territorial Force was created, and was promoted to temporary major on 9 November 1914. Protheroe Beynon must have remained on home service during the war, as no medal card can be found for him. He died at Trewern in 1958, aged 86. His brother David Garrick Protheroe, also served with the Pembroke Yeomanry.

Herbert Swain Pryse, Second Lieutenant. Pryse was born in Cardiff in 1889, the son of David and Annie Pryse. He had originally served in the ranks of the Welsh Regiment, landing in France on 18 December 1915. He served with the Cheshire Regiment as a sergeant before being commissioned into the Welsh Regiment on 27 March 1917. Pryse served with the 1/5th Welsh in Palestine before being transferred to the 24th Welsh on 3 February 1918, and served with the battalion in France. He was promoted lieutenant on 1 September 1918, and remained in the army as a captain after the armistice, joining the 4th Battalion, Somerset Light Infantry. Pryse was awarded the 1914/15 Star, British War and Victory Medals for his services during the war, which were sent to him at 37, Milton Avenue, Wellsway, Bath. He resigned his commission on 10 September 1924, retaining the rank of lieutenant. Pryse died at Bath in 1964, aged 74.

Reverend Hugh Rees MC, Captain. Rees was born at Tregaron in 1877, the son of William and Rachel Rees. He was educated at Lampeter College, before becoming a vicar at Kidwelly prior to the war. He married Florence Emily Stephens in 1908. He volunteered to serve as a Chaplain with the Army Chaplains' Department at the outbreak of war, and was posted to Egypt in 1917, joining the 24th Welsh. Rees was awarded the Military Cross for his services in Palestine. He was awarded the British War and Victory Medals for his services during the war, which were sent to him at The Rectory, Loughor, Glamorgan. He died at Loughor in 1946, aged 69.

John Oswald Rees, Second Lieutenant. Rees was born in 1889, the son of John and Rachel Rees, of 32, Long Oaks Avenue, Swansea. He was commissioned from the Army Cycling Corps into the South Wales Borderers on 16 August 1917, and was attached to the 24th Welsh from the garrison at Zeitoun on 26 August 1917. Rees was wounded during the Third Battle of Gaza, and died of his wounds on 8 November 1917, aged 28. He is buried at Kantara War Memorial Cemetery, Egypt. For his services during the war, he was awarded the British War and Victory Medals, which were sent to his mother at 32, Long Oaks Avenue, Uplands, Swansea.

John Llewelyn Richards MID, Lieutenant. Richards was commissioned into the Pembroke Yeomanry on 1 June 1916. He embarked with the Yeomanry for Egypt, and served with the 24th Welsh after its formation. On 26 July 1917 he was promoted Lieutenant, with precedence from 3 December 1916. He was Mentioned in Despatches on

14 June 1918. He was awarded the British War and Victory Medals for his wartime services, which were sent to his executor.

John Thomas Richards, Second Lieutenant. Richards was the only son of Lewis and Mary Ann Richards, of Penywain, Bedwas, Monmouthshire. He was commissioned from the Royal Fusiliers into the 3rd Welsh on 2 April 1917, and attached to the 24th Welsh in Palestine. He was killed at Beersheba on 6 November 1917, aged 20, and is buried in Beersheba War Cemetery. He was awarded the British War and Victory Medals for his wartime services, which were sent to his mother at Penywain Farm, Bedwas.

George Powell Roch, Captain. Roch was born in Llanboidy, the son of William Francis and Emily Catherine Roch. He married Muriel Thomson, of Bath, in 1899, and was J.P. and D.L. for the County of Carmarthenshire. He had served as a captain in the Royal Garrison Artillery Militia, and on 12 January 1915 was gazetted as a captain in the Pembroke Yeomanry. He was then attached to the 1st Battalion, Kings Shropshire Light Infantry, part of 16 Brigade, 6th Division. He was promoted captain on 26 July 1917, with precedence from 12 January 1915. He was killed during the Second Battle of Kemmel on 21 May 1918, aged 43. He is buried at Nine Elms British Cemetery, Belgium. He was awarded the British War and Victory Medals for his wartime services, which were sent to his widow, Muriel Roch, at 33, Draycote Place, SW3. His brother, William Protheroe Roch, served as a captain in the Welsh Horse, and was killed in the Jordan Valley on 11 March 1918.

John Victor Tweed Roderick, Lieutenant. Roderick was the fourth son of William and Ella Augusta Buckley Roderick, of Goodig, Pembrey. He was educated at Rugby School prior to being commissioned into the Pembroke Yeomanry on 5 July 1915. He served in Ireland before being posted to Egypt, joining the 1/1st Pembroke Yeomanry on the Suez Canal. In March 1917 he transferred to the 1st Battalion, Coldstream Guards, joining the battalion in the Cambrai sector in France, and was promoted lieutenant on 1 July 1917. He was killed in action on 27 August 1918, aged 21, while leading an attack against the village of Moyenneville, and is buried in Bac-du-Sud British Cemetery, Baillieulval, He was awarded the British War and Victory Medals for his wartime services, which were sent to his mother at 45, Brunswick Gardens, Kensington, W8. Two of his brother also fell: Captain Hume Buckley Roderick was killed with the Welsh Guards in France on 1 December 1917; and Lieutenant Allan Whitlock Nicholl Roderick was killed in Gallipoli with the 4th Welsh on 10 August 1915.

Lancelot Duke Conway Rose, Lieutenant. Rose was born in Clevedon, Somerset in 1899, the son of Alfred and Sarah Rose. He was commissioned into the Pembroke Yeomanry from the Inns of Court OTC on 3 April 1915. He embarked for Egypt with the Yeomanry in 1916, and was taken on strength of the 24th Welsh upon its formation in 1917. He was promoted lieutenant on 1 July 1917. He was awarded the British War and Victory Medals for his wartime services, which were sent to him at 32, Windsor Terrace, Uplands, Swansea. He married Daphne Rosemary Williams, of Llandeilo, in 1919. He died in Sussex in 1957, aged 68.

Arthur Rosser, Second Lieutenant. Rosser was the only son of William and Esther Rosser, of Penrhyn, Eaton Grove, Swansea. He was educated at Swansea Grammar School, before joining the Pembroke Yeomanry as a private. He was commissioned from there into the Welsh Regiment in January 1915, and was posted to the 14th Welsh. He was killed during the assault on Mametz Wood on 10 July 1916, aged 19, and is commemorated on the Thiepval Memorial, France. His Commanding Officer wrote: 'Throughout the day he behaved in a most excellent manner, and had he lived would doubtless have received recognition from his King for his bravery. Boy, as he was, he was a man's man, and as such a leader.' He was awarded the 1914/15 Star, British War and Victory Medals for his wartime services, which were sent to his father at Penrhyn, Eaton Grove, Swansea.

George Matthew Rumball MC, Captain (Quartermaster). Rumball was born on 28 May 1867, the son of William and Catherine Rumball, of Westminster. He married Clara Blake on 17 May 1896. He enlisted on 9 February 1889 into the 1st King's Dragoon Guards, and saw service in India and the Boer War, gaining the Queen's South Africa Medal and three clasps, the King's South Africa Medal, and the Long Service Good Conduct Medal prior to the outbreak of the Great War. He was serving as regimental sergeant major with the Dragoon Guards, based at Pembroke Dock, when he was commissioned into the Pembroke Yeomanry on 21 May 1915, and was allotted the post of Quartermaster. He embarked with the Yeomanry for Egypt, and gained the award of the Military Cross in Palestine. He was promoted temporary captain on 21 May 1918. He resigned his commission on 1 April 1921, retaining the rank of captain. He was awarded the British War and Victory Medals for his service during the war, which were sent to him at The Saracen's Head Hotel, Diss, Norfolk. He died at Wandsworth in 1937, aged 69.

Sir Owen Henry Philipps Scourfield, TD, Colonel. Scourfield was born in Camrose, Pembrokeshire on 10 October 1847, the son of Sir John Henry Philipps Scourfield, and Augusta Lort Philipps. He was commissioned into the Pembroke Yeomanry on 2 August 1890, rising to become honorary colonel, Commanding the Pembroke Yeomanry. He married Gertrude Katherine Allen in 1877. He was still in honorary command of the battalion at the outbreak of war, but due to his advanced age command had passed to Lieutenant Colonel Spence-Jones. He died in Burton, Pembrokeshire in 1921, aged 73.

Richard William Serle, Lieutenant. Serle was born in 1891, the son of William Charles Serle and Emily Mary Serle, of Swansea. He was commissioned into the Welsh Regiment on 28 March 1917. He joined the 24th Welsh in Palestine on 7 September 1917, and was promoted lieutenant on 28 September 1918. He relinquished his commission on 30 September 1921. Serle died at Swansea in 1937, aged 45. He was awarded the British War and Victory Medals for his wartime services.

George Alfred Sheridan-Shedden MC, Lieutenant. Sheridan-Shedden was born in Cardiff in 1886, the son of John and Zoe Shedden (née Sheridan). He was commissioned from the Inns of Court OTC into the Pembroke Yeomanry on 3 April 1915. He embarked with the Yeomanry for Egypt in 1916. He later served with the 74th Battalion, Machine

Gun Corps in Palestine, and in France, and was awarded the Military Cross at Épehy (see the Honours and Awards Appendix). He was awarded the British War and Victory Medals for his wartime services. He died in Bristol in 1961, aged 75.

Robert John Richard Cobden Simons, Lieutenant Colonel. Simons was born in Merthyr Tydfil on 2 April 1865, the son of William Vazie Simons and Clara Maria Simons. He was a doctor and a Fellow of the Royal College of Physicians. On 10 June 1896 he was gazetted as Surgeon Lieutenant into the 2nd Glamorganshire Artillery. He married Helen Thomas in 1897. On 9 January 1915 he was appointed Temporary Lieutenant Colonel after being given command of one of the Welsh Field Ambulances of the 38th (Welsh) Division and served with it in France from 1 December 1915. He relinquished his commission due to ill health on 18 January 1917 and was granted the rank of Honorary Lieutenant Colonel. He died in Bath on 15 February 1925 aged fifty nine. For his services during the war he was awarded the 1914/15 Star, British War and Victory Medals.

Douglas Roy Smith, Lieutenant. Smith was born in Maindee on 18 July 1893, the son of Sidney and Elizabeth Smith. He enlisted on 29 September 1910 in the Royal Gloucester Hussars, and had attended annual camp every year from then until the outbreak of war, when he was discharged as medically unfit. He then gained a commission into the Glamorgan Yeomanry, joining the yeomanry in Egypt in December 1916. He was promoted lieutenant on 22 June 1917, with seniority from 20 October 1916. He was awarded the British War and Victory Medals for his wartime services, which were sent to him at Sunningdale, Caerleon, Monmouthshire. He died in Gloucester in 1969, aged 75.

William Arthur Smith, Second Lieutenant. Lieutenant Smith is mentioned in the war diary as being wounded on 31 September 1917. He cannot be identified.

Cecil John Herbert Spence-Jones CMG DSO MID, Lieutenant Colonel. Spence-Jones was born in 1873, the son of Reverend Henry Donald Maurice and Louise M. Spence. In 1908 he married Aline Margaret Colby, of Ffynone Hall, Boncath, Pembrokeshire. On 8 March 1905 he was promoted major in the Pembroke Yeomanry. On 21 October 1914 he was promoted to lieutenant-colonel, in command of the 1/1st Pembroke Yeomanry. He took the battalion to Egypt in 1916, and assumed command of the 24th Welsh upon its formation the following year. He commanded the battalion throughout the war, with spells in temporary command of 230 Brigade interspersed. He retired from the Pembroke Yeomanry with the rank of colonel on 21 October 1918. During the war he was made CMG and was awarded the DSO, as well as being mentioned in despatches several times (see the Honours and Awards Appendix). He was awarded the British War and Victory Medals, as well as the Territorial Force War Medal, for his wartime services, which were sent to him at Ffynone, Boncath, Pembrokeshire. He later resided at Donnington Hall, Ledbury, and was High Sheriff of Herefordshire.

Courtenay Charles Strick, Captain. Strick was born on 24 May 1886, the son of Thomas and Mary Strick. He was commissioned into the Glamorgan Yeomanry on 30 September 1914. On 17 May 1915 he assumed the rank of temporary lieutenant while commanding the South Wales Mounted Brigade Signal Troop, and was promoted lieutenant on 22 June 1917, with seniority from 1 June 1916. On 19 November 1917 he was promoted a captain. He served in France with a signals company, and was awarded the British War and Victory Medals for his wartime services, which were sent to him at Newton, Mumbles, Swansea. He died on 5 November 1958 at Kilgetty, Pembrokeshire, aged 72.

Richard Henry Bowlas Summers, Major. Summers was born on 30 July 1860, the son of James Bowlas and Emma Mary Ann Summers (née Penn), of Walwyn's Castle, Pembrokeshire. He was a well known sportsman, and had played cricket and rugby for Cheltenham College, and rugby for Haverfordwest and for Wales. He played full back in the first ever Welsh international team, which played England in 1881. He was commissioned into the Royal Pembroke Artillery Militia on 29 October 1879, but resigned his commission on 18 April 1885 after six years service. He was promoted temporary major in the Pembroke Yeomanry on 9 November 1914, and was promoted major on 5 December 1916. He served in France from 10 January 1917, attached to the 49th Division Artillery, before being transferred to the 56th Division Artillery. He was awarded the British War and Victory Medals for his wartime services, which were sent to him at Summerville, Haverfordwest. He died in Haverfordwest on 22 December 1941, aged 81.

Wilfred Temple, Second Lieutenant. Temple was born at Cockermouth in 1892, the son of John and Mary Hannah Temple. He was commissioned into the Welsh Regiment on 27 March 1918. He joined the 24th Welsh in France on 6 August 1918, but was later attached to the Sherwood Foresters. Temple was awarded the British War and Victory Medals for his services during the war, which were sent to his wife Hilda at Shakespeare House, Fitz Road, Cockermouth, in 1941. He died in Cumbria in 1958, aged 66.

Arthur Tudor Thomas, Captain. Thomas was born in Taffswell in 1883, the son of William and Ann Thomas. He married Florence Mary Stark in 1909. He was commissioned into the Glamorgan Yeomanry on 2 February 1916. He joined the 24th RWF in France in 1918, and was wounded after the 74th Division had moved back to Flanders from the Somme. He died of his wounds on 29 September 1918 aged 34, and is buried in Pont-d'Achelles Military Cemetery, Nieppe. He was promoted captain whilst commanding a company on 3 July 1918. He was awarded the British War and Victory Medals for his wartime services, which were sent to his widow, Florence Mary Thomas, at 15, Mafeking Road, Cardiff.

Charles William Trevor Trask, Second Lieutenant. Trask was born on 9 April 1899, the son of Colonel Charles James, and Evelyn Trask of Broadshard, Norton sub Hamdon, Somerset. Educated at Connaught House, Weymouth and Sherborne School, he was in the OTC at Sherborne from May 1913 until he left in March 1916. Trask attested for the Inns of Court OTC 26 December 1916, and was posted to the Reserve. He was mobilized on 12 March 1917 and joined 12 Officer Cadet Battalion, being commissioned into the 3rd (Reserve) Battalion Somerset Light Infantry on 27 November 1917. Trask then sailed for Egypt, joining the 24th Welsh on 3 March 1918. He landed with the battalion in France on 7 May 1918, and on 29 June returned to England for leave. Trask rejoined the battalion on 12 July 1918, and was killed in action 18 August 1918, aged 19. He is buried at St Venant-

Robecq Road British Cemetery, Robecq, France. For his services during the war, Trask was awarded the British War and Victory Medals, which were sent to his father at Brondshard, Norton Sub Hamdon, Stoke Under Ham.

Odo Richard Vivian DSO MVO TD, Lieutenant Colonel. Vivian was born in London on 22 April 1875, the son of Henry Hussey and Averil Vivian (née Beaumont). He was commissioned into the Glamorgan Yeomanry on 13 May 1896. He served with the 2nd Volunteer Battalion, Welsh Regiment for a period, before being promoted captain with the Glamorgan Yeomanry on 19 October 1901. He was created a Member of the Victorian Order on 12 August 1904. He married Winifred Hamilton in Ireland on 25 October 1906. He was seconded to the 14th Battalion Royal Irish Rifles on 6 February 1917, and later commanded the 6th Welsh and the 11th Battalion, Cameron Highlanders during the war. For his services during the war, he was awarded the DSO (see the Honours and Awards Appendix). He was awarded the British War and Victory Medals for his wartime services, as well as the Territorial Force War Medal, which were sent to him at Glanogwr, Bridgend. He became lieutenant colonel commanding the 6th Welsh (TA) on 16 February 1920. He became the third Baron Swansea upon the death of his brother in 1932, and died at Builth Wells on 16 November 1934, aged 59. His medals, the Member of the Victorian Order, Distinguished Service Order, British War Medal, Victory Medal with MID emblem, and the Territorial War Medal were sold at auction in 2007, the estimate being £3,000 to £4,000.

Charles Herbert Stanley Wakeford, Lieutenant. Wakeford was born in 1899, the son of Herbert Steele and Mary Wakeford, of Meadow View, Clive Crescent, Penarth. He was commissioned on 27 October 1915 into the Glamorgan Yeomanry, and embarked for Egypt with them in 1916. He was promoted to lieutenant on 1 July 1917, and sailed for France with the battalion in May 1918. Wakefield was killed in action on 7 September 1918, aged 28. He is buried at Tincourt New British Cemetery, France. For his services during the war he was awarded the British War and Victory Medals, which were sent to his father at Meadow View, 54, Clive Road, Penarth.

Francis Reginald Steele Wakeford, Lieutenant. Wakeford was born on 24 May 1893, the son of Herbert Steele and Mary Wakeford, of Meadow View, Clive Crescent, Penarth He was commissioned in the Glamorgan Yeomanry on 25 October 1916, joining the yeomanry in Egypt. He was promoted lieutenant on 25 April 1918. He later transferred to the Royal Air Force as flying officer (Observer). He died on 25 December 1918, aged 25, and is buried in Penarth (St Augustine of Hippo) Churchyard. He was awarded the British War and Victory Medals for his wartime services, which were sent to his father at 54, Clive Road, Penarth.

Howel Cyril Watkins MC, Lieutenant. Watkins was the son of Walter Jones and Nellie Watkins (née Chadwick), of 5, Richmond Villas, Swansea. He was commissioned into the Pembroke Yeomanry on 5 August 1916, and taken on strength in the 24th Welsh after its formation. He was promoted lieutenant on 5 February 1918. He was awarded the Military Cross during the Battle of Épehy, and was wounded and taken prisoner by the Germans during the great offensive, on 21 September 1918. He died of his wounds on 23 October 1918, aged 21, and is buried in Le Cateau Military Cemetery. He was awarded the British

War and Victory Medals for his wartime services, which were sent to his father at 56, Eaton Crescent, Swansea.

Alfred E Welch, Second Lieutenant. Welch was commissioned into the Pembroke Yeomanry on 28 March 1917, and on 7 September 1917 joined the 24th Welsh in Palestine. Little else is presently known of him, but he survived the war and was awarded the British War and Victory Medals for his service.

Cecil Hamlyn Williams MID, Second Lieutenant. Williams was born at Clerkenwell on 23 January 1895, the son of Alfred Hamlyn and Mildred Mercy Williams. He originally served as an able seaman in the Royal Navy, before being commissioned into the Welsh Regiment, and posted to the 24th Welsh. Williams was mentioned in Sir Archibald Murray's Despatches of 28 August 1917. He was later promoted captain, and transferred to the King's Royal Rifle Corps. For his services during the war Williams was awarded the British War and Victory Medals, which were sent to his mother at 35, Dover Street, Piccadilly. He died at Eastbourne in 1976, aged 81.

Hugh Williams, Second Lieutenant. Williams was the son of John and Margaret Williams, of Landers Hook, Treffgarne, Pembrokeshire. He married prior to the war, and lived with his wife Anna Williams at Old Gate House, Robeston Wathen. Williams was commissioned into the Pembroke Yeomanry, but was then attached to the 7th Battalion, King's Shropshire Light Infantry, part of 8 Brigade, 3rd Division. He was killed near Béthune on 28 July 1918 aged 29, and is buried at Sandpits British Cemetery, Fouquereuil. He was awarded the British War and Victory Medals for his wartime services.

James Alexander Wilson MD, Captain (Surgeon). Wilson was commissioned into the Pembroke Yeomanry as Medical Officer on 2 September 1905. Little else is known of him, but he remained in Britain on home service and did not embark for Egypt with the yeomanry.

Richard Cape Wilson, Captain. Wilson was born in Africa in 1892. He was originally commissioned into the Glamorgan Yeomanry on 15 September 1913. He was promoted lieutenant just after the Yeomanry arrived in Egypt, on 26 March 1916, and put in command of No 1 Company. On 11 June 1916 he was promoted captain, with precedence as of 26 March 1916. On 8 March 1917 he was attached to the HQ staff. He was restored to the establishment on 5 March 1918. He was awarded the British War and Victory Medals for his wartime services, as well as the Territorial Force War Medal, which were sent to him at Nash Manor, Cowbridge, Glamorgan. He possibly died in 1959.

Wilfrid Hawthorn Wilson, Second Lieutenant. Wilson was born in St Mellons, Cardiff in 1893, and was brought up by his aunt and uncle, Matthew and Margaret Cope. He was commissioned into the Glamorgan Yeomanry on 30 September 1914, but transferred to the Welsh Brigade, Royal Field Artillery. He served in France from 7 May 1918, and was awarded the British War and Victory Medals for his wartime services, which were sent to him at Edgemont, Derby Road, Nottingham.

John Burrell Holme Woodcock DSO MID, Major. Woodcock was born at Standish, Lancashire in 1885. He was educated at Rugby, before graduating BA, becoming an articled solicitor's clerk. He was commissioned into the Pembroke Yeomanry on 12 May 1906, lieutenant on 22 April 1912, and captain on 26 November 1914. On 24 February 1917 Woodcock was promoted to major, with precedence from 10 August 1916. He assumed temporary command of the 24th Welsh on 19 May 1918 and reassumed command on 14 September 1918, and again on 18 January and 24 February 1919. He was awarded the Territorial Decoration in the Royal Warrant of 13 October 1920, whilst on the staff of 102nd (Pembroke & Cardigan) Field Brigade, Royal Artillery. On 14 April 1926, Major Woodcock DSO TD resigned his commission upon retirement, retaining the rank of major. He was awarded the British War and Victory Medals for his wartime services, as well as the Territorial Force War Medal, which were sent to him at Ashley Manor, Kings Limbourne, Hampshire. He died in South Africa in 1960, aged 75.

William Woolf, Lieutenant. Woolf was born in Cardiff in 1894, the son of Joseph and Rebecca Woolf. He was commissioned from the Royal Engineers into the 17th Welsh in February 1915, and later transferred to the 24th Welsh. He was killed in action at Épehy on 21 September 1918, aged 24, and is buried in Ste. Emilie Valley Cemetery, Villers-Faucon. He was awarded the British War and Victory Medals for his wartime services, which were sent to his parents at 35b Queen's Gate, South Kensington, London.

Charles Frederick Talbot Wyndham-Quin, Major. Wyndham-Quin was born on 12 January 1864, the son of the Fourth Earl of Dunraven, Windham Henry Wyndham-Quin, and of Caroline Tyler. His father had commanded the Imperial Yeomanry during the Boer War. Wyndham-Quin was too old for overseas service, so remained on the home establishment throughout the war. He died in Kensington on 2 April 1926.

John Wyndham, Major. Wyndham was commissioned into the 2nd Welsh in May 1900, and was promoted captain in August 1910. In 1913 he was serving as an assistant district commissioner, South Nigeria, on the Welsh Regiment retired list. At the outbreak of the Great War he first served with the Nigeria Regiment in West Africa and was then posted to the 24th Welsh, serving in Egypt, and later on the staff in France, attached to Fifth Army. On 10 July 1918 he was granted the rank of major on retiring for the second time. He was awarded the 1914/15 Star, British War Medal and Victory Medal for his services, and was also awarded a Silver War Badge. His address on retirement was Williton, Somerset. He died on 24 November 1966 at Bathealton, near Taunton.

Thomas William Yarrow, Major. Yarrow was born in Tottenham in 1854. He enlisted into the 5th Lancers in 1872, and retired in 1906, after thirty four years service. He married the widowed Martha Roberts in Tenby on 7 September 1895. He was Quartermaster and Honorary Major with the Glamorgan Yeomanry at the outbreak of war, and on 9 November 1914 was attached to the Pembroke Yeomanry in the same capacity. He was awarded the Silver War Badge, which was sent to him at 1, Green Hill Avenue, Tenby. He died in Tenby in 1926, aged 72.

James Hamilton Langdon Yorke MC, Captain. Yorke was the son of James Charles Yorke, J.P. and Katherine Ellen Yorke (née Langdon), of Langton, Durnbach, Pembrokeshire, and was educated at Haileybury and at Oriel College, Oxford. He married Violet Mary Vincent, of 8 Argyll Mansions, Chelsea, London, and the couple had two children. Yorke was commissioned into the Pembroke Yeomanry on 3 October 1912, and worked for the British South Africa Company. Upon the outbreak of war he volunteered for overseas service, and embarked for Egypt with the Pembroke Yeomanry in 1916. He was promoted captain in Egypt, joining the 24th Welsh upon formation in 1917. Yorke was killed in action at El Tireh on 27 December 1917. He had just nine days previously been awarded the Military Cross. He was awarded the British War and Victory Medals for his wartime services, which were sent to his widow, at 7, Argyll Mansions, Chelsea, SW3.

Appendix III

Casualties

During the course of the war, 225 men were killed, or died of wounds or illness while serving with the 24th Welsh, the majority of whom fell on the Western Front. Sixteen are buried or commemorated in Egypt; eighty-seven in Palestine; two in Belgium; 107 in France; one in Germany; one is commemorated in Greece; one commemorated in Iraq; three are buried in England; and seven are buried in Wales. Some of the officers were still classed as yeomanry officers, while some were attached from other units. There were also several casualties among the Pembroke and Glamorgan Yeomanry regiments in Egypt before the two merged to form the battalion, so they have been added to the roll; and some men from the 24th Welsh were also attached to other units.

With the formation of the second and third line battalions of each regiment, many of the men who served with these were despatched as reinforcements to other units. As a result, somewhere in the region of 160 further Pembroke Yeomanry and over eighty Glamorgan Yeomanry members were killed while serving with other units, in addition to the members of the 24th Welsh who fell, making an accurate casualty roll somewhat of a challenge.

The following roll of men of the 24th Welsh who fell is considered to be as accurate as possible, and is laid out in alphabetical order, with name, rank, number, unit and date of death:

Name	Rank	Number	Regiment	Date Died
Abraham, G. W. P.	Captain		24th Welsh	19/11/1917
Arrowsmith, Albert	Private	60656	24th Welsh	05/10/1918
Astley, Alexander Gifford Ludford	Captain		14th King's Hussars	05/03/1917
Aylett-Branfill, Capel Lisle	Captain		Glamorgan Yeomanry	11/05/1916
Bagnall, Harry	Private	48295	24th Welsh	04/10/1917
Baguley, Lawrence Smith	Corporal	320595	24th Welsh	11/10/1918
Ball, William	Private	57514	24th Welsh	21/09/1918
Barnacle, David	Private	57756	24th Welsh	18/09/1918
Barritt, Tom Saunders	Private	58975	24th Welsh	01/12/1917
Benjamin, Henry, MM	Private	26532	24th Welsh	01/12/1917
Bennett, Edgar	Private	57511	24th Welsh	20/09/1918
Beynon, Philip Rees	Private	320608	24th Welsh	08/11/1917
Beynon, William	Private	320616	24th Welsh	13/10/1918

Biddle, James Cecil	Serjeant	320692	24th Welsh	20/08/1918
Bloodworth, Edwin Walter	Private	60173	24th Welsh	01/12/1917
Bowen, Thomas	Private	57517	24th Welsh	05/10/1918
Bradshaw, Wilfred John	Private	320599	24th Welsh	31/07/1917
Branfield, Sydney Ernest	Private	320111	24th Welsh	31/10/1917
Brewer, Edmund	2nd Lt	Glamorgan Yeomanry		12/01/1918
Brownhill, William Henry Hugo	Private	55863	24th Welsh	21/12/1918
Bryant, Frank (Byrant)	Private	61692	24th Welsh	21/09/1918
Bullock, John Edward	Private	59956	24th Welsh	20/08/1918
Burns, Christopher	Private	58976	24th Welsh	01/11/1917
Carlisle, Frederick William	Private	57525	24th Welsh	20/08/1918
Cartwright, Albert	Private	60305	24th Welsh	27/12/1917
Churchman, Arthur	Private	57521	24th Welsh	07/09/1918
Clement, Christopher L.	Private	320907	24th Welsh	31/10/1917
Clement, Walter	Private	320573	24th Welsh	15/10/1918
Clemetson, David Louis	Lieutenant		24th Welsh	21/09/1918
Coney, Reginald	Private	320531	24th Welsh	07/10/1918
Conroy, Leo James	Private	57520	24th Welsh	19/09/1918
Cook, Thomas	Private	320301	24th Welsh	06/11/1917
Croston, James William	Private	57524	24th Welsh	07/09/1918
David, William John	Private	320646	24th Welsh	31/10/1917
Davies, Arthur Tudor	Private	320771	24th Welsh	06/12/1917
Davies, David John	Private	73690	24th Welsh	08/11/1918
Davies, Evan Idwal	Private	57545	24th Welsh	21/09/1918
Davies, John	Private	320373	24th Welsh	06/11/1917
Davies, John Henry	Private	320802	24th Welsh	03/03/1918
Davies, John Jenkin	CQMS	320157	24th Welsh	20/10/1918
Davies, Owen	Private	59941	24th Welsh	06/11/1918
Davies, Pryce T.	C.S.M.	320537	24th Welsh	01/12/1917
Davies, Richard Emlyn	Private	60665	24th Welsh	07/11/1917
Davies, Thomas Henry	Private	60663	24th Welsh	27/12/1917
Davies, Watkin Jones	Serjeant	320198	24th Welsh	17/11/1918
Davies, William	Corporal	320952	24th Welsh	04/11/1917
Davies, William	Private	320188	24th Welsh	30/10/1918
Davies, William Thomas	Private	57772	24th Welsh	07/09/1918
Dawson, David John	Private	320494	24th Welsh	21/09/1918
Dayson, Arthur Stanley	L/Cpl	320871	24th Welsh	02/12/1917
Dixon, George	Private	58972	24th Welsh	06/11/1917
Donoghue, Richard	Private	291761	24th Welsh	23/09/1918
Eades, George	Private	25735	24th Welsh	07/09/1918
Eastup, William James	Private	320785	24th Welsh	02/10/1918
Ecob, William Arthur	Private	61032	24th Welsh	10/09/1918
Edwards, Harold Clifford	Private	320779	24th Welsh	20/11/1917
Edwards, William	Lieutenant		24th Welsh	01/11/1917

Armine				
Evans, Aelwyn Christmas (Alcwyn?)	Private	320495	24th Welsh	12/05/1917
Evans, Evan	Private	58520	24th Welsh	06/11/1917
Evans, Evan Charles (Charlie)	C.Q.M.S.	320161	24th Welsh	25/08/1918
Evans, Evan David	Private	61673	24th Welsh	17/10/1918
Evans, Hugh	Private	320718	24th Welsh	21/09/1918
Evans, Morgan	Private	61608	24th Welsh	18/09/1918
Evans, Reginald Charles	L/Cpl	320678	24th Welsh	06/11/1917
Evans, William	Sergeant	320117	24th Welsh	09/03/1918
Evans, William Henry	Private	61652	24th Welsh	21/09/1918
Ferguson, William Henry	Private	57548	24th Welsh	21/09/1918
Frankham, George William	Private	46257	24th Welsh	01/12/1917
Fudge, James	Private	59984	24th Welsh	09/12/1917
Gardner, Reuben	Private	60259	24th Welsh	13/10/1918
Garner, Albert	Private	59208	24th Welsh	04/11/1917
George, Hubert Thomas	Private	320039	24th Welsh	18/09/1918
Giddy, Frederick Edward	Private	320879	24th Welsh	03/10/1917
Glanville, Hugh Slader	Private	320229	24th Welsh	11/11/1917
Goss, James	Private	320849	24th Welsh	01/12/1917
Grady, John	Private	58977	24th Welsh	01/12/1917
Griffiths, David	Private	50312	24th Welsh	31/10/1917
Griffiths, David George	Corporal	320217	24th Welsh	06/11/1917
Griffiths, Evan	Private	320472	24th Welsh	06/11/1917
Griffiths, William Dillwyn	2nd Lieutenant		24th Welsh	18/09/1918
Guest, James Graham	Private	57553	24th Welsh	07/09/1918
Gwilym, David	Private	52896	24th Welsh	10/03/1918
Hadwin, Alfred Litt	Private	57557	24th Welsh	19/09/1918
Hall, James	Private	61612	24th Welsh	23/08/1918
Hanson, Stanley	Private	35824	24th Welsh	01/12/1917
Harries, John Clarke	Private	32040	124th Welsh	03/10/1918
Harries, Seth John	Private	320015	24th Welsh	06/11/1917
Harrington, Henry	Private	320323	24th Welsh	08/10/1918
Heath, Albert	Private	61697	24th Welsh	06/11/1918
Heath, William	Private	48284	24th Welsh	06/11/1917
Hickling, Ernest	Private	285098	24th Welsh	08/11/1918
Hoad, Harry	Private	14332	24th Welsh	06/11/1917
Hollbrook, William Thomas Herbert	Private	320868	24th Welsh	07/09/1918
Holt, John Aspin	Private	60674	24th Welsh	23/09/1918
Horsey, Alfred John	Private	56807	24th Welsh	18/09/1918
Houldsworth, George	Private	57567	24th Welsh	20/09/1918
Howard, Frederick Easton	Private	57555	24th Welsh	07/09/1918
Huish, William Walters	Private	60672	24th Welsh	06/11/1917

James, John	Private	320859	24th Welsh	18/09/1918
Jenkins, David	Private	320385	24th Welsh	06/11/1917
Jenkins, Edwin	C.S.M.	320011	24th Welsh	26/09/1918
Jenkins, Leslie Glanville	Private	320890	24th Welsh	21/09/1918
John, David	Private	320453	24th Welsh	06/11/1917
John, John Higgon	Serjeant	320643	24th Welsh	21/09/1918
John, John James	Private	320374	24th Welsh	21/09/1918
John, William	Private	320285	24th Welsh	27/12/1917
Jones, Cadwallader	Private	320883	24th Welsh	21/09/1918
Jones, David Aaron	Private	320357	24th Welsh	31/10/1917
Jones, David Robert	L/Corporal	320211	24th Welsh	06/11/1917
Jones, Evan Richard	Private	320242	24th Welsh	06/11/1917
Jones, Frederick	Private	320609	24th Welsh	21/06/1917
Jones, Ieuan Cranog (Jenan?)	L/Corporal	320797	24th Welsh	08/12/1917
Jones, John	Private	320234	24th Welsh	06/11/1917
Jones, Moses	Private	320224	24th Welsh	06/11/1917
Jones, Oliver	Private	48144	24th Welsh	06/11/1917
Jones, Peter Emrys	Private	320778	24th Welsh	01/12/1917
Jones, Robert Gwynedd	Private	57571	24th Welsh	21/09/1918
Jones, Sidney George	Private	57651	24th Welsh	13/09/1918
Jones, Thomas	Private	320450	24th Welsh	31/10/1917
Jones, Thomas	Private	60131	24th Welsh	20/09/1918
Jones, Thomas Henry	Private	52907	24th Welsh	30/01/1918
Jones, Thomas John	Private	320238	24th Welsh	06/11/1917
Jones, William Edward	Private	2748	24th Welsh	29/10/1918
Juliff, Alfred James	Private	60255	24th Welsh	24/08/1918
Jury, Thomas	Private	64753	24th Welsh	20/09/1918
Kane, Martin	Private	17335	24th Welsh	06/11/1917
Kelly, Frederick William	L/Corporal	35835	24th Welsh	06/11/1917
Kennedy, Andrew	Private	57572	24th Welsh	18/09/1918
Kershaw, William Henry	Private	57573	24th Welsh	21/09/1918
Knight, Wilfred George	Private	61614	24th Welsh	07/11/1917
Latimer, Henry	Private	38985	24th Welsh	21/09/1918
Leech, Frank	Private	37064	24th Welsh	20/02/1919
Letton, Edward Arthur Thomas	Private	31640	24th Welsh	14/12/1917
Lewis, Albert	Private	320925	24th Welsh	23/09/1918
Leyshon, Arthur William	Private	320910	24th Welsh	29/10/1918
Lind, Howell Jenkins	Private	57577	24th Welsh	23/09/1918
Little, Walter Charles	Private	320352	24th Welsh	21/09/1918
Little, William	Private	57575	24th Welsh	18/09/1918
Llewhellin, John Austin (Jack)	Private	320266	24th Welsh	02/11/1917
Lloyd, David	Private	320277	24th Welsh	07/05/1917
Loosmore, Robert Brinley	Private	320754	24th Welsh	06/11/1917

Manning, Edward	L/Corporal	21609	24th Welsh	19/09/1918
Martin, Philip	Private	10658	24th Welsh	02/09/1918
Masters, Percival	Private	320759	24th Welsh	09/09/1918
Matthews, John Gomer	L/Corporal	25673	24th Welsh	01/12/1917
Mayo, George E.	Private	61618	24th Welsh	06/11/1917
Meade, John Henry	Private	59987	24th Welsh	09/03/1918
Mills, John Rupert	Corporal	61653	24th Welsh	23/07/1918
Morgan, Alan	Private	60219	24th Welsh	04/10/1918
Morgan, Charles Henry	Private	48287	24th Welsh	27/12/1917
Morgan, David Lloyd Popkin, MC.	Captain		24th Welsh	09/03/1918
Morris, Ivor	Private	25427	24th Welsh	23/09/1918
Morris, James	Lieutenant		Glamorgan Yeomanry	27/12/1917
Murray, William Henry	Private	64744	24th Welsh	10/10/1918
Murthwaite, William	Private	59164	24th Welsh	06/11/1917
Newby, Thomas	Serjeant	320513	24th Welsh	01/12/1917
Nicholas, James	Private	320846	24th Welsh	10/10/1918
Norbury, George Llewellyn	Private	57588	24th Welsh	23/07/1918
O'Shea, John	Private	61620	24th Welsh	08/09/1918
Outten, William Henry	Private	60682	24th Welsh	06/11/1917
Owen, Charles	L/Serjeant	58968	24th Welsh	21/09/1918
Park, Frederick	Private	320933	24th Welsh	22/10/1918
Parkinson, John James	Private	58965	24th Welsh	23/07/1918
Phillips, James Howell	Private	320314	24th Welsh	06/11/1917
Phillips, William	Private	52792	24th Welsh	18/09/1918
Postings, Hubert	Private	320305	24th Welsh	10/10/1918
Powell, Alexander	Private	53846	24th Welsh	01/12/1917
Powell, Charles	Private	320978	24th Welsh	23/10/1918
Prichard, Richard Gerald Mansell	Major		Central India Horse	07/06/1918
Pritchard, Thomas Layton	Corporal	320717	24th Welsh	18/09/1918
Prosser, Charles Badam	Private	320262	24th Welsh	08/11/1917
Quirk, Thomas	Private	320804	24th Welsh	18/09/1918
Radcliffe, Clifford George	Serjeant	320614	24th Welsh	18/09/1918
Ravenhill, Edward John	Private	60202	24th Welsh	06/10/1918
Rees, David John	Private	320243	24th Welsh	21/04/1917
Rees, Ezra Howell	Private	320841	24th Welsh	06/11/1917
Rees, James Frederick	Private	320088	24th Welsh	06/11/1917
Rees, John Oswald	2nd Lieutenant		24th Welsh	08/11/1917
Richards, John Thomas	2nd Lieutenant		24th Welsh	06/11/1917
Richards, Maldwyn	Corporal	320175	24th Welsh	31/10/1917
Rieple, William George	Private	320625	24th Welsh	31/10/1917
Roberts, Arthur Thomas	C.S.M.	320533	24th Welsh	23/11/1918
Rockingham, Edward	Private	320155	24th Welsh	21/09/1918
Rogers, Joseph	Private	48975	24th Welsh	27/12/1917

Name	Rank	Number	Unit	Date
Saer, David Charles	L/Corporal	320122	24th Welsh	06/11/1917
Scourfield, Benjamin David	Private	320091	24th Welsh	06/11/1917
Smith, Gilbert James	Private	320258	24th Welsh	06/12/1917
Smith, Hubert George	Private	320057	24th Welsh	06/11/1918
Smith, Joseph	Private	59186	24th Welsh	06/11/1917
Smith, Samuel	Private	37894	24th Welsh	07/09/1918
Smith, William Arthur	Private	320499	24th Welsh	01/01/1917
Southgate, Frederick	Private	320271	24th Welsh	21/04/1917
Stocks, Walter (Wallace) Leonard	Private	291639	24th Welsh	07/09/1918
Swindlehurst, James	Private	57600	24th Welsh	21/09/1918
Tandy, George	Private	28083	24th Welsh	21/09/1918
Taylor, Francis Charles	Serjeant	320613	24th Welsh	19/09/1918
Thomas, David John	Private	320328	24th Welsh	12/11/1917
Thomas, David Lewis	Private	320496	24th Welsh	06/11/1917
Thomas, Edward	Private	60134	24th Welsh	21/09/1918
Thomas, Herbert Nugent	Private	320714	24th Welsh	25/03/1920
Thomas, John James	Private	320114	24th Welsh	18/12/1917
Thomas, Noah	Private	60335	24th Welsh	18/02/1918
Thomas, Thomas	Private	320981	24th Welsh	03/11/1918
Thomas, Thomas James	Corporal	320187	24th Welsh	20/09/1918
Thomas, Walter Rowland	Private	320820	24th Welsh	01/12/1917
Thompson, John	Private	40086	24th Welsh	12/10/1918
Tomkins, Austin William	Private	60195	24th Welsh	01/12/1917
Trask, Charles William Trevor	2nd Lieutenant		24th Welsh	18/08/1918
Tully, Richard Heckels	Private	59196	24th Welsh	07/09/1918
Turner, William	Private	51582	24th Welsh	01/12/1917
Wakeford, Charles Herbert Stanley	Lieutenant		24th Welsh	07/09/1918
Wakeford, Francis Reginald Steele	2nd Lieutenant		Royal Air Force	25/12/1918
Walker, George Robert	Private	59199	24th Welsh	05/03/1919
Watkins, Albert	Private	60200	24th Welsh	18/09/1918
Watkins, Howel Cyril, MC.	Lieutenant		24th Welsh	23/10/1918
Whiting, William Hamlyn	Private	64739	24th Welsh	22/09/1918
Wild, Arthur	Private	57680	24th Welsh	07/09/1918
Williams, David	Private	320254	24th Welsh	21/09/1918
Wiltshire, Reginald John	Private	320983	24th Welsh	23/10/1918
Woodburn, William	Private	58994	24th Welsh	19/12/1917
Woolf, William	Lieutenant		24th Welsh	21/09/1918
Wylie, John	Private	59195	24th Welsh	06/10/1918
Yeandle, Frank	Private	43711	24th Welsh	31/10/1917
Yorke, J. H. L., MC	Captain		24th Welsh	27/12/1917
Young, George E	Private	345194	24th Welsh	27/12/1917

Acknowledgements

It is almost impossible to be able to fully acknowledge all of the people and sources of information that have been used to write this book, as the author has been carrying out research on the 24th Welsh intermittently for over twelve years in between other work, but the following are the notable contributors who come to mind: Mark 'Taff' Collins, who is a mine of information for anything relating to the Welsh Regiment; Nick Powley, for copies of his uncle G. M. Rumball's photographs, which include a particularly fine group photograph of all of the Pembroke Yeomanry officers just after the outbreak of war; John Dart, former curator of the Welsh Regiment Museum at Cardiff, for allowing me to copy the memoires of Ernest Idris Cumpstone; Pembrokeshire Archives for supplying scanned copies of several items in their fine collection, namely the memoirs of Lawrence Marks and Gerald Marston Owen and of J. B. Hitching's 'The Campaigns of the 1/1st Pembroke Yeomanry'; Gal Shaine for supplying modern photographs of the Beersheba battlefield, and the remnants of trenches and defensive positions there; Rhys Davies, for kindly sending me several photographs relating to John Jenkin Davies of Llanfarian. To anyone else who I have missed out who has sent me photographs in the past, I apologise, as my referencing technique leaves a lot to be desired!

The photographic collection of the Library of Congress (USA), several of which are used in this book, contains a large number of items relating to Turkish occupied Palestine, and these photographs are available copyright free via the Library's website.

The fine newspaper archive collection held by the National Library of Wales at Aberystwyth, most of which is now freely available online, has been of great importance, proving to be an important source of portraits of some of the men and also being a great source of information from the myriad of letters from men of the 24th Welsh published in various newspaper during the course of the war.

The archives of the Commonwealth War Graves Commission (CWGC) are a standard source for any work of this type, and we sometimes forget what an important role the CWGC plays in commemorating these brave men. Also related to this is the Soldier's Died in the Great War CD (SDGW), which contains details of all of the officers and men of the British army who fell.

The availabilty of the surviving service papers on Ancestry and Find My Past, together with other available medal rolls and census records, is of great value when researching individual men.

The author has also made use of his own personal collection of photographs, war diaries, trench maps and letters for this book.

Select Bibliography

The History of the Welsh Regiment, 1914-1918, by T.O. Marden.

History of the 53rd (Welsh) Division, by Major C.H. Dudley Ward.

The 74th (Yeomanry) Division in Syria and France, by Major C.H. Dudley Ward.

The Story of the Fourth Army (The Battles of the Hundred Days), by Major General Sir A. Montgomery.

Sir Archibald Murray's Despatches, by J.M. Dent. (Also freely available on the *London Gazette* website).

Sir Douglas Haig's Despatches, by J.M. Dent. (Also freely available on the *London Gazette* website).

The Fife and Forfar Yeomanry 1914-1919, by D.D. Ogilvie.

The Diary of a Yeomanry M.O., by Captain O. Teichman, DSO, MC.

How Jerusalem was Won, by W.T. Massey.

The War Diary of the 24th Battalion, Welsh Regiment. National Archives Ref. WO95/3154-3.

The War Diary of 231 Brigade H.Q. National Archives Ref. WO95/3154-1.

Index